INTERLANGUAGE PRAGMATICS

Exploring Institutional Talk

Second Language Acquisition Research
Theoretical and Methodological Issues
Susan M. Gass and Jacquelyn Schachter, Editors

INTERLANGUAGE PRAGMATICS

Exploring Institutional Talk

Edited by

KATHLEEN BARDOVI-HARLIG
BEVERLY S. HARTFORD
Indiana University

2005

LAWRENCE ERLBAUM ASSOCIATES, PUBLISHERS
Mahwah, New Jersey   London

The camera copy for the text of this book was supplied by the editors.

Copyright © 2005 by Lawrence Erlbaum Associates, Inc.
All rights reserved. No part of this book may be reproduced in
any form, by photostat, microform, retrieval system, or any other
means, without the prior written permission of the publisher.

Lawrence Erlbaum Associates, Inc., Publishers
10 Industrial Avenue
Mahwah, New Jersey 07430
www.erlbaum.com

Cover design by Kathryn Houghtaling Lacey

Library of Congress Cataloging-in-Publication Data

Interlanguage pragmatics: exploring institutional talk / edited by Kathleen Bardovi-Harlig,
Beverly S. Hartford.
p. cm.
Includes bibliographical references and index.
ISBN 0-8058-4890-8 (cloth: alk. paper) — 0-8058-4891-6 (pbk. : alk. paper)
1.   Discourse analysis—Social aspects. 2. Conversational analysis. 3. Pragmatics.
4. Interlanguage (Language learning) I. Bardovi-Harlig, Kathleen, 1955- II. Hartford, Beverly S.

P302.84.I584 2004
306.44—dc22

2004053192

Books published by Lawrence Erlbaum Associates are printed on acid-free paper,
and their bindings are chosen for strength and durability.

Printed in the United States of America
10 9 8 7 6 5 4 3 2 1

Contents

113157

Introduction

Kathleen Bardovi-Harlig
Beverly S. Hartford
Indiana University

Discussions of research design in interlanguage pragmatics reveal a tension between the desire for highly controlled production tasks that yield comparable language samples and the desire to integrate the investigation of authentic discourse into studies of interlanguage pragmatics. In spite of the interest the field has expressed in authentic discourse, controlled elicitation tasks still dominate data collection. This book introduces interlanguage pragmatics researchers to institutional talk, talk that occurs in the course of carrying out an institution's business, usually between an institutional representative and a client. The collection and analysis of institutional talk—one form of authentic, consequential discourse—meets the field's methodological requirements of comparability, predictable occurrence of pragmatic features, high rates of occurrence, and relative ease of data collection. Other advantages of exploring institutional talk include the availability of participants for retrospective interviews and of consultants for interpretation. The investigation of institutional talk can be used to study the influence of context, the interaction of pragmatic features, the effect of timing and escalation, the comparison of goals and outcomes, and acquisition of linguistic and pragmatic features. Institutional settings also afford researchers the opportunity to observe the acquisition of institutional rules themselves, which represent a microcosm of culture.

In order to explore these advantages fully, we have assembled previously unpublished studies in this volume that address both interlanguage pragmatics and institutional talk. Taken together, these studies demonstrate the benefits of studying—the context of authentic and consequential talk—the traditional variables of status, directness, social distance, imposition, and others typically investigated in interlanguage pragmatics. Many chapters in this volume introduce new concepts, thus expanding the range of interlanguage pragmatics research beyond what can be investigated in production questionnaires. Additional concepts that are investigated include trust, individual variation across multiple turns and interactions, authority and equality (in balance to dominance and solidarity), and discourse style. The chapters also challenge readers to reconsider the primacy of the dichotomy between native speaker and nonnative speaker. Importantly, these chapters demonstrate that success (and lack of success) is found on both sides of this linguistic divide. We are hopeful that these fine-grained analyses will contribute to a better integration of the nonnative speaker in pragmatics research. The potential for extended analysis of both native and nonnative pragmatics in authentic interaction helps place emphasis on individual pragmatic strategies that are (un)successful which may be more or less prevalent in one speaker group than another. This will lead to a greater sophistication in our description of why native speakers may be more

1

successful, but avoids the pitfall of attributing "pragmatic competence" to native speakers (NS) and "lack of pragmatic competence" to nonnative speakers (NNS).

To this end, the studies reported in this volume are set in a variety of institutions in which both NS and NNS participate as institutional representatives and clients. The range of settings investigated in this volume include a university writing center, a university physics laboratory, a variety of secondary school classrooms, an employment agency, and a four-star conference hotel. The different settings show the importance of locating research in talk that native and nonnative speakers actually perform. Speakers engage in talk in settings that are important to them and studies of situated language observe people engaged in talk in institutions which they frequent. This then eliminates the methodological question of constructing relevant scenarios in elicitation tasks and provides the opportunity to observe actual outcomes.

Cataloguing differences between NS and NNS is ultimately insufficient: We must also understand which differences are important (Kasper, 1997). One way to do this is to study outcomes. The study of consequential talk found in institutions furthers that goal: Native and nonnative differences can be understood in light of what pragmatic strategies seem to contribute to and which seem to impede the interlocutor's success at the institution. Institutional events have outcomes. An advising session may result in a signed registration form, a writing tutorial may result in a better paper, an interview at an employment agency may result in a job referral—or not. Outcomes viewed as endpoints are not the only measure of success, however. There may be characteristics of the encounter itself that indicate a felicitous or infelicitous interaction: how long it takes to negotiate, what follow-up questions are asked during the encounter, and speaker dominance, for example.

Whereas a predetermined research design may set up a dichotomy between native and nonnative speakers, we may find by observing authentic interactions that such a dichotomy is only one variable among many. The NS–NNS speaker division may be less important than shared interests or common background, education, job types, gender, as studied by Kerekes, individual styles, investigated by Yates, or expertise, as discussed by Tarone and Gibbs. Some of these differences in viewing the participants are evident in the descriptors used by the various authors, including the familiar NS–NNS designation, as well as NE (Native English) and L2 Writers used by Williams, and novice and expert members of a discourse community, employed by Tarone and Gibbs. Participants may also be referred to by their roles, such a student and teaching assistant, as in the chapter by Davies and Tyler.

This volume is organized into eight chapters. The first chapter provides an overview of research that has been done in interlanguage pragmatics in the context of institutional talk. This is followed by six chapters that report on studies conducted at institutions and that illustrate a number of advantages to using institutional talk as a source of information informing the acquisition of

L2 pragmatics. The volume ends with a chapter that addresses the practical considerations of conducting research on pragmatics at institutions.

In the first chapter, "Institutional Discourse and Interlanguage Pragmatics Research," we survey research in interlanguage pragmatics that is situated in institutional talk. We argue the main thesis of the book, namely that institutional talk is a rich setting for the investigation of interlanguage pragmatics, and that such work/investigations can easily be accomplished in the framework of interlanguage pragmatics. We review 13 studies that were available at the time of this writing that illustrate the benefits of the approach. We demonstrate that such studies can and do address the typical concerns of interlanguage pragmatic analysis such as the realization of a range of speech acts, while at the same time addressing concerns such as miscommunication, input, communicative success, and conversational strategies.

In her chapter, "Writing Center Interaction: Institutional Discourse and the Role of Peer Tutors," Williams studies 10 writing tutorials that take place between four writing tutors and five students at a university. This design allows each student to be observed in two tutorials with different tutors. Stimulated recall interviews were also conducted. Williams reports that the input to the NE and L2 writers is not always the same. There are both quantitative and qualitative differences. Tutors produce more supportive interruptions of L2 writers, but more advice for NS writers. Directives to nonnative speakers get more upgraders than directives to native speakers. One possible explanation may be the effort on the part of the tutors to facilitate L2 writer comprehension. This may also be a factor in the simpler and more explicit directive forms that the tutors use with these students. Though characteristics of both dominance and solidarity are present in the writing center sessions, the data suggest that both participants willingly take on nonreciprocal roles in their interaction. The balance is toward tutor dominance and authority, as shown through turn length, floor management, and their use of potentially face-threatening speech acts.

In the next chapter, Yates investigates the directives used by 18 teacher trainees doing their practice teaching in secondary schools in Australia. In "Negotiating an Institutional Identity: Individual Differences in NS and NNS Teacher Directives," Yates compares the directives produced by nine Australian background teachers and nine Chinese background teachers each in two full class sessions in a variety of school subjects that include ESL, business, math, music, science, and swimming. Teacher directives are compared by group (Australian and Chinese, male and female) and by individuals. Although, in general, Australians employ a greater variety of mitigators than Chinese background teachers, the production data also shows that the Australian female teacher trainees use more mitigators than the Australian males and that the Chinese background female teachers use more than the Chinese background males. In addition to gender and background, individual differences also play a role. Individuals vary in the way in which they project themselves through language use, in this case, in how they mitigate directives in the social identity of novice teacher. The variation found here is a useful reminder that all speakers of a language, both native and nonnative, are actively engaged in projecting themselves as individuals in relation to cultural norms with such resources as they have at their disposal.

In chapter 4, Kerekes situates her study, "Before, During, and After the Event: Getting the Job (or not) in an Employment Interview," in the office of an employment agency that specializes in placing applicants in temporary employment. Kerekes follows 48 job applicants, 24 NS and 24 NNS, also balanced for gender and type of job they seek, and 4 female middle-class staffing supervisors who conducted the interviews that constitute the primary data of the investigation. Kerekes also conducted background interviews with the staffing supervisors and debriefing interviews with both staffing supervisors and applicants after each employment interview. The outcomes of the interviews show that nonnative speakers have an equal chance of success, which in this case means getting a referral for a job. Kerekes finds that comembership is likely to influence a staffing supervisor's choice of questions to the applicant as well as her more generous interpretations of the applicant's responses. This ultimately leads to the greater likelihood of a placement in cases of high comembership. In this chapter, we see that, whereas clerical candidates have a higher success rate than their light industrial candidates, and female candidates are more successful than their male counterparts, there is no obvious advantage to being either a NS or NNS of English; neither was there an advantage for the NNSs in having a particularly high level of L2 ability. As was recounted by the supervisors in their follow-up interviews with Kerekes, successful encounters were related to sociolinguistic factors such as the ability to demonstrate desirable employee characteristics, which proved equally possible for job candidates with a variety of language backgrounds.

Chapter 5, "Discourse Strategies in the Context of Crosscultural and Institutional Talk: Uncovering Interlanguage Pragmatics in the University Classroom" is set in a university physics lab. In the first part of their study, using an interaction between a Korean teaching assistant and an American undergraduate, Davies and Tyler present an interactive microanalysis of a negotiation about cheating. In the second part, they investigate the possible sociolinguistic factors which might influence the nature of the negotiation. In order to do so, they utilize six Korean and three American judges, all of whom have teaching experience, ranging from one semester to several years. They ask the judges to determine whether or not the exchange would be acceptable or expected in their respective university settings. Both groups seem to have schemas for how a teacher might deal with a student suspected of cheating, but neither group suggested the schema in evidence in the Korean teaching assistant's talk. This leads Davies and Tyler to conclude that L1 influence is not the primary factor in shaping the negotiation. Rather, each crosscultural situation is potentially a new context in the interface between cultural and linguistic systems. They interpret the interaction a complex construction built of L1 pragmatics and of a partial understanding of the target language pragmatics, filtered through his perception of the target culture, and further shaped by resources and constraints of particular institutional contexts.

In her chapter, "English for Specific Purposes and Interlanguage Pragmatics," Tarone outlines work based on genre analysis and introduces readers familiar with the interlanguage pragmatics research to the English for specific purposes (ESP) literature, which is typically overlooked in interlanguage pragmatics. Research on ESP examines ways in which members of particular discourse communities use language varieties (genres) to communicate with one another in their pursuit of common goals. Pragmatic effects are often at the center of ESP research, which stresses the way discourse communities agree to use language. A discourse community is a group of individuals who share a set of common public goals, use mechanisms of intercommunication to provide information, use one or more genres to pursue their goals, use some special lexis, and include members with content and discourse expertise. Fundamental to this approach is the expert–novice distinction among members of a discourse community. Particularly important for the study of the development of pragmatics is that all newcomers or novice participants must learn the rules of the discourse community, regardless of their status as native speakers or nonnative speakers. In fact, a NNS can as easily be an expert in a discourse community as a NS. This would apply, for example, to the novice teachers in Yates' study, learning to become representatives of the institutions, and to the clients in Kerekes' study learning to be successful job applicants. Both groups included NS and NNS participants, all of whom sought to be successful within the relevant discourse community. We can see that the genre analysis challenges us to look beyond the assumption that the native–nonnative divide is the most important one in learning pragmatics in a new setting.

Tara Gibbs illustrates genre analysis in the setting of a four star conference hotel in her chapter, "Using Moves in the Opening Sequence to Identify Callers in Institutional Settings." Gibbs investigates the *call-in*, part of a class of communicative events with the single goal of requesting another department to do something at the hotel. She demonstrates that novice housekeepers who use the structure of a conversational opening are misidentified by other hotel employees, whereas the experts who use the opening moves distinct to the call-in are immediately recognized as housekeepers. That is, the former are not viewed as members of the discourse community, whereas the latter are. Gibbs analyzes the call-ins of one primary novice and one expert with examples drawn from other novices and experts. She compares the call-ins of novices before instruction modeled on the expert call-in to the same novices' call-ins after instruction. Novices show successful outcomes after instruction that involves modeling; that is, they are appropriately identified by the other employees whom they are required to call as part of their job. The use of expert models helps novices become more like the normative members of the discourse community.

In chapter 8, "Practical Considerations," Bardovi-Harlig and Hartford discuss the fundamentals of getting started on a project involving institutional talk. As an adjunct to the material contained in the chapters of this volume, we asked the authors of those chapters and other researchers who have written on institutional talk to share their practical advice and experiences with us. Their insights helped us develop a set of guidelines to conducting research on institutional talk, which we illustrate with their first-hand accounts. These guidelines are intended to help the researcher when setting up a project on institutional research. Some of the guidelines deal with the daily minutiae required to carry out such research successfully; details such as being thorough with checking equipment and locateons, and listening/viewing recordings as soon as they are available. Other guidelines are intended to help the researcher gain access to the institution and carry out the work in such a way as to have things run as smoothly as possible for all concerned. They suggest ways to approach the institution, ways to accommodate the potential participants as well as the institution itself; and they address what still remains to be done after data gathering is complete. Among other things, these latter guidelines contain some simple politeness suggestions, perhaps commonsensical for many. Sometimes, however, researchers forget to practice these niceties as they carry out the project, even though they unconsciously do so in their daily lives. These guidelines serve as reminders.

We hope the reader will find that this volume serves as a handbook for interlanguage pragmatic research utilizing one type of authentic data. Not only does it contain practical suggestions for how to gather the data for such research, the chapters illustrate various ways in which the data might be approached in order to address the research queries of the investigator. Close linguistic analysis of the discourse, consideration of sociolinguistically relevant factors such as gender, status, and L1 background, the relation of various outcomes to the discourse observed, and practical applications of the project are all presented as avenues of investigation expanding the current practice in interlanguage research.

REFERENCE

Kasper, G. (1997). The role of pragmatics in language teacher education. In K. Bardovi-Harlig & B. S. Hartford (Eds.), *Beyond methods: Components of language teacher education* (pp. 113-136). New York: McGraw Hill.

1

Institutional Discourse and Interlanguage Pragmatics Research

Kathleen Bardovi-Harlig
Beverly S. Hartford
Indiana University

Interlanguage pragmatics research investigates the acquisition of pragmatic knowledge in second languages, deriving its research methods from comparative cross-cultural studies and second language acquisition research. Both disciplines place a high value on the control of variables that facilitate comparison across speakers, whether across cultures and languages, between native and nonnative speakers, or among learners at different stages of acquisition. The orientation of these disciplines exerts a strong pull toward experimental data collection procedures. However, the fundamental nature of the very object of study–language use–argues for the study of situated authentic discourse. This tension between the controlled and the authentic has been pointed out in a number of discussions of research methods in interlanguage pragmatics research. As Kasper and Dahl (1991) observe:

> IL pragmaticists are caught between a rock and a hard place. With the exception of highly routinized and standardized speech events, sufficient instances of cross-linguistically and cross-culturally comparable data are difficult to collect through observation of authentic conversation. Conversely, tightly controlled data elicitation techniques might well preclude access to precisely the kinds of conversational and interpersonal phenomena that might shed light on the pragmatics of IL use and development. Clearly there is a need for more authentic data, collected in full context of the speech event. (p. 245)

The identification of the problem and the call for greater use of authentic conversation as data has done little to shift the balance toward the study of authentic talk in interlanguage pragmatics research, however. As we show in the following discussion, tightly controlled elicitation tasks are still the norm.

The problem that we address in this chapter is how interlanguage pragmatics research can retain the highly valued replication and comparability of experiments that have dominated interlanguage pragmatics studies and at the same time meet the expressed desire of incorporating authentic data into the interlanguage pragmatics corpus. The goal of this chapter is to introduce interlanguage pragmatics researchers (and students of interlanguage pragmatics) to institutional talk and to demonstrate that it is a source of authentic discourse that helps fulfill the expressed needs of the field. Institutional talk may be understood as talk between an institutional representative and a client (e.g., a faculty advisor and a graduate student, or an interviewer at a job agency and an applicant) or between members of the same institution (also called workplace talk, such as talk between a nursing supervisor and a nurse, or among hotel or factory employees). We return to a more technical definition in the next section.

We are well aware that some linguists in other areas need no introduction to institutional talk or other forms of conversation. In this chapter we address ourselves specifically to interlanguage pragmatics and interlanguage pragmatics researchers as we adopt and adapt this source of data as our own. We do not intend to provide a comprehensive overview of research on institutional talk, but rather to review recent interlanguage pragmatics studies that have investigated institutional and workplace talk and to demonstrate their contribution to the field of interlanguage pragmatics. In the next section we provide a definition of and introduction to institutional talk, and in the following section provide a brief survey of data collection in interlanguage pragmatics research.

INSTITUTIONAL DISCOURSE

Although there are varying definitions of institutional discourse in the field, we draw upon those offered by Sarangi and Roberts (1999) and Drew and Heritage (1992). Sometimes referred to as workplace talk or institutional interaction, interaction, these authors agree, "is institutional insofar as participants' institutional or professional identities are somehow made relevant to the work activities in which they are engaged" (Drew & Heritage, 1992, pp. 3–4). For our purposes this includes two main categories: interactions between institutional representatives and clients, and interactions between members of the institution.

A few of the former contexts, referred to as *frontstage* by Sarangi and Roberts (1999, p. 20) in which institutional discourse has been studied include settings such as business, as in employment interviews (Akinnaso & Ajirotutu, 1982; Gumperz, 1982a); legal, especially court testimonies (Conley & OBarr, 1990; Gumperz, 1982b; Philips, 1990); educational, including school counseling sessions of students (Erickson & Schultz, 1982; He, 1994) and teacher–student discourse (Mehan, 1994); and medical, including interviews between doctors and patients (Fisher & Todd, 1983; Labov & Fanshel, 1977; Tannen & Wallat, 1993).[1]

The second category, interaction that takes place among workers of the institutions rather than between client and institutional representative (*backstage* for Sarangi & Roberts, 1999, p. 20), has been less widely studied. However, some work can be cited: ODonnell (1990) discusses the interaction in disputes between labor and management; Linde (1988) examines pilot and air traffic controller discourse; Erickson (1999) discusses physician–apprentice discourse; and Cook-Gumperz and Messerman (1999) study professional collaboration.

---

[1] Drew and Heritage (1992) covers a wide range of these settings, as does Sarangi and Roberts (1999).

Institutional discourse differs from ordinary conversations in three primary ways: goal orientation, constraints, and frameworks (Levinson, 1992). Drew and Heritage (1992, p. 22) summarize these facets of institutional discourse as follows:

1. Institutional interaction involves an orientation by at least one of the participants to some core goal, task or identity (or set of them) conventionally associated with the institution in question. In short, institutional talk is normally informed by *goal orientations* of a relatively restricted conventional form.
2. Institutional interaction may often involve *special and particular* constraints on what one or both of the participants will treat as allowable contributions to the business at hand.
3. Institutional talk may be associated with *inferential frameworks* and procedures that are particular to specific institutional contexts.

These three characteristics are those which make institutional discourse suitable data for interlanguage pragmatics research: They contribute to the comparability of multiple interactions. Whereas conversations do not tend to have such constraints and are therefore not so easily comparable, institutional interactions often include expected norms of interaction such as turn-taking, constant social relations/roles, and asymmetrical power relationships.[2] Sarangi and Roberts (1999) also list as additional constraints on institutional talk the following: "decision-making and problem-solving; the production and regula-tion of professional knowledge and activities concerned with professional credibility, role relationships around issues of identity and authority" (p. 11).

TYPES OF DATA IN INTERLANGUAGE PRAGMATICS RESEARCH

Interlanguage pragmatics research has been slow—and even reluctant—to embrace conversational or other authentic data, as an inventory of the data collection methods used in published volumes of interlanguage pragmatics research shows. The survey of methods in use in interlanguage pragmatics done by Kasper and Dahl in 1991 shows that out of 34 production studies, reporting 35 data collection procedures, only 2 (6%) used authentic data, 19 (54%) used discourse completion tasks (DCTs), and 14 (40%) used role plays. In *Interlanguage Pragmatics* (Kasper & Blum-Kulka, 1993), seven chapters report data collection. One uses a role play and five use some type of DCT (4 DCTs and one written dialogue construction). One uses authentic dinner table conversations (Blum-Kulka & Sheffer, 1993). In *Speech Acts across Cultures: Challenges to Communication in a Second Language* (Gass & Neu, 1996), 11 chapters report 13 data collection techniques. No chapters report spontaneous

---

[2] Although most of this work investigates face-to-face oral discourse, there is some work on written institutional discourse, particularly on business writing (Moran & Moran, 1985; Yli-Jokipii 1991).

conversation: One study collected TV commercials (Schmidt, Shimura, Wang, & Jeong, 1996), and one used talk generated in the course of a puzzle-solving task performed by dyads (Geis & Harlow, 1996). The remaining 11 used controlled elicitation tasks: Five used DCTs (3 written, 2 oral), 4 used role plays, and 2 used retrospective interviews to collect reports of speech acts. A monograph entitled *Interlanguage Refusals* (Gass & Houck, 1999), reports on role plays in which participants play themselves (EFL students visiting the United States and staying with host families) faced with a number of undesirable offers, invitations, or suggestions.

Although many readers will be familiar with the elicitation tasks used in interlanguage pragmatics, we will briefly review the major types here. Production questionnaires are the most commonly used elicitation task in interlanguage pragmatics. In fact, Rose (2000, p. 111) characterizes the dominance of production questionnaires as reflecting the field's "overwhelming reliance on one method of data collection." Production questionnaires include any of a variety of questionnaires that elicits speech act production data (Johnston, Kasper, & Ross, 1994, 1998; Rose, 1997). Among production questionnaires, the most common type is the DCT. DCTs, often described as written role plays, present a description of a situation (called a scenario) and ask the participant to respond. There are at least two types of DCTs: open questionnaires in which no turns are provided, and dialogue completion tasks in which an initiating turn or a rejoinder is provided (Kasper, 1991). Production questionnaires have developed to include oral as well as written DCTs (Murphy & Neu, 1996; Yuan, 1998), computer-interactive DCTs where the computer gives and takes up to three turns (Kuha, 1997), the cartoon oral production task (COPT) designed for younger L2 learners (Rose, 2000), and dialogue writing (Bergman & Kasper, 1993).

Two types of role plays are distinguished in the literature: closed and open role plays (Gass & Houck, 1999; Kasper & Dahl, 1991). Closed role plays are more commonly known as oral DCTs; in these a respondent replies to a scenario provided by the researcher on tape. Such oral DCTs do not offer the opportunity to study interaction. Open role plays (or simply, role plays) describe a scenario provided by the researcher which two or more participants act out. The outcome of the interaction is often unspecified so that participants have some flexibility in their contributions.

In contrast to responses to production questionnaires and role play scenarios, authentic discourse takes place without the instigation of a researcher. We note that authentic discourse may be either oral or written, and either monologic, dyadic, or multipartied. Conversational data constitutes the most familiar form of authentic discourse and the one most generally referred to in discussions of data collection in interlanguage pragmatics research. In this chapter we focus on oral dyadic exchanges that are the intended target of most interlanguage pragmatics research, but include one example of interactional e-mail institutional discourse that has been investigated in interlanguage pragmatics (Hartford & Bardovi-Harlig, 1996a).

The major data collection techniques have received numerous assessments in the literature (e.g., Cohen, 1996; Cohen & Olshtain, 1994; Gass & Houck, 1999; Houck & Gass, 1996; Kasper & Dahl, 1991; Rose, 1997; Wolfson, 1989). We draw on these discussions to compare the resulting language samples by three main features: comparability, interactivity, and consequentiality. These three features reflect the articulated values of the field (Bardovi-Harlig, 1996; Gass & Houck, 1999; Kasper & Dahl, 1991, among others). *Comparability* assures that language samples can be reasonably compared. Comparability is seen to be the result of *control* in the collection of production data (cf. Kasper & Dahl, 1991). *Interactivity* characterizes language samples in which speakers have the opportunity to take turns. *Consequentiality* refers to the fact that there is a real world outcome, or *consequence*, to naturally occurring talk, which often extends beyond the verbal exchange to establish itself in order to accomplish goals (Drew & Heritage, 1992; Sarangi & Roberts, 1999).

In Table 1.1 we use these three features to characterize the data yielded by the major collection techniques (i.e., production questionnaires, role plays, conversations, and institutional talk). We use the conventional notation of indicating that a feature is present or absent, (e.g., [+/- comparable]), although we note that this is a shorthand because these features likely represent continua rather than binary categories. Production questionnaires, by virtue of the fact that they are highly controlled tasks, yield language samples of high comparability. However, as widely noted, they are neither interactive, nor consequential. Role plays retain the experimental control of production questionnaires, resulting in comparable language samples, and they have the additional advantage of being interactive. Kasper and Dahl (1991) observe that open role plays "represent oral production, full operation of the turn-taking mechanism, impromptu planning decisions contingent on interlocutor input, and hence negotiation of global and local goals, including negotiation of meaning" (p. 228). On the other hand, role play talk is not consequential; Gass and Houck (1999, p. 29) report, "Role plays are just that, role plays, with few, if any, real or real life consequences." Aston (1993, p. 229) also notes that "it is difficult for this technique to reproduce the interpersonal context of naturally occurring talk."

An additional type of interactive language sample that is collected by experimental techniques is the simulated task as shown in the second column of Table 1.1. In simulated tasks speakers are brought together by researchers in an experimental setting and asked to complete a task such as puzzle solving (Geis & Harlow, 1996) or teaching a computer program (Woken & Swales, 1989) for the purpose of observing their talk in methods other than role play. Although simulated tasks are rarely used in interlanguage pragmatics—of the volumes reviewed, the sole representative is the puzzle-solving task used by Geis and Harlow (1996)—they are familiar in studies of NS–NNS conversation (e.g., Gass & Varonis, 1985; Selinker & Douglas, 1985; Woken & Swales, 1989; Zuengler, 1989). Like role enactments used by Gass and Houck (1999), but unlike some role plays, simulated tasks have the advantage that participants

Table 1.1. Analysis of Language Samples by Source

Production questionnaires	Role plays simulated tasks	Conversation	Institutional talk
+ comparable	+ comparable	- comparable	+ comparable
- interactive	+ interactive	+ interactive	+ interactive
- consequential	- consequential	+ consequential	+ consequential

speak as themselves rather than assuming a hypothetical role. Nevertheless, simulated tasks are generally undertaken by speakers with no social connection, in contrast to spontaneous conversations in which the speakers have some social link to their interlocutors.[3] Finally, like role plays, simulated tasks lack consequences beyond the task itself.

Moving to the third column of Table 1.1, conversation is characterized as both interactive and consequential. Whereas role plays have few consequences, every conversation has socioaffective consequences. In real-world conversations speakers negotiate face, they take turns, and they attend to aspects such as topic and key (Hymes, 1964) in the process of being cooperative speakers (Grice, 1975). Deviations from the accepted norms can result in changed evaluations by the participants of each other, or in the need to reinterpret contributions. These may be long-lasting consequences or fleeting; no matter which, participants in conversations are invested and therefore affected by any interaction. Such consequences have been frequently reported in the literature: Socioaffective consequences were documented by Beebe and Cummings (1985, 1996) in their corpus on refusals in telephone calls. In 1985, TESOL was held in New York and the local organizing committee called local members to volunteer. However, TESOL had been scheduled during Passover, a major Jewish holiday and many TESOL members declined to volunteer during the holiday. As Beebe and Cummings observed, "It is extremely unlikely that a hypothetical situation could evoke such strong emotion as the actual scheduling of TESOL during Passover in 1985" (1996, p. 79). A second example of socioaffective consequence is found in research on conversational openings and closings. Research on conversational openings reports that when speakers engage in these openings, they (re-) establish their relationship with their interlocutors, reveal information about the state of the relationship, establish status relations, and ascertain whether an interaction will be friendly or not (Irvine, 1974). Closings on the other hand, not only serve to organize the termination of a conversation, but they also reinforce relationships and support future interactions as they anticipate lack of access to each other after the closing (Button, 1987; Goffman, 1971; Hartford & Bardovi-

---

[3] Note that the lack of social connection between speakers in simulated tasks provides a counterpoint to Aston's (1993) observation that real-world relationships between actors in role plays who are assigned other roles "might constitute an additional, and unplanned, influence on the role play" (p. 229). The generalization that we draw from these two observations is that relationships that are invented or imposed on participants add another layer of complexity to the interpretation of talk that is not present when authentic relationships are in play.

Harlig, 1992; Omar, 1992; Schegloff & Sacks, 1973). Such work on relationships cannot be observed in simulated tasks.

The advantages of studying conversation for interlanguage pragmatics research derive from the fact that conversation is a natural occurrence, as noted above: It is spontaneous authentic language use by speakers who are speaking as themselves, in genuine situations, with socioaffective consequences. In addition, conversations exhibit a variety of speech acts and attributes in a single encounter and constitute a rich source of data. From the interlanguage pragmatics perspective, however, conversational data is seen as being insufficient from the standpoint of comparability of the language sample. Except for the most routine and superficial exchanges, conversational samples are not viewed as being comparable and role plays are seen as more desirable for interlanguage pragmatics research with respect to that feature: "Role plays have the advantage over authentic conversation in that they are replicable" (Kasper & Dahl, 1991, p. 229). In fact, many reviews of interlanguage pragmatics research design do not include conversation and only compare experimental methods. Furthermore, it is generally accepted that observation does not yield enough tokens of a particular attribute to constitute a reasonably sized language sample (Wolfson, 1986, 1989).

Thus far in the literature, there has been a perceived trade-off between comparability and consequence. However, as the last column of Table 1.1 shows, there is at least one type of talk which is authentic and consequential, and at the same time can be compared to many other samples taken from the same setting: institutional talk.

The goal-oriented nature of institutional talk allows for comparison across speakers in the same way that experimental interactions allow researchers to compare speakers (e.g., Selinker & Douglas, 1988; Woken & Swales, 1989; Zuengler, 1989). Comparison is facilitated because similar conversations recur both with the same participants (the institutional representatives) and with different participants (the clients), in similar settings, and on similar topics. Furthermore, as Agar (1985) and Erickson and Schulz (1982) have noted, many institutional encounters have very similar structures, which are quite different from informal, spontaneous conversations. Within one type of interaction, similar time frames are maintained: For example, writing tutorials last about an hour; advising sessions are scheduled in 15-minute intervals. Clients and institutional representatives may draw on their shared knowledge of the structure and goals of institutional events to assure success, as Cameron and Williams (1997) show in interviews between a NNS nurse and her NS patients. The institutional setting makes it possible to control for some of the variables that are troublesome when working with spontaneous events, and makes it possible to compare results.

An example regarding comparability of institutional encounters is found in the closings of advising sessions studied by Hartford and Bardovi-Harlig (1992). Nonnative speakers sometimes had difficulty closing the conversations. Since all sessions had a similar structure and known time frame (about 15 minutes), this shared information about the session might serve as background knowledge, which all participants could utilize and assume of each other. Additionally, because faculty advisors participated in multiple sessions, they served as constants: It was possible to examine how they interacted in both successful and less successful closings with both native speakers and nonnative speakers. Native speaker students could be compared to the nonnative speaker students in order to determine what the similarities and differences were across subjects and speech events, and thus discover how the unsuccessful closings differed from the successful ones. Kasper and Dahl (1991) observed that the advising sessions yielded authentic language samples that could be compared with each other "as NSs and NNSs interacted with the same interlocutors and in the same status relationship, comparability of the data was ensured" (p. 231).[4]

In the following section we demonstrate the benefits of using institutional talk for interlanguage pragmatics research.

INSTITUTIONAL TALK AS A SOURCE OF AUTHENTIC DISCOURSE FOR INTERLANGUAGE PRAGMATICS RESEARCH

In this section we discuss the advantages of utilizing institutional talk as a source of spontaneous discourse in interlanguage pragmatics research. In the last 10 years there have been a small but significant number of studies that have examined interlanguage pragmatics through institutional talk and that illustrate its benefits as a tool for the study of interlanguage pragmatics. Data collected from institutional talk offer a good balance of authenticity and consequence on the one hand and potentially large data sets resulting from predictable occurrences and control of variables on the other. Table 1.2 summarizes interlanguage pragmatics studies of institutional talk that takes place between an institutional representative and a client.[5] Table 1.3 summarizes the smaller set of interlanguage pragmatics studies that investigate talk between institutional members. One study appears on both tables: Cameron and Williams (1997) report on a nurse in training who is a nonnative speaker of English interviewing two patients in a hospital psychiatric unit (institutional talk) and talking to her nursing supervisor (workplace talk).

As Tables 1.2 and 1.3 show, authentic discourse may be studied from multiple perspectives and a variety of analytic frameworks. To date, the theoretical framework that has dominated interlanguage pragmatics has been speech act analysis, and thus it is also a common—but not the exclusive—method of analysis of institutional talk. Perhaps the most important point we can make here is that interactive data are not restricted to any one type of analysis, including

---

[4] They also note, however, that the advising sessions might be "confronting the limits of cross-cultural comparability" (p. 231) because institutions and hence the talk might be culture specific. We return to this point later in the chapter.

[5] In Table 1.2 we include only studies that investigate discourse directly. Studies based on interviews in which learners and their interlocutors report on speech behaviors in institutional settings, such as Li (2000), have not been included.

speech acts. Although this argument is beyond the scope of this chapter, it could be that once researchers see the richness of authentic discourse and possibilities for investigation, the dominance of the speech act model might naturally lessen.[6]

Methodological Considerations:
Institutional Talk as a Natural Experiment

The advantages of studying authentic discourse are often sacrificed because of the perceived difficulty of data collection. Unpredictability of occurrence, lack of control of variables (Beebe, 1994; Beebe & Cummings, 1996), and paucity of sufficient features in a sample (Wolfson, 1986) are often cited as methodological problems of studying authentic data. In addition, advantages of experimental data (to the exclusion of authentic data) have included the availability of retrospective interviews (Cohen, 1996; Cohen & Olshtain, 1994). In this section we begin by investigating these methodological points in order to argue that institutional talk yields authentic language samples that can inform interlanguage pragmatics research. In the following sections we move on to the additional characteristics of language use and development that can be studied in such data.

Institutional talk usually takes place in relatively fixed locations within the institution, and this aids in data collection. For example, advising sessions occur in the advisors' offices, writing tutorials occur at the writing center, and psychiatric interviews take place at the hospital. Because institutional talk takes place in predictable locations and often at predictable times through the scheduling of appointments or the hours of operation, offices and other settings can be prepared for data collection before the speech event. In the larger settings of the workplace, Clyne (1994) identified areas within factories that were sites of predictable talk and were relatively quiet enough for recording. We should also note that there are some types of institutional encounters which change location, but which could still be investigated. Sarangi and Roberts (1999, p. 5) point out that workplaces may vary, and in some cases the institutional representative may go to the client, as do, for example, nurses who deliver homecare. In this case, the actual physical setting will vary, but still, the essential psychological setting does not, and so the nature of this discourse is much the same, that is, institutional.

Moreover, in addition to the sites of occurrence of the institutional talk itself, the nature of institutional talk is such that discourse topics and attributes of talk can be anticipated in advance of the data collection. Because of the goal-oriented nature of institutional discourse, specific speech acts can be anticipated in the course of the speech event. Thonus' (1999) data on writing tutorials

---

[6] Readers who are interested in analyses other than or in addition to the speech act framework should note Cameron and Williams, 1997; Gass and Houck, 1999; Hartford and Bardovi-Harlig, 1992; Kerekes, 2003; Tarone and Kuehn, 2000, Tyler, 1995, and Tyler and Davies, 1990, and many chapters in this volume.

Table 1.2. ILP Studies of Institutional Discourse

Study	Focus	Institutional representative	Client	Institutional setting
Bardovi-Harlig & Hartford (1990, 1993a)	Suggestions and Rejections (refusals)	NS	NS and NNS graduate students	Academic advising sessions
Tyler & Davies (1990)	Communication missteps	NNS teaching assistant	NS undergraduate student	Physics lab
Hartford & Bardovi-Harlig (1992)	Closings	NS	NS and NNS graduate students	Academic advising sessions
Ellis (1992)	Requests	NS teachers	2 child learners of ESL	Classroom discourse
Tyler (1995)	Miscommunication	1 NNS international teaching assistant	NS student	Tutoring session
Bardovi-Harlig & Hartford (1996)	Input	NS	NS and NNS graduate students	Academic advising sessions
Hartford & Bardovi-Harlig (1996a)	Requests	2 NS faculty members	NS and NNS students	E-mail messages to faculty
Cameron & Williams (1997)	Communicative success	1 NNS nurse	2 NS patients	Hospital psychiatric unit
Thonus (1998, 1999)	Directives	NS writing tutors	NS and NNS undergraduates	Writing tutorials
Churchill (1999)	Requests	NS and NNS teachers	Learners of EFL in partial-immersion	Academic setting
Kerekes (2001)	Linguistic behaviors and conversational strategies	4 NS staffing supervisors	48 applicants 22 NS, 22NNS, 4 bilinguals	Employment interview
Yates (2000)	Directives (mitigation)	9 NNS and 9 NS student teachers	Students	Classroom teaching

Table 1.3. ILP Studies of Workplace Discourse

Study	Focus	Institutional employee	Workplace interlocutor	Institutional setting
Clyne (1994) Main corpus, 150 hours. Secondary corpus, 32 hours (meetings)	Speech acts (complaints/ whinges, directives, commissives, apologies), turn-taking, small talk	37 NNS employees in supervisorial, equal, and subordinate positions. Secondary corpus combined w/primary, 39 NNS	NNS employees in supervisorial, equal, and subordinate positions. Secondary corpus, NS and NNS interlocutors at meetings	Main corpus, Nipponcar, Amcar, Weaver, Elektro, Catering. Secondary corpus, Weavers, Employment Office, Parents Group
Cameron & Williams (1997)	Communicative success	1 NNS nurse	Nurse's clinical supervisor	Hospital psychiatric unit

included problem statements by the students and suggestions by the tutors. Students make requests that help them complete their assignments in the course of being students, whether they be elementary school-aged children (Ellis, 1992) or teenagers in high school (Churchill, 1999). Another such example is the occurrence of directives in the talk of student-teachers addressed to secondary school pupils (Yates, 2000).

Participants in an institution can generally be identified, and this allows researchers to describe speakers according to the variables relevant to a given study. The institutional speaker is generally known to the researcher, and information about the institutional client can be ascertained. Moreover, the roles of the participants are institutionally proscribed and the relationships are generally fixed. In her study of writing tutorials, Thonus (1998) balanced the institutional representatives by selecting 12 tutors from among the 20 employed at the Writing Tutorial Services, including six tutors who met with students whose paper topic was the same as their area of expertise and six tutors who met with students whose paper topic was not. She further balanced the client-participants so that seven of the tutorials took place between students and tutors who had met with each other before, and five tutorials took place with participants who had not yet met their tutors. In this way, Thonus was able to compare the tutorials for familiarity with topic on the one hand and familiarity between the participants on the other. Only tutorials for which students presented drafts of their papers were selected for inclusion in the study, which somewhat restricted the stage of the writing process at which the student sought assistance, thus further assuring the similarity of the tutorial sessions. This illustrates one way institutional roles and attributes can be used to balance participants in a study.

The concentration of occurrences of talk particular to given institutions leads naturally to a corpus with a substantial number of tokens for analysis. For example, Yates' (2000) study of student-teachers yielded 2,973 directives (1,527 from 9 Anglo-Australian teachers in 13 hours, 18 minutes of classroom recordings, and 1,446 from 9 Chinese background NNS teachers in 12 hours and 18 minutes of recording). Thonus' (1998) study of 12 writing tutorials yielded 441 directives addressed to NS students and 343 to NNS students. The size of the corpora—as realized by number of tokens of the targeted speech act— allowed both Thonus and Yates to establish pragmatic profiles for each of the individual participants. Understanding differences among speakers rather than reporting group data is a necessary step to understanding acceptable usage and variation in the target language by both native speakers and nonnative speakers.

Two longitudinal studies of the use of requests in a school setting also resulted in good-sized corpora. Ellis (1992) recorded 410 requests made by two children, and Churchill (1999) reported 184 requests of 37 participants. It is worth noting that even within the institutional setting, certain individuals may not produce the target speech acts, even if the majority of the participants do, and this, too, is revealing. Churchill reported that only 27 of the 37 participants in his study produced requests. The nonproduction of requests by 10 learners reveals a type of contextualized opting out not available in experimental tasks and perhaps not obvious in conversations where comparability among conversations is hard to establish.

Cohen (1996) and Cohen and Olshtain (1993, 1994) advocate the use of retrospective interviews to provide insight into production and perception in the area of L2 pragmatics. Retrospective interviews constitute one type of external evidence on which analysts may draw (Tyler & Davies, 1990) and have been used successfully in the study of institutional talk (Erickson & Shultz, 1982, for native speakers; for work in interlanguage pragmatics, Clyne, 1994; Kerekes, 2001, 2003; Thonus, 1998; Tyler, 1995; Tyler & Davies, 1990) as well as in experimental studies (e.g., Cohen & Olshtain, 1993).

In the tutoring session investigated by Tyler (1995), retrospective interviews with both participants reveal insights into the motivation behind several turns in which the student and tutor each intended to establish expertise regarding the basic knowledge that underpins the assignment under discussion. The student had to write a computer program that could score a bowling game. When the student asked "Do you know how to score the game?" and the tutor answered "Yeah approximately", we learn from the student that she interpreted that to mean that the tutor was not fully knowledgeable about scoring procedures. We learn from the tutor that he believes he has given an unequivocal statement of expertise. In order to remain modest he added a tag "approximately." He asserted that any Korean would understand that his response meant, "Yes, I know how to score bowling." The interpretation of this turn proved to be absolutely crucial to the tutoring session, and the session never fully recovers from the misinterpretation by both parties.

Related to retrospective interviews of the participants is the use of nonparticipant consultants to interpret the data of others. An additional benefit of the institutional setting is the potential availability of consultants to interpret the data of others. This may prove to be extremely valuable in areas in which the analysts do not have subject expertise or institutional membership. (See Selinker & Douglas, 1989 and Douglas & Selinker, 1994, on the use of the subject-specialist informant in their work on discourse domains.)

The judgments or interpretations of consultants provide a second type of external evidence for an analyst. Tyler and Davies (1990) studied a conversation between a Korean teaching assistant and an American undergraduate involving a negotiation over poor grades. Tyler and Davies enlisted the help of American undergraduates and two Korean graduate students to interpret the conversation between the teaching assistant and the undergraduate. Both sets of consultants provided insightful comments on both the structure and the content of the interaction. The American undergraduate consultants' responses confirmed the researchers' own expectations for the structure of a negative evaluative exchange (i.e., why the student had earned a low grade): They expected the teaching assistant's first turn to provide a general overview of the problem or refer to the most important error. In contrast, the Korean graduate-student consultants felt that the strategy used by the Korean teaching assistant, beginning the explanation of the poor grade by referring to the more minor errors and building to the main one (called the "inductive/collaborative strategy," p. 401), is less threatening and more face-saving than the strategy expected by the Americans. However, the Korean teaching assistant's strategy led many American undergraduate consultants to conclude that the teaching assistant did not really know why he had given the poor grade he had. In contrast, in his retrospective interview, the teaching assistant reported that he knew that the student was upset and had wanted to soften the effect of his statement concerning the student's failure. The American consultants rejected the sympathetic interpretation.

A second study to use consultants was a study of requests which were made of faculty by students via e-mail (Hartford & Bardovi-Harlig, 1996a).[7] The requests were presented to faculty consultants who rated the degree of imposition of the content of each request. There was a high degree of agreement on the level of imposition among the faculty. The use of such consultants helped confirm the validity of the analysis. In a follow-up to the study the same questionnaire about level of imposition was administered to domestic and international (NS–NNS) graduate students in the same department as the faculty. The results of the graduate student survey revealed that the students did not seem to have the same perception as faculty concerning the imposition of the requests, particularly for some of the high imposition categories. Requests that students assumed were simply a part of the faculty member's job were generally seen as low imposition, even if they required extra time and effort on the part of the faculty member. Using such students in a consultancy role helped to explain some of the lack of politeness markers in e-mail requests: Often they were lacking just where the faculty and the students perceived the imposition differently.

As we have shown, the investigation of institutional talk addresses many of the methodological issues that researchers have raised and discussed in the interlanguage pragmatics literature. However, the fact that studying institutional talk offers the advantage of studying comparable and authentic discourse is only part of what the study of institutional talk offers interlanguage pragmatics research. The study of institutional talk opens the possibilities of studying more features of language, language use, and language acquisition than have generally been considered in interlanguage pragmatics previously.

What We Can Learn From Institutional Talk

In this section we discuss how the study of institutional talk leads to an enriched understanding of interlanguage pragmatics. We examine five main areas: understanding language in context, interaction of multiple features, timing and escalation, understanding goals and outcomes of talk, and acquisition of pragmatics and the institutional rules themselves.

---

[7] We realize e-mail is not oral like the other studies discussed. However, it is interactional and natural. We include it here in order to discuss the use of consultants.

Understanding Language in Context. Understanding the role of context is crucial to understanding language use and development. In controlled elicitation tasks such as production questionnaires and role plays, context translates into developing credible and culturally appropriate scenarios to which speaker-writers respond (Rose & Ono, 1995). However, many scenarios seem to present a rather simplified context and the attempts to deliver subtle differences in the details in a verbal description often meet with respondent fatigue, inattention, or insufficient language proficiency (Bardovi-Harlig, 1999a). Attempts to overcome the limits of verbal delivery include the use of drawings (Rose, 2000), photographs (Rodriquez, 2001), and film (Bardovi-Harlig & Dörnyei, 1998; Leary, 1994; Rose, 1997). Native speakers seem to need less fully specified scenarios than do nonnative speakers who are often not as familiar with certain settings and rely more heavily on details of the scenarios (Bardovi-Harlig & Hartford, 1993b). Regardless of the scenario delivery however, individual scenarios (i.e., contexts) continue to emerge in study after study as an important variable (Bergman & Kasper, 1993). No matter how carefully a scenario is presented to respondents in an experimental task, context will remain an underexplored variable because analysts can never be sure that respondents recognize the setting presented to them. Instead, the study of authentic discourse captures speakers as they engage in meaningful interactions. The results of recent studies suggest that speakers, and especially learners, who have not experienced interactions in settings presented in experimental tasks (such as attending school in the host environment, living in a dorm, or going to cafes), are more likely to guess at a response rather than to produce one based on other experience which might be relevant (Garton, 2000; Rodriguez, 2001). In authentic interaction, conversational as well as institutional, speakers are observed in settings in which they have opted to interact. Although some institutional interactants may be more familiar with the institution than others, the fact of the matter is that, in an authentic institutional interaction, it is necessary that they participate and achieve some outcome. Thus, even if they are not fully versed in the norms of that particular institution's interactions, outcomes are arrived at through negotiation and feedback, which may in turn contribute to the acquisition of those norms by the participants.

The range of institutional settings provides a broad context for the investigation of institutional talk. Moreover, any single setting can provide a rich background for investigation. Medical interviews, for example, occur whenever patients come to medical establishments seeking health-related care. Such interviews may be between doctors and patients or between nurses or receptionists and patients. In addition, talk between institutional members is common in this setting: talk between doctors and nurses, between nurses and supervisors, and between nurses, to name only a few interactions. Cameron and Williams (1997) studied the interactions between an NNS nurse and her supervisor (talk between institutional members), which occurs naturally in a supervisory setting, and interactions between the nurse and two patients (talk between an institutional representative and her clients). Other general contexts for institutional talk that have been studied in interlanguage pragmatics include writing tutorials, employment interviews, and social service interviews (Tables 1.2 and 1.3). Like the scenarios developed for controlled elicitation tasks, the contexts within an institution may shift subtly to allow for the investigation of variables. In addition to the most obvious variables in interlanguage pragmatics studies—the differences between native and nonnative speaker, and differences in L2 proficiency (not to mention the commonly investigated factors of age and status)—the influence of context-based variables can be compared. For example, Kerekes (2001, 2003) examines the difference in talk and resolution of mis-communication when interviewers regard job candidates as being trustworthy and when they do not. Thonus (1998, 2002) explores the characteristics of writing tutorial sessions that tutors and students rated as successful and those that they rated as unsuccessful.

A second type of context that is offered by the study of institutional talk is found in the talk itself. The contextualization of turns at talk is not available in data from production questionnaires. Sequential contributions and negotiations can be observed in role plays but these are not located in a larger authentic context. Taking a speech act perspective as an example, the definable contexts allow us to understand how speech acts are realized, how they are elaborated and negotiated, and how and why they eventually reach a resolution between the speakers. One promising area of investigation is the difference in speech addressed to native- and nonnative-speaker clients by institutional represent-tatives (Tarone & Kuehn, 2000). Tarone and Kuehn observe that financial workers may word questions differently with native speakers than with language learners, thus changing the interaction locally at the level of the turn for the language learner. Although they point out that they could not follow that line of investigation because different financial workers interviewed the native speakers and the language learner, this is an important point of comparison that could even be addressed by analyzing the pivotal turns of institutional representatives in existing larger corpora (e.g., Bardovi-Harlig & Hartford, 1993a; Thonus, 1998, 1999).

We make no claim that these contexts are simple; in fact, they can be quite complex. On the other hand, institutional contexts are identifiable, and in spite of their complexity, they are describable. More importantly for interlanguage pragmatics research, these contexts are replicable within an institution resulting in a background against which it is possible to study other variables such as age, gender, education, native language, language proficiency, and severity of the problem presented to the institution by the client or to the client by the institution.

Multiple Pragmatic Features and Their Interrelations.   Like conversations, institutional talk also exhibits a number of structures in any one encounter. In medical settings, for example, institutional representatives ask questions, give directions, and make diagnoses. Clients may also ask questions, and in addition they are responsible for answering questions and acknowledging directions. The corpus of talk from academic advising sessions alone has been a rich source of data for the investigation of many aspects of discourse including the construction of student identity (Bardovi-Harlig & Hartford, 1993c), conversational structure and closings (Hartford & Bardovi-Harlig, 1992), and numerous speech acts that have included suggestions (Bardovi-Harlig & Hartford, 1990, 1993a), refusals (Bardovi-Harlig & Hartford, 1991, 1993a), and requests for advice (Bardovi-Harlig & Hartford, 1990). Similarly, in a single conversation between institutional members, Clyne (1994) identifies complaints, apologies, directives, and commissives.

In addition, a complete, multifaceted interaction allows researchers to understand particular exchanges in light of subsequent ones. For example, online interpretations can be readjusted if information that occurs later in a conversation demands it. In the advising interviews, Bardovi-Harlig and Hartford (1993a) showed that there were times when the advisor had understood student responses to advice on course schedules to be agreements at the time that they were negotiated; however, later in the interviews the students indicated that they had not actually agreed to those suggestions, but were only giving what they believed were polite backchannels, and so schedule renegotiations had to take place. Thus, occurrences of multiple features within any single institutional interaction not only provide a potentially rich source of data, but may also provide a view of the participants' interpretations of the interaction.

Timing and Escalation. There are often multiple occurrences of the same features within a single encounter of institutional talk. This facilitates the study of both the features and the effect of timing. For example, the talk of student-teachers not only contained directives to students (predictably), it also contained multiple directives addressing the same issue (Yates, 2000). Thus, the institutional sample yields important information on escalation resulting from repeated requests. Yates found that in the classroom, the simple imperative is the unmarked form of a routine directive. In a series of directives given to a class which was waiting outside a room at the beginning of a lesson, a teacher said, "So come in quietly. Quietly/ Year seven." As they got more unruly, with loud talking and jostling, the teacher switched to a more polite, more deferential form, increasing the distance between herself and her students saying, "Excuse me Year seven/ could you go back outside and line up please" (p. 134). Yates's data also show how a series of requests can escalate over a class period (in contrast to directives issued in direct succession as in the previous example), moving from two uses of an unmarked imperative (" R/ go on with your work" and "S/ turn around"), to a warning ("If you don't stay X and do your work/ I'm going to have to send you out the back to talk to Mr. X, /alright?/ and do your work out there"), to the discipline phase delivered with a question ability strategy and a requestive politeness marker please, "R and S/ can both of you please take your book/ and go and speak to Mr. X in the back room" (p. 134).

Goals and Outcomes. Hymes (1964) distinguishes between goals and outcomes in interactive language speech events. These are particularly relevant for institutional language. In such speech events, there may be conventional goals and conventionally expected outcomes. For example, in a consultation in a doctor's office, the conventional goal and expected outcome for both participants is diagnosis of the patient. A further expectation, or goal, on the part of the patient participant is generally advice from the physician regarding treatment. However, such expectations are not always met. It may be the case that the physician cannot offer treatment advice, or even that the advice is contrary to what the patient expects. In this case, the goals of the patient may not be met, although there is certainly an outcome to the speech event. Thus goals and outcomes may not always be the same, or may differ for each participant. There is then, in institutional talk, usually some real world, expected, tangible gain to at least one of the participants, seen as the purpose of the conversation itself. In the institutional encounters studied in the interlanguage pragmatics literature, goals have included receiving a signed registration form in an advising session, help with a writing assignment in a writing tutorial, a placement in a job interview, financial assistance in a social service interview, or a psychiatric assessment in a psychiatric evaluation.

Comparing goals to outcomes affords one independent measure of success of the interaction. Goals are often stated by clients during the course of the institutional speech event and outcomes are generally observable. Tyler (1995) reports on participant goals in a tutoring session in which the student had voluntarily sought out the tutor for help on a major computer programming assignment in order to increase her chances of success. Tyler reports that the student "genuinely needs to successfully complete the assignment" (p. 139). The tutor, an international graduate student in Computer and Information Science, was enrolled in an advanced, elective English oral skills course. Graduate students enrolled in the course offered free tutoring to U.S. undergraduates as part of the course. The graduate student tutor knew that all tutoring sessions were videotaped and reviewed with the students by the professor. The tutor also desired to do his best, be evaluated favorably by the instructor, and improve his English skills. The outcome was quite different, however. Both participants found the session so unsatisfactory that each complained to the supervisor about the other.

Another feature of institutional talk is that the outcomes are often recorded in written form. This is so common that Agar (1985) identified report writing as the third and final stage of the institutional interview. There were many examples of written documentation in the studies reviewed here. The advisors in the academic interviews (Bardovi-Harlig & Hartford, 1990, 1993a) entered the agreed-upon classes on a registration ticket and in the student's departmental file. The interviewers for the temporary job agency filled in an action document that recorded the interviewers decision on whether the job candidate should be hired (Kerekes, 2003). In the writing tutorial, the tutor filled in both an assignment sheet and a session evaluation (Thonus, 1998). In the psychiatric interview, the nurse took notes to which she later referred in meeting with her supervisor (Cameron & Williams, 1997). In the case of the tutoring session described earlier, an oral report in the form of a complaint was registered by both of the participants (Tyler, 1995). The existence of such documentation provides an additional external record of the outcome of the encounter—at least as far as the institutional representative understood it.[8]

Observing institutional outcomes may be one way to begin to understand what pragmatic features are particularly significant in particular types of interactions. Kasper (1997, 1998) discusses the importance of determining whether divergence from the pragmatic norm is problematic or not, where *problematic* may include miscommunication as well as resultant negative social perceptions. As Kasper (1998) notes, "pragmatic divergence itself is not problematic if the social values indexed are acceptable or perhaps even valued by the recipient" (p. 198). Regarding the outcome of the tutoring session between the Korean tutor and the undergraduate (Tyler, 1995), the interaction and negotiation of face were so unsatisfactory that both participants complained about the other to the tutor supervisor. In contrast, Cameron and Williams (1997) report that the outcome of the consultations between the nurse and her supervisor were more satisfactory because of their mutual cooperation: The nurse and her supervisor drew on professional knowledge and goals to assure successful communication in spite of the limited linguistic competence of the NNS nurse. In studies of multiple speakers, mixed outcomes were reported. Student and tutor participants evaluated the success of the sessions (Thonus, 1998), and in employment interviews NNS showed equal or better rates of being hired than native speaker applicants (Kerekes, 2001).

The Study of Acquisition. Interlanguage pragmatics has been defined as the intersection of the study of pragmatics and the study of second language acquisition (Kasper, 1998). The study of institutional talk allows researchers the opportunity to study contextualized linguistic and pragmatic development on the one hand and the acquisition of institutional rules on the other. Neither area has been fully explored within interlanguage pragmatics or studies of institutional talk, but both are promising areas of investigation.

One area of investigation is the acquisition of second-language pragmatic and linguistic features. As research interlanguage pragmatics increases its emphasis on acquisition, it will be necessary to involve learners at different levels of proficiency (Bardovi-Harlig, 1999a, 1999b; Kasper & Schmidt, 1996: Rose, 2000). Thus far, interlanguage pragmatics has concentrated on advanced level learners due at least in part to the fact that many of the controlled tasks favor higher proficiency learners. Whereas special tasks can be developed for lower level learners (see Rose, 2000 for an example), such a practice is not yet

---

[8] Two of the studies (Kerekes, 2003; Tarone & Kuehn, 2000) examined encounters with another type of written record, the application. The applications are filled out by the job or social service applicants prior to the encounter and feature prominently throughout the interview.

in place. Because second language learners of all levels of proficiency interact with institutions both as clients and as institutional members, the study of institutional talk expands the study of language use to include lower proficiency speakers both as clients or members of institutions. Academic settings are particularly good sources for learners at various levels of grammatical and pragmatic proficiency, as illustrated by Ellis's (1992) longitudinal study of classroom requests and by Bardovi-Harlig and Hartford's cross-sectional study of learner talk during advising sessions in an academic intensive ESL program (Bardovi-Harlig & Hartford, 1997; Hartford & Bardovi-Harlig, 1996b). Churchill's (1999) longitudinal study of institutionally situated requests is noteworthy because it does not take place in the host environment, but rather in an EFL setting, in a partial immersion high school in Japan in which English is used outside of class. Whereas academic settings often include language learners ranging from relatively low proficiency to higher proficiency, interactions outside academic settings are by no means limited to higher proficiency learners, as can be seen in the case of both clients (Tarone & Kuehn, 2000) and institutional representatives (Cameron & Williams, 1997).

An additional type of development that can be observed in the institutional setting is the learning of the institutional rules and the type of talk, or genre (Tarone & Kuehn, 2000), that is associated with the institution. Kasper and Dahl note that the advising sessions might be "confronting the limits of cross-cultural comparability" (1991, p. 231) because the practice of academic advising and hence the talk associated with it might be culture specific. To the extent that institutions have no equal in other cultures, this creates a natural laboratory in which the acquisition studies of interlanguage pragmatics can observe how L2 speakers learn new cultural-institutional rules in addition to learning the language that goes with them. Moreover, nonnative speakers are not alone in having to learn institutional rules and institutional talk. Erickson and Schultz (1982) observed that academic counselors taught the interview to native-speaker students during the sessions themselves. (See also Tarone, chapter 6, this volume.) Bardovi-Harlig and Hartford (1993a, 1996), Tarone and Kuehn (2000), and Li (2000) observe the fact that new participants must learn the rules of the institution. Tarone and Kuehn distinguish between novice and expert clients. The social service interviews studied by Tarone and Kuehn, like the advising sessions studied by Bardovi-Harlig and Hartford, are normally private and thus "the only way for a novice to become an expert is by participating in an interview" (Tarone & Kuehn, 2000, p. 100). The fact that institutional talk has to be learned by all clients—native speakers and nonnative speakers alike—affords us the opportunity to observe the learning processes of native speakers as well as those of nonnative speakers in institutions where both are clients and/or members. This includes settings such as graduate students enrolled in a particular graduate program (Bardovi-Harlig & Hartford, 1990, 1993a, 1996; Hartford & Bardovi-Harlig, 1992, 1996a), social service applicants (Tarone & Kuehn, 2000), and job applicants at temporary staffing agencies (Kerekes, 2001, 2003). For example, Tarone and Kuehn show that even native-speaker applicants must learn that the interviewer does not want to hear the story of why an applicant is applying for assistance; instead, the interviewer needs to have other information to make the determination of eligibility. In this example from Tarone and Kuehn (2000, p. 112), the interviewer cuts off the applicant's explanation of why he is applying for assistance and moves to the next stage of the intake interview, the explanation of an applicant's rights and responsibilities.

(1) Social services interview

> Applicant: Right, I've been having a problem trying to get it, and so-
> Interviewer: OK. We'll go over your rights and responsibilities

Examples of such teaching are found throughout the reports on institutional talk. In the exchange between the teacher and the student reported by Churchill (1999, p. 16), the teacher indicates that he expects a student to say something when turning in an assignment, and the student responds by constructing a request with the help of her friend.

(2) Mariko attempts to hand in her homework assignment to her teacher

> Teacher: What? You have nothing to say?
> Mariko: Could (looks at Yukiko)
> Teacher: Could you...
> Mariko: Could you check my homework.

Advisors in academic advising interviews also provide opportunities for graduate students to take an appropriate turn by providing competency slots. Advisors open the core of the advising session (the "directive" phase, Agar, 1985) with questions that indicate to the student-participants that they are expected to have suggestions ready; and through these questions, the students may learn that they should perform such a speech act in this context, as in the following examples from Bardovi-Harlig & Hartford (1996, p. 175):

(3) Competency slots

> a. Now, what do you want to take in the fall?
> b. Okay....so you looked through the list of courses, so you pretty much know what you want to take?
> c. Do you have some idea of what you would want to take?

At the same time, students are given specific opportunities by the advisor to display their competence as graduate students through institutional talk. An advisor may also express his approval of turns taken by a student as the advisor did in Example (4) (Bardovi-Harlig & Hartford, 1996, p. 176). This may also serve to indicate to the student that he or she is learning the rules of the genre.

(4)   Explicit acknowledgment of the rules of the genre

> Advisor: I wish I had people come in with, that knew what, that knew what they wanted to do, like you. That helps me.

These exchanges are examples of the input available to institutional participants to help them learn the rules of institutional talk. Transcriptions of employment interviews and the accompanying retrospective interviews that reveal unresolved miscommunication stemming from either lack of knowledge or conflicting beliefs about employment interviews (Kerekes, 2001, 2003), suggest that some types of institutional talk, or some institutional representatives, might be less likely to assist novices in learning the genre. We do not yet know what type of input is particularly effective or how learners (i.e., novice clients or members, whether language learners or not) might interpret certain rules for their own purposes (for example, Tarone & Kuehn, 2000, report that even experienced applicants try to tell the reasons for their application), but the study of novices engaged in institutional talk will lead to answers of these important questions and perhaps to important insights regarding learning and input more generally.

Institutional talk provides a microcosm of culture, and observing novice participants as they become experts allows researchers to observe how institutional talk and institutional rules are taught and learned. Because institutions form closed and definable systems (or relatively more easily definable systems compared to the whole of culture) and are culture specific, researching the learning of institutional rules through institutional talk breaks the study of cultural rule learning into manageable proportions.

ADDITIONAL CONSIDERATIONS

Generalizability

The features that ensure a high level of comparability are also those features that might restrict a broader interpretation of studies of institutional talk to other discourses. In institutional talk, as we have shown, participants have fixed roles and fixed goals, and while this promotes comparability across interactions, findings may not apply to other settings. In institutional talk participants generally have a single institutional status within an individual encounter, and even within a series of encounters. For example, the advisor is always of higher institutional status than the student within the academic advising session. In addition, Ellis (1992) and Churchill (1999) note that students talk to a limited range of addressees, namely the teacher and other classmates. Participants have generally fixed roles, as determined by the nature of the institutional context itself: For example, within a single psychiatric interview, the nurse does the assessment, and the patient responds to her questions; within the social services interview, the financial worker asks questions to verify the financial status of the applicant and the applicant supplies the information. We do not generally have the opportunity to observe the interviewers switch roles and become the respondent, as we might in casual conversations. However, following a single institutional participant through multiple types of interaction balances the data for the effect of fixed roles in a single type of interaction. For example, Cameron and Williams's (1997) study of talk in a hospital psychiatric unit shows one speaker in two institutional roles each with a different status. The main speaker, an NNS nurse, is the institutional representative and higher status speaker when she interviews her NS patients, and is a nurse-trainee of lower status when she discusses her case load with the nursing supervisor. Clyne's (1994) corpus of talk among institutional members includes key participants talking to both supervisors and peers. Thus, as the work by Clyne (1994) and Cameron and Williams (1997) shows, solutions to some of the limitations in design can be found in the institutional setting itself.

There is no doubt that institutional talk is different from casual conversation in many ways, as outlined earlier. In casual conversations, establishing comity, or friendly relations, is key (Ashton, 1993). Therefore, what we learn from the study of institutional talk should only be applied with great caution to conversation more generally. At the same time, however, observations of institutional talk could serve to generate research hypotheses that can be tested against casual conversation in interlanguage pragmatics research.

Discourse within individual institutions may be generalizable within the institutions themselves. It is important to note that the study of institutional talk for its own sake in interlanguage pragmatics is not trivial. Institutional encounters occur fairly frequently in the lives of people and should not be regarded as rare or unusual types of speech events. The number of nonnative speakers at institutions in the anglophone world is significant and growing. At our research university alone, in the 2002-2003 academic year, there were more than 3,320, or 8.5% international students, and the expectation is that that number will grow to one student in ten in coming years. The number of international students at several major research universities in California and New York exceeded 4,500, eclipsing the 10% figure (Opendoors, 2001). The number of international students studying in the United States during the same period was 514,723 (Opendoors, 2001). This is not an incidental population. With increasing numbers of nonnative speakers engaged in institutions in the areas of education, health care, social services, and the workplace, institutional talk becomes a significant area of investigation in its own right. Although the number of international students in the United States and other anglophone countries is significant, it does not even begin to approach the number of immigrants in these (and other) countries who most certainly will have numerous institutional encounters.

Finally, although it may seem that institutional discourse represents only a very narrow set of linguistic and pragmatic activities in which native and nonnative speakers might engage, in fact, many of the activities may be representative of a more general type of discourse, such as seeking help and solving problems, so that the practice of such activities could be carried beyond these settings by language learners (as well as native speakers).

Ethical Issues

The last methodological consideration is also an ethical one. Most research institutions require that the researchers obtain approval from the appropriate committee to conduct research with human subjects. In addition, the institutions which are the objects of research may also have some concerns. Often the talk which is targeted for research is regarded as "private" or in some other way to be protected from public view. For the researcher, in practical terms, this means getting consent from all of the participants, some of whom will be bound by certain institutional concerns. Furthermore, as Sarangi and Roberts (1999, pp. 41–42) point out, there is concern among researchers about whether or not such research should have tangible benefits for the people being studied. This includes the questions of how research findings should be disseminated: Is the audience other academics and research communities, with no access available for the institutional participants?[9] It seems to us that in the field of applied linguistics, these concerns of application and dissemination may be less trouble-some than for "pure" researchers. That is, one of the purposes of applied linguistics dissemination is to educate language teachers about the discourses of such institutions, where, in turn, they will educate their learners who are potential participants, both as clients and workers. (See, for example, Li, 2000; Tarone & Kuehn, 2000). It is less obvious, perhaps, how the institutions will directly benefit, and here it would be up to the researcher to make that clear to the institution in question.

Although such concerns must be taken into consideration by the investiga-tors, we should note that it is possible to conduct such research in hospital or medical settings, even though concerns for privacy might seem especially relevant and perhaps major obstacles. The study by Cameron and Williams (1997), for example, was a result of the second author participating in a language needs analysis for nonnative speaking graduate nursing students, so that the application, or benefit, "preceded" the later analysis (p. 423). In a footnote, however, these authors discuss a number of the problems related to research on institutional discourse and medical discourse, in particular (pp. 439-440, fn 5). These difficulties include real-world concerns such as opening the institution to legal actions such as being sued, the possibility of the institution withdrawing support at any time, limited access to follow-up interviews with participants, and numerous other considerations. Tarone and Kuehn (2000) also discuss the issues of privacy in the social service interview. In contrast, studies by Bardovi-Harlig and Hartford (1990, 1993a), Bouton (1995), Churchill (1999), Thonus (1998, 1999), Tyler (1995) and Tyler & Davies (1990), while

---

[9] By "access" we mean that the academic field may employ a discourse that is so particular to the field that nonprofessionals are not able to easily engage it.

maintaining the anonymity of their informants, point to the advantage of securing permission to study discourse at one's own institution.

Nevertheless, institutions and the people who make up institutions often do agree to be studied, and in a remarkable array of settings. In addition to the settings described in Tables 1.2 and 1.3, other institutional settings include those cited earlier this chapter, some of which can be found in other chapters of this book. Any serious researcher can approach an institution. It need not be only researchers with years of experience. Among the studies listed in Tables 1.2 and 1.3, a number were carried out by doctoral candidates for their doctoral theses. We discuss in some detail the practical considerations of conducting institutional research in the final chapter of this volume.

CONCLUSION

In this chapter we have addressed a primary concern in research on interlanguage pragmatics: the pull between replicable, comparable data and authentic, situated data. We have argued that one promising avenue of compromise, institutional discourse, yields data that are both comparable and authentic, and which meet the three primary requirements of comparability, interactivity, and consequentiality. Institutional discourse is comparable because institutional speech events contain similar attributes within institutions and sometimes across them: They tend to have similar time-frames, similar structuring, similar topical selection, and similar participant roles. They are interactive because they include at least two participants who exchange talk for the institutional purposes for which they meet. Finally, they are consequential because they are situated in authentic situations and have goals and outcomes of concern to all the interactants.

We have also demonstrated that institutional discourse may be utilized in interlanguage pragmatics research not only for the investigation of a single aspect of pragmatics, speech acts, but for other aspects as well, including conversational structuring, turn contributions, placement and timing of contributions, and politeness strategies.

Institutional discourse can be utilized to investigate the acquisition of interlanguage pragmatics as well as instances of usage. We have shown that often both native and nonnative speakers have to learn such discourses, and argue that this is an excellent opportunity for the researcher to compare acquisitional strategies across native and nonnative speakers.

Institutional discourse can also be investigated for its own sake within interlanguage pragmatics because of the number of nonnative speakers who may be involved in such events. We have argued that the information gained from the analysis of institutional discourse has practical application. It is a type of discourse that almost all second language learners will have to engage in in the real world at some point in their learning histories. Pedagogical usages can be developed which will be meaningful to the learners' lives. Although not all learners will encounter all institutional events, there are some which may be seen as occurring and recurring for them and for which they can acquire some expertise.

Finally, although the investigation of institutional talk is not a substitute for the examination of casual conversation which interlanguage pragmatics studies will eventually need to undertake, it can lead to fruitful investigation on a number of planes for interlanguage pragmatics research. Furthermore, it will help bring interlanguage pragmatics research in line with work already being carried out by other discourse analysts. Clearly, the amount of research focusing on the discourse of institutional talk which is done from frameworks other than interlanguage pragmatics suggests that it is an important and promising area for such research. There is every reason to believe that the same holds true for interlanguage pragmatics research.

REFERENCES

Akinnaso, F. N., &. Ajirotutun, C. (1982). Performance and ethnic style in job interviews. In J. Gumperz (Ed.), *Language and social identity* (pp. 145-62). Cambridge, England: Cambridge University Press.

Agar, M. (1985). Institutional discourse. *Text, 5*, 147-168.

Aston, G. (1993). Notes on interlanguage comity. In G. Kasper & S. Blum-Kulka (Eds.), *Interlanguage pragmatics* (pp. 224-250). Oxford, England: Oxford University Press.

Bardovi-Harlig, K. (1999a). Researching method. In L. F. Bouton (Ed.), *Pragmatics and language learning* (Vol. 9, pp. 237-264). University of Illinois, Urbana-Champaign: Division of English as an International Language.

Bardovi-Harlig, K. (1999b.) The interlanguage of interlanguage pragmatics: A research agenda for acquisitional pragmatics. *Language Learning, 49*, 677-713.

Bardovi-Harlig, K. (1996). Pragmatics and language teaching: Bringing pragmatics and pedagogy together. In L. F. Bouton (Ed.), *Pragmatics and language learning* (Vol. 7, pp. 21-39). University of Illinois, Urbana-Champaign: Division of English as an International Language.

Bardovi-Harlig, K., & Dörnyei, Z. (1998). Do language learners recognize pragmatic violations? Pragmatic vs. grammatical awareness in instructed L2 learning. *TESOL Quarterly, 32*, 233-259.

Bardovi-Harlig, K., & Hartford, B. S. (1990). Congruence in native and nonnative conversations: Status balance in the academic advising session. *Language Learning, 40*, 467-501.

Bardovi-Harlig, K., & Hartford, B. S. (1991). Saying "No": Native and nonnative rejections in English. In L. F. Bouton & Y. Kachru (Eds.), *Pragmatics and language learning* (Vol. 2, pp. 41-57). University of Illinois, Urbana-Champaign: Division of English as an International Language.

Bardovi-Harlig, K., & Hartford, B. S. (1993a). Learning the rules of academic talk: A longitudinal study of pragmatic development. *Studies in Second Language Acquisition, 15*, 279-304.

Bardovi-Harlig, K., & Hartford, B. S. (1993b). Refining the DCT: Comparing open questionnaires and dialogue completion tasks. In L. F. Bouton & Y. Kachru (Eds.), *Pragmatics and language learning* (Vol. 4, pp. 143-165). University of Illinois, Urbana-Champaign: Division of English as an International Language.

Bardovi-Harlig, K., & Hartford, B. S. (1993c). The language of comembership. *Research on Language and Social Interaction, 26*, 227-257.

Bardovi-Harlig, K., & Hartford, B. S. (1996). Input in an institutional setting. *Studies in Second Language Acquisition, 18*, 171-188.

Bardovi-Harlig, K., & Hartford, B. S. (1997, April). *Academic Advising Sessions with Students in an Intensive English Program.* Paper presented at the Eleventh International Conference on Pragmatics and Language Learning, Urbana, IL.

Beebe, L. (1994, March). *Notebook data on power and the power of notebook data.* Paper presented at the Twenty-eighth Annual TESOL Conference, Baltimore, MD.

Beebe, L., & Cummings, M. C. (1985). *Speech act performance: A function of the data collection procedure?* Paper presented at the Nineteenth Annual TESOL Conference, New York, NY.

Beebe, L., & Cummings, M. C. (1996). Natural speech act data versus written questionnaire data: How data collection method affects speech act performance. In S. M. Gass & J. Neu (Eds.), *Speech acts across cultures: Challenges to communication in a second language* (pp. 65-86). Berlin: de Gruyter.

Bergman, M. L., & Kasper, G. (1993). Perception and performance in native and nonnative apology. In G. Kasper & S. Blum-Kulka (Eds.), *Interlanguage pragmatics* (pp. 82-107). Oxford, England: Oxford University Press.

Blum-Kulka, S., & Sheffer, H. (1993). The metapragmatic discourse of American-Israeli families at dinner. In G. Kasper & S. Blum-Kulka (Eds.), *Interlanguage pragmatics* (pp. 196-223). Oxford, England: Oxford University Press.

Bouton, L. F. (1995). A cross-cultural analysis of the structure and content of letters of reference. *Studies in Second Language Acquisition, 17,* 211-244.

Button, G. (1987). Moving out of closings. In G. Button & J. R. E. Lee (Eds.), *Talk and social organization* (pp. 101-151). Clevedon, England: Multilingual Matters.

Cameron, R., & Williams, J. (1997). Senténce to tén cents: A case study of relevance and communicative success in nonnative–native speaker interaction in a medical setting. *Applied Linguistics, 18,* 415-445.

Churchill, E. F. (1999, October). *Pragmatic development in L2 request strategies by lower level learners.* Paper presented at the Second Language Research Forum, Minneapolis, MN.

Clyne, M. (1994). *Inter-cultural communication at work: Cultural values in discourse.* Cambridge, England: Cambridge University Press.

Cohen, A. D. (1996). Speech acts. In S. L. McKay & N. H. Hornberger (Eds.), *Sociolinguistics and language teaching* (pp.383-420). Cambridge, England: Cambridge University Press.

Cohen, A. D., & Olshtain, E. (1993). The production of speech acts by EFL learners. *TESOL Quarterly, 27,* 33-56.

Cohen, A. D., & Olshtain, E. (1994). Researching the production of second language speech acts. In E. E. Tarone, S. M. Gass, & A. D. Cohen (Eds.), *Research methodology in second-language acquisition* (pp. 143-156). Hillsdale, NJ: Lawrence Erlbaum Associates.

Conley, J., & OBarr, W. (1990). *Rules versus relationships: The ethnography of legal discourse.* Chicago: University of Chicago Press.

Cook-Gumperz, J., & Messerman, L. (1999). Local identities and institutional practices: constructing the record of professional collaboration. In S. Sarangi & C. Roberts (Eds.), *Talk, work and institutional order: Discourse in medical, mediation and management settings* (pp. 145-182). Berlin: de Gruyter.

Douglas, D., & Selinker, L. (1994). Research methodology in context-based second-language research. In E. E. Tarone, S. M. Gass, & A. D. Cohen (Eds.), *Research methodology in second-language acquisition* (pp. 119-131). Hillsdale, NJ: Lawrence Erlbaum Associates.

Drew, P., & Heritage, J. (1992). (Eds.) *Talk at work.* Cambridge, England: Cambridge University Press.

Ellis, R. (1992). Learning to communicate in the classroom: A study of two learners requests. *Studies in Second Language Acquisition, 14,* 1-23.

Erickson, F. (1999). Appropriation of voice and presentation of self as a fellow physician: Aspects of a discourse of apprenticeship in medicine. In S. Sarangi & C. Roberts (Eds.), *Talk, work and institutional order: Discourse in medical, mediation and management settings* (pp. 109-144). Berlin: de Gruyter.

Erickson, F., & Shultz, J. (1982). *The counselor as gatekeeper.* New York: Academic Press.

Fisher, S., & Todd, A. (Eds.). (1983). *The social organization of doctor–patient communication.* Norwood, N.J.: Ablex.

Garton, M. (2000). *The effect of age, gender, and degree of imposition on the production of native speaker and nonnative speaker requests in Hungarian.* Unpublished doctoral thesis, Indiana University, Bloomington, Indiana.

Gass, S. M., & Neu, J. (1996). (Eds.). *Speech Acts across cultures: Challenges to Communication in a Second Language.* Berlin: de Gruyter

Gass, S. M., & Houck, N. (1999). *Interlanguage Refusals.* Berlin: de Gruyter

Gass, S. M. & Varonis, E. M. (1985).Variation in native speaker speech modification to nonnative speakers. *Studies in Second Language Acquisition, 7,* 37-57.

Geis, M. L., & Harlow, L. L. (1996). Politeness strategies in French and English. In S. M. Gass & J. Neu (Eds.), *Speech acts across cultures: Challenges to communication in a second language* (pp. 129-153). Berlin: de Gruyter.

Goffman, E. (1971). *Relations in public.* New York: Basic Books.

Grice, H. P. (1975). Logic and conversation. In P. Cole & J. Morgan (Eds.), *Speech acts* (Syntax and Semantics, Vol. 3, pp. 41-58). New York: Academic Press.

Gumperz, J. (1982a). Fact and inference in courtroom testimony. In J. Gumperz (Ed.), *Language and social identity* (pp. 163-194). Cambridge, England: Cambridge University Press.

Gumperz, J. (1982b). *Language and social identity.* Cambridge, England: Cambridge University Press.

Hartford, B. S., & Bardovi-Harlig, K. (1992). Closing the conversation: Evidence from the academic advising session. *Discourse Processes, 15,* 93-116.

Hartford, B. S., & Bardovi-Harlig, K. (1996a). "At your earliest convenience": Written student requests to faculty. In L. F. Bouton (Ed.), *Pragmatics and language learning,* (Vol. 7, pp. 55-69). University of Illinois, Urbana-Champaign: Division of English as an International Language.

Hartford, B. S., & Bardovi-Harlig, K. (1996b, August). *Cross-sectional study of the acquisition of speech acts by non-native learners of English: The use of natural data in an intensive English program.* Paper presented at AILA, Finland.

He, A. W. (1994). Withholding academic advice: Institutional context and discourse practice. *Discourse Processes, 18,* 297-316.

Houck, N., & Gass, S. (1996). Non-native refusals: A methodological perspective. In S. M. Gass & J. Neu (Eds.), *Speech acts across cultures: Challenge to communication in a second language* (pp. 45-64). Berlin: de Gruyter.

Hymes, D. (1964). Models of interaction of language and social life. In D. Hymes & J. Gumperz (Eds.), *Directions in Sociolinguistics: The Ethnography of Communication* (pp. 35-71). New York: Holt, Rinehart, and Winston.

Irvine, J. (1974). Strategies of status manipulation in Wolof greetings. In R. Bauman & J. Scherzer (Eds.), *Explorations in the ethnography of speaking* (pp. 167-191). Cambridge, England: Cambridge University Press.

Johnston, B., Kasper, G., & Ross, S. (1994). Effect of rejoinders in production questionnaires. *University of Hawaii Working Papers in ESL, 13,* 121-143.

Johnston, B., Kasper, G., & Ross, S. (1998). Effect of rejoinders in production questionnaires. *Applied Linguistics, 19,* 157-182.

Kasper, G. (1991, October). *(More on) Methods of data collection in interlanguage pragmatics.* Paper presented at the Conference on Theory Construction and Methodology in Second Language Acquisition Research. East Lansing, MI.

Kasper, G. (1997). The role of pragmatics in language teacher education. In K. Bardovi-Harlig & B. S. Hartford, (Eds.), *Beyond Methods: Components of language teacher education* (pp. 113-136). New York: McGraw Hill.

Kasper, G. (1998). Interlanguage pragmatics. In H. Byrnes (Ed.), *Learning foreign and second language: Perspectives in research and scholarship* (pp. 183-208). New York: The Modern Language Association.

Kasper, G., & Blum-Kulka, S. (1993). (Eds.). *Interlanguage pragmatics.* Oxford, England: Oxford University Press.

Kasper, G., & Dahl, M. (1991). Research methods in interlanguage pragmatics. *Studies in Second Language Acquisition, 13,* 215-247.

Kasper, G., & Schmidt, R. (1996). Developmental issues in interlanguage pragmatics. *Studies in Second Language Acquisition, 18,* 149-169.

Kerekes, J. (2001) *The co-construction of a successful gatekeeping encounter: Strategies of linguistically diverse speakers.* Unpublished doctoral thesis, Stanford University, Stanford, California.

Kerekes, J. (2003). Distrust: A determining factor in the outcomes of gatekeeping encounters. In S. Ross (Ed.), *Misunderstanding in spoken discourse* (pp. 227-257). London: Longman/Pearson.

Kress, G., & Fowler, R. (1979). Interviews. In R. Fowler, B. Hodge, G. Kress, & T. Trew (Eds.), *Language and control* (pp. 63-80). London: Routledge and Kegan Paul.

Kuha, M. (1997). The computer-assisted Interactive DCT: A study in pragmatics research methodology. In L. Bouton (Ed.) *Pragmatics and language learning, Monograph* 8 (pp. 99-127). University of Illinois, Urbana-Champaign: Division of English as an International Language.

Labov, W., & Fanshel, D. (1977). *Therapeutic Discourse.* New York: Academic Press.

Leary, A. (1994). *Conversational replicas on computer for intermediate-level Russian: A Theoretical Model of a Design Paradigm.* Unpublished masters thesis, University of Iowa, Iowa City.

Levinson, S. (1992). Activity types and language. In P. Drew., & J. Heritage. (Eds.), *Talk at work* (pp. 66-100). Cambridge, England: Cambridge University Press.

Li, D. (2000). The pragmatics of making requests in the L2 workplace: A case study of language socialization. *Canadian Modern Language Review, 57,* 58-87.

Linde, C. (1988). The quantitative study of communicative success: Politeness and accidents in aviation discourse. *Language in Society, 17,* 375-400.

Mehan, H. (1994). The role of discourse in learning, schooling, and reform. In B. McLeod (Ed.), *Language and learning: Educating linguistically diverse students* (pp. 71-94). Albany, NY: State University of New York Press.

Moran, M. H., & Moran, M. G. (1985). Business letters, memoranda, and résumés. In M.G. Moran & C. Journet (Eds.) *Research in technical communication* (pp. 313-52). Westport, CT: Greenwood Press.

Murphy, B., & Neu, J. (1996). My grade's too low: The speech act set of complaining. In S. M. Gass & J. Neu (Eds.), *Speech acts across cultures: Challenges to communication in a second language* (pp. 191-216). Berlin: de Gruyter

ODonell, K. (1990). Difference and dominance: How labor and management talk conflict. In A. Grimshaw (Ed.), *Conflict talk* (pp. 210-40), Cambridge, England: Cambridge University Press.

Omar, A. S. (1992). *Opening and closing conversations in Kiswahili: A study of the performance of native speakers and learners.* Unpublished doctoral thesis, Indiana University, Bloomington, Indiana.

Phillips, S. (1990). The judge as third party in American trial-court conflict talk. In A. Grimshaw (Ed.), *Conflict talk* (pp. 197-209), Cambridge, England: Cambridge University Press.

Rodriquez, S. (2001). *The perception of requests in Spanish by instructed learners of Spanish in the second- and foreign-language contexts: A longitudinal study of acquisitional patterns.* Unpublished doctoral thesis, Indiana University, Bloomington, Indiana.

Rose, K. (1997). Film in interlanguage pragmatics research. *Perspectives* (Working Papers of the Department of English, City University of Hong Kong), *9,* 111-144.

Rose, K. (2000). An exploratory cross-sectional study of interlanguage pragmatic development. *Studies in Second Language Acquisition, 22,* 27-67.

Rose, K., & Ono, R. (1995). Eliciting speech act data in Japanese: The effect of questionnaire type. *Language Learning, 45,* 191-223

Sarangi, S., & Roberts, C. (Eds.). (1999). *Talk, work and institutional order: Discourse in medical, mediation and management settings.* Berlin: de Gruyter.

Schegloff, E. A., & Sacks, H. (1973). Opening up closings. *Semiotica, VIII,* 289-327.

Schmidt, R., Shimura, A., Wang, Z., & Jeong, H. (1996). Suggestions to buy: Television commercials from the U.S., Japan, China, and Korea. In S. M. Gass & J. Neu (Eds.), *Speech acts across cultures: Challenges to communication in a second language* (pp. 285-316). Berlin: de Gruyter

Selinker, L., & Douglas, D. (1985). Wrestling with 'context' in interlanguage theory. *Applied Linguistics, 6,* 75-86.

Selinker, L., & Douglas, D. (1988). Using discourse domains in creating interlanguage: Context, theory, and research methodology. In J. Klegraf & D. Nehls (Eds.), *Essays on the English language and applied linguistics on the occasion of Gerhard Nickels 60th birthday* (pp. 357-379). Heidelberg: Julius Groos.

Selinker, L., & Douglas, D. (1989). Research methodology in context-based second-language research. *Second Language Research, 5,* 93-126.

Tannen, D. (1986). *Conversational style: Analyzing talk among friends.* Norwood, NJ: Ablex.

Tannen, D., & Wallat, C. (1993). Interactive frames and knowledge schemas in interaction: Examples from a medical examination/interview. In D. Tannen (Ed.), *Framing in discourse* (pp. 57-78). Oxford, England: Oxford University Press.

Tarone, E., & Kuehn, K. (2000). Negotiating the social service oral intake interview: Communicative needs of nonnative speakers of English. *TESOL Quarterly, 34,* 99-126.

Thonus, T. (1998). *What makes a writing center tutorial successful: An analysis of linguistic variables and social context.* Unpublished doctoral thesis, Indiana University, Bloomington, Indiana.

Thonus, T. (1999). How to communicate politely and be a tutor, too: NS–NNS interaction and writing center practice. *Text, 19,* 253-279.

Thonus, T. (2002). Tutor and student assessments of academic writing materials: What is "success?" *Assessing Writing, 8,* 110-134.

Tyler, A. (1995). The coconstruction of cross-cultural miscommunication: Conflicts in perception, negotiation and enactment of participant role and status. *Studies in Second Language Acquisition, 17,* 129-152.

Tyler, A., & Davies, C. (1990). Cross-linguistics communication missteps. *Text, 10,* 385-411.

Woken, M. D., & Swales, J. M. (1989). Expertise and authority in native-nonnative conversations: The need for a variable account. In S. Gass, C. Madden, D. Preston, & L. Selinker (Eds.), *Variation in second language acquisition* (Discourse and Pragmatics, Vol. 1, pp. 211-222). Clevedon, England: Multilingual Matters.

Wolfson, N. (1986). Research methodology and the question of validity. *TESOL Quarterly, 20,* 689-699.

Wolfson, N. (1989). *Perspectives: Sociolinguistics and TESOL.* Cambridge, MA: Newbury House.

Yates, L. (2000, July). *"Ciao, Guys!": Mitigation addressing positive and negative face concerns in the directives of native-speaker and Chinese background speakers of Australian English.* Unpublished doctoral thesis, LaTrobe University, Bundoora, Victoria, Australia.

Yli-Jokipii, H. (1991). Running against time and technology: Problems in empirical research into written business communication. In K. Sajavaara, D. March, & T. Keto (Eds.), *Communication and discourse across cultures* (pp. 59-72). Jyväskylä, Finland: Kopi-Jyvä Oy.

Yuan, Y. (1998). *Sociolinguistic dimensions of the compliment speech event in the southwest Mandarin dialect spoken in Kunming, China.* Unpublished doctoral thesis, Indiana University, Bloomington, Indiana.

Zuengler, J. (1989). Performance variation in NS–NNS interactions: Ethnolinguistic difference, or discourse domain? In S. Gass, C. Madden, D. Preston, & L. Selinker (Eds.), *Variation in second language acquisition* (Discourse and Pragmatics, Vol. 1, pp. 228-244). Clevedon, England: Multilingual Matters.

2

Writing Center Interaction: Institutional Discourse and the Role of Peer Tutors

Jessica Williams
University of Illinois

There are many different interactional settings in a university, including large, teacher-fronted classes, seminars, advising sessions, and student–teacher conferences, and new students must learn the pragmatic rules for each of these settings. They will interact with fellow students, teaching assistants, tutors, professors, and administrators, and with each, expectations and norms for interaction may differ. For second language (L2) learners, this poses a particular challenge, with high language proficiency no guarantee of pragmatic success (Bardovi-Harlig, 2001; Bardovi-Harlig & Hartford, 1990, 1993b; Fiksdal, 1989; Harris, 1997; He, 1993; Kasper & Rose, 1999; Storch, 2002; Thonus, 1999a, 1999b; Tyler, 1995). One setting that L2 learners may encounter with increasing frequency is the university writing center. The focus of this study is the interaction between tutors and writers seeking their assistance. Specifically, it addresses the institutional nature of this interaction, the status of tutors within those sessions, and whether they behave differently when they work with L2 writers versus native English (NE) writers[1].

Writing centers or labs have been established at many if not most major universities in the country to provide assistance and support for writers across the institution. There are a variety of models for writing centers (Kinkead & Harris, 1993), but one common model uses peer tutoring, that is, the tutors who provide assistance are themselves students. Most writing centers that operate in the peer-tutoring tradition trace their roots to the work of Bruffee (1984), who maintained that tutoring is essentially an interaction between peers who share similar backgrounds, experience, and status, one that creates a different and powerful context for learning. Trimbur (1987), in his discussion of the apparent contradiction of being both a peer and a tutor, sees the writing center conference as a colearning situation, where the tutor and writer collaborate and negotiate means and goals as equals. The value of peer tutoring is that it allows unfettered conversation. The peers are not miniteachers; rather, they represent a different set of eyes and ears, another voice in the writing process. They are often interpreters who have one foot in the teacher's discourse community and another

---

[1] The term NE writer is used here since the normal term, native speaker, is not a suitable description. Some L2 writers are indistinguishable from native speakers in their oral production.

in the students' (Harris, 1995). Importantly, these peers have recently gone through similar experiences, are closer to the writers' experiences, and therefore may better understand the challenges they face. The literature on writing centers in general, and peer tutoring in particular, is extensive (e.g., Bouquet, 1999; Gillespie, Gillam, Brown, & Stay, 2002; Kinkead & Harris, 1993; Murphy & Law, 1995; two dedicated journals: *Writing Lab Newsletter* and *Writing Center Journal),* yet there has been relatively little investigation of L2 writers' experiences in the writing center, specifically, the interaction between L2 writers and their tutors (though see Blau, Hall, & Strauss, 1998; Ritter, 2002; Thonus 1999a, 1999b, 2001, 2002). Much of the writing on L2 writers in the writing center is limited to a cautious set of do's and don'ts (e.g., Gadbow, 1992; Harris & Silva, 1993; Kennedy, 1993; Moser, 1993; Powers, 1993; for a somewhat different perspective, see Blau & Hall, 2002).

The role of the peer tutor can be ambiguous and delicate, combining as it does a status that is equal yet somehow unequal to the writer–client. Most literature on peer tutoring, at least among children, assumes that that the two participants "do not have equal status in their instructional relationship. Their engagement, therefore, is low on equality, at least relative to other forms of peer discourse" (Damon & Phelps, 1989, p. 11). The notion of peerness, however vexed it may be when applied to tutors of native speakers, becomes even more problematic in interaction with L2 learner. It is an open question whether native speaking tutors, who bear the inherent authority of native speaker status, and L2 writers can really be said to operate on an equal footing, a question that will be explored in this study.

WRITING CENTER INTERACTION AS INSTITUTIONAL DISCOURSE

"Conversation" is a popular word in academia, composition studies, and writing centers. The handbook for the University of Illinois at Chicago's Writing Center opens with the following statement, "Our goal is to help each other conduct meaningful *conversations* with students who come to us for help with writing." (Aleksa, Bednarowicz, Smith, Brecke, & Huang, 2000, p. 5, emphasis added). In fact though, writing center sessions are not really conversations in the everyday sense; rather, they are more characteristic of *institutional discourse.* The literature on institutional discourse distinguishes between classic institutional discourse (between institutional representatives and service seekers) and workplace talk (between institutional workers) (Bardovi-Harlig & Hartford, chapter 1, this volume). Interaction between writers and tutors falls into the first category. Within this category, we can again distinguish between two kinds of pairings: The first consists of experts providing some sort of service to a client seeking this service. This is typical, for instance, of interaction in medical settings (e.g., Fisher & Todd, 1983; Cameron & Williams, 1997; Tannen & Wallat, 1993) and gatekeeping encounters (e.g., Erickson & Schultz, 1982; He, 1994; Kerekes, chapter 4, this volume; Tarone & Kuehn, 2000). Second is the pairing between expert and novice, more frequent in educational or training settings, perhaps between teacher and student or apprentice (e.g., Lave & Wenger, 1991; Mehan, 1985; Rudolph, 1994; Woken & Swales, 1989). The current study is of interest for two reasons. First, writing center sessions stand at the intersection of these two types of interaction: Writers come to the center seeking services, as they might in a medical encounter, yet they are also potentially in the position of novice or apprentice academic writer. Second, there has been relatively little research done on this kind of institutional discourse involving L2 speakers (see Bardovi-Harlig & Hartford, chapter 1, this volume, for a review). The study has three parts: It begins with an examination of the structure of writing center interaction from the perspective of institutional discourse, then addresses how tutor status informs and is informed by this inter-acttion, and finally, explores the extent to which the interaction between tutors and L2 and NE writers is comparable.

Data Collection

The corpus for this study consists of 10 writing center sessions. There are four tutor participants, all fluent speakers of English. One is a monolingual native speaker, two are bilingual native speakers (L2s = Spanish, Tagalog), and one is a highly fluent, bilingual L2 speaker of English (L1 = Russian). The writer participants include two NE writers, both of whom turned out to be bilingual as well (L2s = Korean, Greek), though neither their oral nor spoken production showed signs of the nonEnglish language, and three L2 writers (L1s = Chinese (2), Khmer). This kind of ethnic and linguistic diversity is the rule rather than the exception on this urban, largely commuter campus, where white mono-lingual English speakers are in the minority. Furthermore, white middle-class, monolingual speakers with good high school preparation often test out of the composition classes from which the participants were drawn. It is therefore not surprising that even the "NS baseline" group as well as the tutors present a multicultural, multilingual profile. Each writer participated in two sessions, in all but one case, with different tutors. Both tutors and writers were paid for their participation in the study. Writers were recruited from the basic English compo-sition classes required of all undergraduates who place into it. Tutors were recruited from the regular staff at the University Writing Center.

The corpus brings together several types of data in an effort to provide a complete view of the session as well as the real life consequences of the sessions: background interviews, tutoring sessions, and stimulated recalls. All participants were initially interviewed about their backgrounds, their expec-tations as writers or tutors, and their past experience tutoring L2 writers/using the writing center. All tutoring sessions were videotaped, transcribed, and coded by the researcher and a research assistant. Finally, the corpus includes a modified stimulated recall of the session with the writer and the tutor. Each participant was interviewed separately on audiotape within 3 days of each session while watching the videotape (Gass & Mackey, 2000). This final step in the triangulation of the data was included in order to analyze the participants' motivation for their contributions to the interaction and their understanding of, and reactions, to their partners' contributions. The combination of the videotapes and recall sessions helped to determine, first with quantitative measures, and then through participant reflection, the roles that the participants played and how they viewed the role of their partner in the session. In addition to the transcribed videotapes, the preliminary drafts or predraft work that the writer brought to the session were copied and collected. The writers were also asked to submit a copy of any subsequent draft that emanated from work during the session. Analysis of the written data is not presented in this article (see Williams, in press).

THE STRUCTURE OF INTERACTION

One of the identifying characteristics of institutional discourse is its predictable structure (Agar 1985; Drew & Heritage, 1992; Sarangi & Roberts, 1999). There are a number of reasons for this, the primary one being its task or goal-orientation. The topics that can be discussed are narrowly constrained and the roles of the participants, though subject to negotiation, are usually clearly drawn and generally of unequal status. Agar maintains that the goal orientation and specific procedures associated with institutional discourse result in a predictable sequence of moves. He proposes that institutional discourse generally has three phases, *diagnosis, directive,* and *report.* These are widely reported in medical and management settings, but also in advising and tutoring sessions (Bardovi-Harlig & Hartford, 1993a; Ritter, 2002; Thonus, 1999a). Even before the diagnosis phase, however, in writing center sessions, there is often an overt goal-setting phase that may be absent from other institutional interaction. After introductions, tutors will elicit the writer's goals for the session. They normally will also extend an offer of help, which contains the implicit claim to their ability to provide that help, that is, their expertise. In example (1) the writer, a NE writer, provides a statement of her problem, and an admission of her novice status.

(1)   T = tutor (Joe)   W = writer (Esther)[2]

      T: OK. My name is Joe[3].
      W: My name is Esther (shake hands)
      T: *How can I help you today?*
      W: *Well, I have to write.like.a compare and contrast paper on religion.* How two authors have wrote.and I have to write a paper about.what I think um.whether or not we need religion….um. But I'm kind of stuck. *I don't know really how to write a compare and contrast paper. I need some help with that.*
      T: Do you have um.the assignment sheet that your teacher handed out?
      W: Yes. This is uh.the assignment sheet. She emailed us.

---

[2] Complete transcription conventions are provided in the appendix.
[3] All the names are pseudonyms.

T: Oh, this is the sheet? OK. Lemme just read it over a little bit (reads silently)…Have you read the section on comparing and contrasting?

Writing center discourse generally includes the first two phases suggested by Agar: *diagnosis*[4] and *directive*, though the importance of the final phase, *report*, is relatively minor.[5] Although the data from this study do not reveal the tight sequences reported by Thonus (1999a, 1999b), the basic phases are identifiable in most sessions. In fact, the first phase, diagnosis, appears to dominate writing center sessions, a characteristic that is even more apparent in sessions with L2 writers. A diagnosis can be offered in a very general sense by writers themselves, as in the example (1) above. This is essentially a statement of the problem, of what has brought the writer to the center, rather than a diagnosis of what is wrong. In research on revision processes, this phase is often referred to as *identification* or *detection* and precedes *diagnosis* (Bereiter & Scardamalia, 1987; Cumming & So, 1996; van Gelderen, 1997). The latter task almost always falls to the tutor, as in the excerpts below, both from sessions with L2 writers. It may be a global diagnosis, as in (2), in which the tutor points out where the writer is moving in the wrong direction, or a local diagnosis, as in (3), in which the tutor focuses on an error in inflectional morphology.

(2)   T (Eugenia); W (Evelyn, L1 = Chinese)

   T: OK.but again, if you write that, that's going to be the same thing as this paper.
   W: What do you mean?
   T: *That's not really what the teacher's looking for.* He wants you to take Willams and O'Rourke and tie them together and say why they are either the same or why are they different. Or what is the correlation between them?..Do you see what I'm saying?
   W: mmhm.

(3)   T   (Eugenia); W (Sammy, L1 = Chinese)

   W: More than *three hundreds* teachers from all over the country come to Chicago, Illinois to participate in the show.
   T: More than *three hundreds* teachers
   W: More than *three hundreds* teachers from all over the country come to Chicago, Illinois to participate in the show.
   T: Ok, now let's look at..these two words…OK, Can '*hundreds*' be a plural?
   W: mm.
   T: Can the word '*hundred*' be a plural?
   W: ..Maybe. (laughs) ..No?
   T: No, it can't.

---

[4] The use of the term *diagnosis* is perhaps unfortunate, given the widespread rejection of the medical metaphor in the writing center literature (e.g., North, 1984). However, since Agar's description of institutional discourse has proven useful in other settings, I will pursue it here.
[5] Tutors submit a report after each session, and writers are also asked to provide a brief written evaluation of their experience. This phase is not part of the interaction, however.

In some cases, the diagnosis comes relatively early in the session, perhaps prompted by teacher comments on the draft. The structure of some sessions, especially ones with L2 writers that include some attention to sentence-level issues, is a series of diagnosis–directive cycles. There are other instances in which the entire session is devoted to establishing a diagnosis. It is interesting to note that in the current data, this happens only with L2 writers. In these cases, although the tutor may be able to detect surface or even more general problems in the student's writing, it is not immediately clear what is at the root of the problem. For the most part, the writers have either not understood the assignment or the readings they are required to incorporate into the assignment, as in this exchange (4) between a tutor and a L2 writer.

(4)   T   (Eugenia); W (Evelyn)

> T: OK, so.in this paper, did you write about the similarities or the differences?
> W: I wrote um..*Actually, I wrote, after I wrote this essay, then I reread it, then I found out that.that.it.it doesn't meet the assignment* (laughs)
> T: OK, so what did you write about in your essay?
> W: I wrote, I wrote Williams, Williams think there shouldn't be any racism and ..um.and then I gave some example why she thinks so.
> T: And then you also did PJ and the other side of it, right?
> W: but PJ, I did,…we should keep the bias in our language. *And it doesn't..it doesn't um.meet the assignment* (laughs).

In this particular session, the diagnosis phase was quite lengthy. It took more than 30 minutes to discover that that writer had completely misinterpreted one of the essays she was to analyze. She understood the author's statement that "neutrality hides racism" to be a recommendation of neutral language, rather than an indictment of bland politically correct language. Part of her misunderstanding was the result of her lack of familiarity with cultural institutions, such as the purpose and process of writing letters to the editor, the widespread fear of litigation in this country, and the function of a university law review. It is almost three-quarters of the way through the session that the eureka moment occurred. The tutor had explained of the process of sending a letter to the editor of a newspaper and an editor's prerogative to edit the content of any letter submitted if it is deemed inflammatory. In fact, the author's (Williams') letter describing an incident of racial discrimination had been drastically cut for this very reason, but the writer had not understood this. At the beginning of this excerpt, she is still clinging to her original interpretation of the essay, that the author is recommending the use of neutral language. By the end, after considerable explanation by the tutor, she comes to realize that the two authors (Williams and O'Rourke), whose work she is comparing, have similar rather than contrasting views.

(5)   T (Eugenia); W (Evelyn)

W: But um, didn't we discuss earlier that Williams should keep neutral -keep um don't keep the bias in language? If the editor did that, then she will be happy about it?

T: OK, is this 'try to be neutral' the idea behind Williams or the idea behind her story?

W: Behind her story.

T: OK, so it's not necessarily the way she feels, right? It's the way you see the story...Do you see how these two aspects are different? Williams..I haven't read this article, again.and I am just telling you, y'know, what I think from the information I have gotten from you. This is what I am understanding: that Williams um..wrote a very. like active. letter to the editor, expressing her feelings about how she was treated at the store, right? And it had all the ..what the editor would call .like negative aspects.

W: mmhm

T: In that it had racism and sexism and all the other y'know, her feelings in it. Right? So what the editor tried to do is the editor sent her back the edited letter that was completely neutral, right? So the idea behind this letter, the editor or whoever wanted to publish it, doesn't make it seem like it's a really big deal..by um..by making it simple, right? So the idea behind the letter is trying to be neutral hides racism. That's the idea behind the letter.

W: ..oh...OK

T: Do you see how those two things can be different?

W: uh huh (smiling) If this..if this idea is behind the story.behind um..um what we came up with--that idea--then that would make sense.

T: OK..OK, so now, how do you think this is related to O'Rourke?

W: ....um.........hm

T: OK, so O'Rourke says we've gone too far in trying to avoid bias in language, right? OK, so do you think he is choosing the same side as Williams? Which is a different side from the editor?

W: ....mmmm

T: How do you think these two are similar or different?

W: *He said um..um. if he was the editor, he will publish her her essay.*

T: *Alright! Great!*

In fact, this session consists almost entirely of one long diagnosis sequence, with the directive portion at the very end only implicit in the tutor's reinterpretation of the text. The L2 writer must infer that she should now revise based on this new interpretation. Although this nondirective style was not typical in sessions with L2 writers, it was not uncommon. Indeed, writing center tutors are taught that much of their job entails guiding writers to discover meaning for themselves, to identify problems in their writing, and to figure out ways to improve it (e.g., Brooks, 1991). Thus, the diagnosis phase is often a deliberately collaborative and lengthy process, compared to say doctor–patient interaction, in which the doctor does not generally invite the patient to participate in the diagnosis. Tight sequences of organized question–answer adjacency pairs, though represented in the present data, are not the norm in writing center sessions. In excerpt (6), the tutor tries to get the L2 writer to see that her thesis and introduction do not lead the reader to the body paragraphs she has written. In this case, the teacher, in her comments, had offered an initial diagnosis that the writer's paragraphs lacked logical development, yet, again, it took almost the entire session to translate this into ideas that the writer could understand.

(6)   T (Oscar); W (Min; L1 = Khmer)

> W: This paragraph I just write.it's about …mm..telling about how he expl.how he found that.his father told him the false stories.
> T: mmhm.   Right..now..um.so what did you wanna. Why did you include that in your essay about finding out that his father told false stories?
> W: ..m. to see.his father denies the past.
> T: OK.
> W: yeah.
> T: *so.um. what's..why'd you include that in your introduction? How does that relate to your introduction?*..You just said..you just said his father wanted to talk about.I mean, the author wanted to talk about how his father—
> W: —lost his identity
> T: mmm. Lost his identity.um..OK, so, *which one is your thesis here in the introduction?*
> W: uh. My thesis is.about how his father lost..his father lost his identity..the effect on his son.

Thus, one typical feature of writing center discourse is extended diagnosis sequences, a characteristic accentuated in sessions with L2 writers.

THE STATUS OF INTERACTANTS

Institutional discourse structure also involves identification of participant role and status, often designating on participant as dominant. However, as Thonus (1999a, 2001) and Ritter (2002) point out, once again, writing center sessions present a possible exception to, or at least a hybrid of this view. Although the tutors are consulted as relative experts, they are also presented as peers, ostensibly as status equals, at least when interacting with NE writers. Indeed in any context, the marking of relative status is complex, and interactionally achieved. Yet, there are some structures and signals that are generally associated with expert status that can begin to give a picture of the tutor's more dominant role in writing center interaction (see Tarone, chapter 6, this volume). These are shown in Table 2.1.

Table 2.1. Markers and Conversational Moves Generally Associated with Expertise/Dominance

Dominance markers in interaction
    Longer turns
    Interruptions
    Topic initiation
Dominant speech acts
    Suggestions/requests
    Rejections/challenges
Lexical markers of dominance
    Lack of mitigation/modulation
    Aggravators

Interactional Features of Writing Center Sessions That Suggest Tutor Dominance

Turn Length. Tutor talk shows many signs of interactional dominance, a finding that corroborates those of earlier studies (Cumming & So, 1996; Ritter, 2002; Thonus 1999a, 2001; Young, 1992). Among these are significantly longer turn length, as seen in Table 2.2. In general, tutors have longer turns than writers. There is a single exception in the data, in a session with a NE writer. In sessions with the L2 writers, the trend toward longer tutor turns is even stronger, suggesting greater dominance by tutors in their sessions with L2 writers.

Table 2.2. Turn Length in Number of Words

Writer-name	Tutor-name	Writer mean turn length	Tutor mean turn length	Writer–tutor difference
Esther-NE writer	Joe	15.5	27.0	6.5
Esther-NE writer	Oscar	13.4	10.1	-3.3
Annie-NE writer	Robert	13.8	19.6	5.8
Annie-NE writer	Joe	16.2	22.1	5.9
Evelyn-L2 writer	Eugenia	7.1	26.2	19.1
Evelyn-L2 writer	Eugenia	12.7	21.9	9.2
Min-L2 writer	Eugenia	6.6	27	20.4
Min-L2 writer	Oscar	8.8	16.8	8.0
Sammy-L2 writer	Joe	12.1	29.6	17.5
Sammy-L2 writer	Eugenia	11.3	22.2	10.9

Table 2.3. Interruptions by Tutors

Writer-name	Tutor-name	Mean interruptions per turn	Mean interruptions - tutor completes turn
Esther-NE writer	Joe	.081	.098
Esther-NE writer	Oscar	.071	.100
Annie-NE writer	Joe	.085	.098
Annie-NE writer	Robert	.182	.063
Evelyn-L2 writer	Eugenia	.092	.126
Evelyn-L2 writer	Eugenia	.088	.136
Min-L2 writer	Eugenia	.106	.128
Min-L2 writer	Oscar	.077	.131
Sammy-L2 writer	Joe	.088	.109
Sammy-L2 writer	Eugenia	.119	.111

Interruptions and Overlaps. Interruptions have also often been suggested as a marker of speaker dominance (West & Zimmerman, 1985; Zuengler & Bent, 1991, though see Goldberg, 1990, for a summary of findings to the contrary). The relative rate of interruptions in the writing center data shows tutors wielding authority (Table 2.3). All of the figures in the table are interruptions of the writer by the tutor. Interruption in the other direction, by the writer, occurs very rarely, often only once or twice during a session and sometimes not at all.

It has been frequently noted that not all interruptions are necessarily dominating (Goldberg, 1990; Makri-Tsilipakou, 1994; Murata, 1994; Zuengler & Bent, 1991). Tannen (1989) and Murray (1985) have also disputed the equating of interruption with speaker dominance, on both theoretical and methodological grounds, yet there are clear cases in the data in which the tutor intrudes into the writer's turn in mid-sentence. Column three of Table 2.3 contains interruptions in which the learner cuts off the speech of the other interlocutor, either by changing the topic (7a), or dismissing or challenging the contribution (7b), moves that may be considered dominating. These have also been referred to as *intrusive* (Murata, 1994) or *disaffiliative* (Makri-Tsilipakou, 1994) interruptions. Among these, there is little difference between tutor interaction with NE writers and L2 writers. Differences seem to be more a matter of individual style or the product of the specific interaction between the two interlocutors.

(7a) T (Oscar); W (Min)

   W: um..this one I already had a grade on it. But uh..I don't satisfy-I am not
       satisfy with the grade I--
   T: --What about the writing?

(7b) T (Oscar); W (Min)

> W: This is uh..one pages. If you take out, it's uh--
> T: --No, no, I'm not saying take it
> out..but uh.. no, but um..how would this be a reflection of his father's changing
> beliefs? Do you see what I'm asking now?

The last column in Table 2.3 includes interruptions that might be considered more collaborative or supportive.[6] Tannen (1984, 1989) suggested that certain types of simultaneous speech demonstrate active participation and solidarity rather than dominance. It is possible that there is some effort on the part of the tutors to reduce social distance by engaging in overlapping speech; however, the postsession interviews suggest a somewhat different interpretation. These exchanges consist of instances in which the tutor finishes the writer's thought, often after at least a second of wait time. In many cases, the writer also chimes in with the end of the utterance, producing an overlap. These might be better considered *rescues* than interruptions. In retrospective accounts, tutors reported that they were trying to guess what the writers intended to express and offered the utterance ending as a way of minimizing their struggle and embarrassment, especially in sessions with L2 writers (e.g., ex. 8). Writers, when questioned on this point in the videotape, usually claimed that the interruption was helpful.

(8)   T   (Oscar); W (Min)

> W: and then I use.the next paragraph is about the example about when he went
>   to the movies and he saw white people...
> T: looking glamorous//
> W: //glamorous and perfect.

It is interesting to note that there are far more of these rescues of L2 writers than of NE writers. Thus, it may be that these moves are at once dominating, in that they demonstrate the expertise of the tutors, and supportive, in that they attempt to follow the conversational aims of the writer. This is further evidence of the hybrid status of the tutor in writing center interaction.

Directives and Suggestions.   Although the diagnosis phase of institutional discourse is usually the lengthiest in writing center sessions, particularly in those with L2 writers, because most writers come to the writing center looking for direction and advice, it is no surprise that almost all sessions include a directive phase as well. The directive phase of institutional interaction is one in which experts can demonstrate their authority and, as a result, their higher status. The experts make suggestions and give advice. The client or novice often collaborates to facilitate this dominance. Bardovi-Harlig and Hartford (1990) describe

---

[6] Other terms for this type of interruption include *cooperative* (Murata, 1994) or *affiliative* (Makri-Tsilipakou, 1994).

situations in which contributions between status unequals must be congruent with the roles that they recapitulate during interaction. In Bardovi-Harlig and Hartford's work, faculty members advise students on course selections. It is the job of the faculty to give advice. Students may make suggestions, or even reject those made by faculty, but they must do so in a way that appears congruent. In conferences with writing teachers, this pattern of dominance has also been demonstrated (Newkirk, 1995; Pathey-Chavez & Ferris, 1997; Sperling, 1991; Ulichny & Watson-Gegeo, 1989).

In the writing center, however, this is a more delicate situation as the status of tutors is not always clear. According to accepted writing center practice, tutors are not supposed to appropriate student writing, or directly tell writers to make changes in their writing (see e.g., Blau & Hall, 2002; Brooks, 1991; Capossela, 1998; Harris, 1982, 1995; Thonus, 1999b, 2001). In practice though, tutors often do give direct advice. And, as has been found repeatedly, this is what some writers, especially L2 writers, expect and want them to do (Blau & Hall, 2002; Clark, 2001; Harris, 1997; Thonus, 1999c; Young, 1992). All of the L2 writers in postsession interviews explicitly stated that their purpose in coming to the writing center was to have tutors make suggestions about how to improve a specific piece of writing. Perhaps for cultural reasons, or simply out of politeness, few wished to voice their concern that they had not received as much advice as they had hoped. All but one remained noncommittal on the issue, saying that their tutor was "nice" or "helpful." The one writer with strongly voiced complaints about the session was a NE writer who received the least and least explicit advice on how to improve her paper. Instead, the tutor engaged the writer in a general discussion of the ideas that were developed in the essay. The student was visibly disgruntled during the session, and in the postsession interview declared that the tutor had been "no help," that he had "just rambled on and on."

There are many ways to make suggestions. Thonus (1999a, 1999c, 2002) addresses this issue first in terms of form: declarative, imperative, interrogative modal (1st and 2nd person) and then goes on to examine how these all might be mitigated, based on work by Blum-Kulka, House, and Kasper (1989). However, this approach does not always capture the way in which mitigators or aggravators can accumulate to mark status relations. In particular, modality can be used either to highlight the dominant status of the tutor or to mitigate it (e.g., *you should* vs. *you could*) (He, 1993). Modal operators (*should, might*) and modal adjuncts (*maybe, I think*, conditionals, such as *If you want*) generally fulfill two functions: to mark logical possibility or to signal features of the social situation and interaction. In terms of their capacity to mitigate the potentially face-threatening act of a directive, only some modals are suitable. The following generalization can be made: Modals of logical possibility that fall below certainty—*might, may, probably, I think, maybe*—have a mitigating or softening effect on directives. Modals of social interaction—*should, have to, need to* (though negated modals present a special case)—and modals of certainty—*will, gonna*—aggravate or heighten directives.

Modality is not the only way to adjust the force of directives. An interrogative tends to lessen the force of an utterance (*Should we end it here?*) whereas an imperative increases it (*End it here.*). The use of *we* tends to mitigate directives (Rounds, 1987; Thonus, 2002). The force of the directive can be upgraded with the addition of qualifiers such as *really, more,* and softened with checks for agreement or comprehension, such as *y'know?, right?* (Rudolph, 1994). Often these modulators are not used singly but in combination for a cumulative effect. The following examples of tutor suggestions illustrate some of the possibilities, with mitigators and aggravators marked with subscripts:

(9a) T (Oscar)

> T: Do you see how.places where you *could$_1$ maybe$_2$* clear that up for me?$_3$
> (Oscar)

(9b) T (Eugenia)

> T: Okay, because 'studies' is *really$_1$* an awkward word to use here. You *should$_2$* use..m..

In the first example, the cumulative effect of the three signals is one of mitigation, in the second, escalation. Of course, it is also possible that a directive could contain modulation in both directions, and this does indeed occur. In the following examples, the modulations with numeric subscripts mitigate the force of the directive whereas those with the alphabetic subscripts augment them.

(10a)T (Eugenia)

> The introduction *is supposed$_1$* to tell us everything *we$_a$* are going to read about, *right$_b$*?

(10b)T (Joe)

> Once *we$_a$* include your thesis at the end of. once *we$_a$* include your thesis at the end of your introductory paragraph, then *we$_a$'re gonna$_1$* start talking about how *we$_a$* came to your thesis.

Thus, consistent with their ambiguous status, tutors often do a delicate dance of exerting authority and reducing status difference though their linguistic choices. Table 2.4 shows tutor suggestions in terms of the degree to which their force is either mitigated or heightened through the use of the devices described earlier. A score of 1+ means that the suggestion contains one aggravator; 2+, two aggravators. A score of 1- means one mitigator and so forth. "Mixed" means that the suggestion contained both types of modulators.

Table 2.4. Modulation of Tutor Suggestions

Tutor	Sug-gestions N	1+ N	1+ %	2+ N	2+ %	1- N	1- %	2- N	2- %	3- N	3- %	Mix N	Mix %	Other N	Other %
NE writers															
Joe	49	5	10.2	1	2.0	12	24.5	19	38.8	5	10.2	7	14.3	0	0
Oscar	39	5	12.8	0	0	8	20.5	18	46.2	4	10.3	4	10.3	0	0
Robert	38	2	5.3	0	0	17	44.7	14	36.8	3	7.9	2	5.3	0	0
Joe	47	6	12.8	0	0	11	23.4	19	40.4	6	12.8	5	10.6	0	0
Total NE writers	*173*	*18*	*10.4*	*1*	*0.6*	*48*	*27.7*	*70*	*40.5*	*18*	*10.4*	*18*	*10.4*	*0*	*0*
L2 writers															
Eugenia	27	8	29.6	3	11.1	10	37.0	4	14.8	0	0	2	7.4	0	0
Eugenia	32	7	21.9	2	6.3	12	37.5	5	15.6	1	3.1	4	12.5	0	0
Eugenia	39	9	23.1	3	7.7	17	43.6	4	10.3	0	0	5	12.8	1	2.6
Oscar	23	7	30.4	0	0	8	34.8	5	21.7	0	0	3	13.0	0	0
Joe	28	10	35.7	2	7.1	13	46.4	1	3.6	0	0	1	3.6	01	3.6
Eugenia	34	14	41.2	3	8.8	10	29.4	3	8.8	0	0	2	5.9	20	5.9
Total L2 writers	*183*	*55*	*30.1*	*13*	*7.1*	*70*	*38.3*	*22*	*12*	*1*	*.05*	*17*	*9.3*	*4*	*2.2*

A writer may also request advice from the tutor. Although this does put the writer in the dominant position of controlling the flow of discourse, this position is immediately relinquished when the tutor begins to offer advice. Furthermore, writers usually only make these requests when authorized to do so by the tutor.

(11) T (Joe); W (Esther)

> T: *How can I help you today?*
> W: Well, I have to write.like.a compare and contrast paper on religion. How two authors have wrote.and I have to write a paper about.what I think um.whether or not we need religion....um.but I'm kind of stuck. I don't know really how to write a compare and contrast paper. *I need some help with that.*

Only in rare instances does a writer make an unlicensed request. In the following excerpt, the writer is quickly cut off when she does so and is told that it is not the job of tutors to give direct advice. In fact, however, this tutor had done so repeatedly in this and other sessions.

(12) T (Eugenia); W (Min)

> W: oh..mmm.cause I just can't say 'disadvantage' because 'disavantage' is just like < > Just like one point—
> T: —OK. Um, let's see if we can look up a similar word for 'disadvantage' (looks up in dictionary) [softly] It's not in here (puts book back).
> W: *Can you just give me some like—*
> T: —*Well, I can't really <u>give</u> [loud] you an idea.* Um. How 'bout you think of a title for it?
> W: Title, yeah. *Can you give me a title this column?*
> T: *I can't really give you a title* (laughs).
> R: OK.

Or more gently:

(13) T (Eugenia); W (Min)

> W: *Today I would like to work on my grammar.*
> T: Okay.
> W: um...*Just my grammar..um..and..and please tell me if there's any..um..if there's any area I need to explain so I can have a clearer idea—*
> T: —*Okay. Well, let's work on that first and then we can put off the grammar until like..the last ten or fifteen minutes.*
> W: uh huh, okay.

Here, ironically, the tutor uses the nondirective philosophy of the center to maintain her authoritative stance.

Topic Shifts/Leading Moves. The dominant interlocutor controls the flow of the discourse, pursuing or shifting topics. Topic shifts are difficult to quantify, or sometimes even identify in writing center sessions because, in some cases, the tutor and writer seem to pursue the same topic the whole time. Therefore, the analysis will focus specifically on moves that push the interaction forward, what Gass and Varonis (1986) call *leading moves*. Although it is possible for an interlocutor to push the conversation forward in a more implicit fashion, for instance, with body movement or gaze direction, only explicit moves in which the movement forward is marked linguistically, are counted here (14a,b).

(14a)T (Joe); W (Sammy)

> T: I think that pretty much is going to improve your um..first page a lot more. *Is there anything else you want to work on the first page on?*

(14b)T (Eugenia); W (Eveyln)

> T: OK..um. *let's put off the question for a second. How bout O'Rourke?* What was his story about?

Table 2.5 shows that tutors use far more leading moves than writers. Again, the tutor dominance is evident in their control over the flow of the session, though there is no clear difference between their interaction with L2 and NE writers.

Rejections and Challenges. Rejections and challenges are risky and face-threatening acts (Gass & Houck, 1999). Learning to challenge suggestions made by others, especially those of potentially higher status takes more than knowledge of the language. It has been amply demonstrated that grammatical competence is not a guarantee of pragmatic competence (Bardovi-Harlig, 2001; Bardovi-Harlig & Dörnyei, 1998) and that developing this competence takes a long time (Bardovi-Harlig & Hartford, 1993b; Salsbury & Bardovi-Harlig, 2000). Because of the status difference between the participants, it is not surprising that challenges are relatively rare in the data. When the tutor offers advice, generally it is either accepted or briefly acknowledged (though in the end, often ignored). Only rarely do writers explicitly reject a tutor's suggestion or request, and when they do, they use some form of mitigation, such as downgraders or an excuse or explanation (see Bardovi-Harlig & Hartford, 1991; Gass & Houck, 1999). Tutor response varies from acceptance of the challenge to gentle rebuff to mild anger. In (13) the tutor offers the highly mitigated (mitigation in italics) suggestion that one paragraph in the writer's essay may not fit. The writer rejects the suggestion that it be cut with explanation that the resulting essay will be then too short to fulfill the assignment. The tutor backs off and revises the suggestion.

Table 2.5. Leading moves

Tutor-name	Leading moves	Writer-name	Leading moves
Joe	4	Esther-NE writer	1
Oscar	6	Esther-NE writer	1
Joe	3	Annie-NE writer	0
Robert	5	Annie-NE writer	1
Eugenia	4	Evelyn-L2 writer	0
Eugenia	6	Evelyn-L2 writer	0
Eugenia	4	Min-L2 writer	0
Oscar	3	Min-L2 writer	1
Joe	4	Sammy-L2 writer	0
Eugenia	3	Sammy-L2 writer	0

(15) T (Oscar); W (Min)

> T: Because that's the only one. Either that one sticks out or this one sticks out, right? But it's about..if you're talking about um.. changing.changing beliefs, you said?
> W: mmhm
> T: Awright. I guess the one paragraph that sticks out if you're talking about changing beliefs is this first one, right? *Or no*? Or with the father *at least*.
> W: *This is uh..one pages. If you take out, it's uh--*
> T: —*No, no, I'm not saying take it out*..but uh..no, but um..how would this be a reflection of his father's changing beliefs? Do you see what I'm asking now?
> W: mmhm mhhmm… yah…

Excerpt (16) contains a rejection of a request rather than of a suggestion. Earlier in this session, the tutor had asked the writer to read aloud, but she returned with a request that he read it instead. Here, he presses her, not accepting her excuse of poor pronunciation. He does, however, provide a justification for his rejection of her initial challenge, that he needs her to read it aloud in order to evaluate it.

(16) T (Oscar); W (Min)

> T: OK..um..Actually, *I need to hear it…It helps me to think.* Can you—
> W: *Because*
> T: Or does it take--
> W: *I get so..It's get a lot from .I get a lot of evidence from the book and some of the evidence, I don't know how to pronounce.*
> T: Oh, that's fine.
> W: *Can you?*
> T: When you get to that part, you can just-.I'll read it to myself, but I want to hear you read your writing…OK?

In the final example of challenges, (15), the writer had repeatedly met the tutor's suggestions for changes in grammatical form and word choice—the focus of the session at his request—with the response "maybe," a modal expression that Salsbury and Bardovi Harlig (2000) found was favored by low-proficiency L2 learners in challenges and refusals. In this excerpt, toward the end of the session, the tutor loses patience. In fact, this is the only writer in the corpus who offers barely mitigated rejections, perhaps serving as a challenge to the tutor's authority. This may explain the tutor's somewhat explosive response.

(17) T (Eugenia); W (Sammy)

> T: See, you did it right here. It is more than just a noun, right?
> W: yeah
> T: So you should have done the same thing here, right?
> W: *Maybe.*
> T: [loud] *What do you mean, maybe? Maybe?* If you take out the "more" here, "It is just a noun"..right? It's the same sentence as you have right here.
> W: mhm.
> T: OK, go on.

In the postsession discussion, this writer was described by his tutor as difficult and uncooperative. She expressed frustration that after she had acquiesced to his request to go over grammatical problems in his paper, against her better judgment, he seemed to show little willingness to accept her advice. "Why did he bother to ask if he didn't want my advice?" she asked. It was her view that he had agreed to come to a session simply in order to collect the payment offered for participation in the project. Indeed, of the writers who participated in the study, he is the only one who did not return to the writing center after the project ended.

Negotiating Interactional Status

Floor Management. So far, our primary focus has been how tutors show interactional dominance. However, it has been pointed out that because status can be interactionally achieved, the nondominant party in interaction often collaborates to allow the dominant party to lead and to hold the floor (Dyehouse, 1999; Rudolph, 1994). One way in which this can be achieved is through back-channeling. This practice shows that the listener is interested and attending but is not attempting to claim the floor.[7] Like the leading moves, these were coded conservatively, with only audible signals counted. Most instances are single word utterances (*yeah, OK*), or simply verbalizations such as *uh huh* or *mmm*. These are considered backchannels when they follow the other speaker's turn

---

[7] In fact, however, backchanneling, especially minimal signals by L2 writers, may not be signal of comprehension or agreement. Williams (in press) demonstrates that tutor suggestions that meet with minimal signals of L2 writer attendance are rarely taken up in subsequent revisions.

with little or no pause, and there is no subsequent speech from that speaker. Often the turns are simultaneous, that is, the first speaker continues with the turn while the back channel is offered.

Here again we see that the writers regularly yield to tutors (Table 2.6). However, there is no clear trend differentiating NE writers from L2 writers; instead, there is more individual variation across pairs. Among the tutors, for example, Joe backchannels very little whereas Oscar does so extensively, once even more often than the writer with whom he was working. Both of these styles hold across writer partners. Sammy, the writer described above, who displays a variety of uncooperative behaviors, shows the lowest level of backchanneling of all of the writers. It is important to underscore that though the writers consistently occupy the nondominant position in these interactions, they are active participants in constructing this role for the tutors.

We have seen the tutors generally dominate the interaction in the writing center sessions, that they more freely offer face-threatening speech acts, such as suggestions and advice, that most backchannel less than the writers, and that they hold the floor for longer. All of this suggests they perceive themselves and that the writers perceive them as experts–authorities rather than peers, much as has been described in work on institutional interaction between experts and clients. In the case of writing center tutors, however, roles can be ambiguous and goals become fuzzy. Thus, in addition to markers of interactional dominance, we also see moves that may be intended to decrease status difference and increase solidarity with the writer. In addition to displaying their expertise and authority, tutors may try to establish comembership to show that they are status equals with their interactants. We have already seen some of this in the backchanneling behavior of tutors and the mitigation of face-threatening speech acts.

Small Talk. Tutors may also try to reduce status differences and personal-ize the interaction with small talk (Erickson & Schultz, 1982; Thonus, 2002) and the establishment of common experience and of a personal stake in the outcome

Table 2.6. Backchanneling

Tutor-name	Backchannel cues	Writer-name	Backchannel cues
Joe	8	Esther-NE writer	46
Oscar	69	Esther-NE writer	59
Joe	6	Annie-NE writer	34
Robert	37	Annie-NE writer	52
Eugenia	9	Evelyn-L2 writer	39
Eugenia	14	Evelyn-L2 writer	59
Eugenia	17	Min-L2 writer	61
Oscar	21	Min-L2 writer	47
Joe	3	Sammy-L2 writer	8
Eugenia	17	Sammy-L2 writer	24

of the process. This can establish comity (Aston, 1993) or more specifically, what Bardovi-Harlig and Hartford (1993) describe as *social comembership*. This contrasts with *role comembership*, which tutors and writers cannot claim since the institution has assigned them different roles. Again, there is considerable variation across tutors, with some more comfortable in an authoritative role and others gravitating toward a peer relationship. In the first excerpt (18a), the tutor empathizes with the writer's situation, calling on their common student status. In the second (18b), the tutor alludes to their shared status as Asian-Americans.

(18a)T (Oscar); W (Esther)

> W: I just finished my paper so I'm like—
> T: *yeah, you're kickin' back.*
> W: yeah...I should start.
> T: *And you don't--so this is kind of hard for you to talk about it now? Cause you wanna relax?*
> W: yeah.

(18b)T (Oscar); W (Esther)

> W: And they got a little bit more freedom than me and sometimes I was like.you know.oh.just because I'm Korean, I'm like this.
> T: mmhm
> W: because I'm Korean, I can't go out as much..other people—
> T: *—It's also because you're a girl. If you were a Korean boy, they probably would let you.*
> W: yeah.also like when I go like when I come come in a little bit past my curfew. My parents will be like, if you were a—like again-
> T: *—oh, what's your curfew?*
> W: Curfew? Curfew is like 12:00.
> T: *Oh, OK, that's not different. Cause my friends have like 10:00.*

In the next example (19), the tutor's strategy for reducing status differences is a little different. In this exchange, he develops a small talk sequence to demonstrate a personal interest in her cultural heritage, specifically, Korean food. He pursues this topic, providing information about his own personal experience and preferences, even when the writer displays little inclination to pursue the topic.

(19) T (Oscar); W (Esther)

> T: But what about when like when they came over..and they didn't know Korean? Did they ever come over?
> W: um..yeah..they came over and...it was weird.like I tried to show them like Korean I tried to tell them about like.you know.my Korean. Sometimes they were like they would be like.they wouldn't really understand.
> T: *What about the food?* (laughs)
> W: yeah..They wouldn't understand...Yeah, the food is different, too..Um..

T:　*I like it.*
W:　yeah
T:　[softly] *It's great* (laughs)
W;　oh yeah.Korean food?
T:　Only, *it's only thing I know is-I can't pronounce it..forget it.*
W:　OK
T:　*the meat*
W:　*bulgogi?*
T:　*yeah! That one!*

In some cases, this contradiction between peer and expert status can be confusing. In this final excerpt (20), the tutor senses—perhaps signaled by the writer's minimal response—that he has breached the normal constraints of the session by providing too much personal information, and he apologizes.

(20) T (Oscar); W (Min)

T:　Mkay.....um..Ok well, are there any physical details about the house.that you.that you
W:　mm
T:　or you can't think of that?
W:　it's uh…physical [softly]
T:　Anything that.well, if it doesn't stick out in your head, then maybe, y'know, you can leave it alone.
W:　OK
T:　like…*my house has red carpet (laughs)*
W:　oh
T:　yeah, *my parents like red, so we have red furniture, red carpet, a red car, so I like.that's what I would write about.*
W:　mm..OK
T:　or pets and plants-*we have a lot.well not pets, we have a lot of plants.*
W　[softly] oh
T:　Ok, *I'm sorry.* Let's keep going...um so we go on faith.

COMPARABILITY OF INTERACTION WITH NE AND L2 WRITERS

We have already noted that some characteristics of tutor–writer interaction are more prominent in sessions with L2 writers: Both the diagnosis phase and tutor turn length tends to be longer in interaction with L2 writers. In addition, the nature of tutor interruptions of NE and L2 writers differs somewhat, with tutors more likely to make supportive interruptions that "rescue" L2 writers. One other clear trend, shown in both quantitative and qualitative terms, is apparent in the directives and suggestions made by tutors. First, the density of advice is far greater in NE writer sessions than in L2 writer sessions (Table 2.7). When questioned about the smaller number of suggestions or advice in their sessions with L2 writers, two of the tutors maintained that they wanted to make sure that the writer understood and concentrated on the main issues, and that they did not want to confuse the writers by "giving them too many ideas or directions." It is

Table 2.7. Tutor Suggestions

Writer-name	Tutor-name	Number of tutor turns	Number of tutor suggestions	Mean suggestions per turn
Esther-NE writer	Joe	142	49	.35
Esther-NE writer	Oscar	138	39	.28
Annie-NE writer	Joe	102	47	.46
Annie-NE writer	Robert	141	33	.23
Evelyn-L2 writer	Eugenia	118	27	.23
Evelyn-L2 writer	Eugenia	162	32	.20
Min-L2 writer	Eugenia	181	39	.22
Min-L2 writer	Oscar	129	23	.18
Sammy-L2 writer	Joe	156	28	.18
Sammy-L2 writer	Eugenia	167	34	.20

Note: These are suggestions for improving the text, and do not include directives such as "Please read me your essay."

important to note the differences between NE writer and L2 writer sessions cannot be attributed exclusively to what one might call "grammar help." Many L2 writers go to the writing center for help with second language issues, which they usually refer to as "grammar." Of course, NE writers also often request help with sentence-level correctness. However, since the philosophy of the writing center is to work on the writing process, not simply the surface accuracy of the product, tutors are often inclined to deflect or delay any discussion of grammar. In fact, only one session in this corpus addressed grammar issues as a primary focus, at the insistence of the writer. There are references to grammatical issues in most of the sessions with NE writers and L2 writers alike, but they do not constitute a major part of the sessions.

Second, there are qualitative differences in tutor interaction with NE writers and with L2 writers. In contrast to Thonus' findings, tutors in this study are generally more direct in their suggestions to L2 writers than to NE writers. The differences across suggestion types for NE writers and L2 writers are considerable: Just 12.6% of the suggestions made to NE writers are heightened, in contrast to 37.2% of those made to L2 writers; 75.6% of the suggestions made to NE writers are mitigated, compared to 55.3% for the L2 writers. In addition, L2 writers seem to get simpler suggestions, with fewer modulations of any kind. Figure 2.1 shows the percentage of suggestions made with one, two and three modulations, combining the mitigators and aggravators. It shows that suggestions to L2 writers tend to be simpler than those aimed at NE writers.

Bardovi-Harlig and Hartford (1993a) suggest that more elaborate encodings come in interaction between speakers of closer status, in which roles and authority have to be negotiated, whereas status unequals are likely to be more indirect, consistent with the Bulge Theory, originally suggested by Wolfson (1988). If one argues that native speaker status brings these writers closer into comembership with their tutors, then these findings are consistent with those of Bardovi-

Figure 2.1. Number of Modulations in Tutor Suggestions

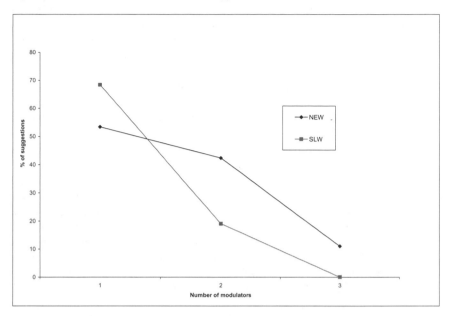

Harlig and Hartford. With L2 writers, tutors take on the authority of the status more easily, displaying it more frequently through unmitigated or more forceful suggestions. Another possibility is pointed out by Thonus (1999b), that tutors use these simpler modulation strategies in an effort to increase the comprehensibility of their suggestions to L2 writers. It may be that the multiple use of upgraders, though perhaps less polite, serves comprehensibility. Tutors are far more likely to use at least one upgrader with the L2 writers than with NE writers, and even more likely to use two. This may make tutor directives clearer. This interpretation is consistent with post-session interviews with tutors. When they were questioned about the form of their suggestions, at first, most seemed unaware that they were behaving any differently with L2 writers than with NE writers. On reflection, two tutors thought that they might have used simpler and more direct and unmitigated suggestions because they thought that the writer would be more likely to understand the advice expressed in this way and consider it seriously.

CONCLUSIONS AND IMPLICATIONS FOR SLA

The structure of the writing center sessions clearly reflects patterns and features reported for institutional discourse. It has a predictable structure; it has set roles for participants and a narrow range of topics. Within this generalization, there is some variation. Although almost all sessions contain goal-setting, diagnosis and directive phases, sessions with L2 writers tend to favor a very lengthy diagnosis stage, perhaps as the interlocutors struggle to come to a mutual understanding of their task. The range of permissible topics is limited. For example, although a small amount of initial and closing small talk is tolerated and even expected, if a participant ventures too far or too long outside of the established range of topics, the other participant usually reigns him in with signals of discomfort or lack of interest in response.

Roles are negotiated during the sessions, but again, only within a predictable range. Tutors' interactive style blends characteristics of dominance and solidarity, underscoring their dual roles as experts and peers relative to the writers they are assisting. Tutors must consistently maintain this balance between authority and equality. One possible way of describing their role is offered by Vygotsian approaches to education, that of the *more capable peer* (Moll, 1989). A growing body of research into peers assisting one other in the construction and internalization of new knowledge has demonstrated the benefit of collaboration with true peers (Donato, 1994; Storch, 2002; Swain, Brooks, & Tocalli-Beller, 2002; Swain & Lapkin, 1998; Villamil & De Guerrero, 1998; see Lantolf, 2000, for a review). Collaboration with writing center tutors is somewhat different, and potentially even more beneficial since they lay claim to some expertise and authority as well as commonality of experience with the writers, hence the term, *more capable* peer. Writing center interaction is consistent with what Storch (2002) calls an *expert–novice* pattern, in which one interlocutor (the tutor) generally controls the flow of discourse, demonstrating a lack of equality. Yet, there is moderate *mutuality,* that is, the expert actively encourages the participation of the novice.

Though characteristics of both dominance and solidarity are present in the writing center sessions, the data here suggest that both participants willingly take on nonreciprocal roles in their interaction. The balance is toward tutor dominance and authority, as shown through turn length, floor management, and their use of potentially face-threatening speech acts. This trend is more pronounced in sessions with L2 writers on many, but not all measures. Although this tendency toward dominance may be linked to their native speaker knowledge, it is not generally manifested in a display of linguistic knowledge. That is, the content of the sessions does not usually emphasize their superior native speaker competence, so this is not a compelling explanation for the difference between L2 writer and NE writer sessions. One possible explanation again, may be the effort on the part of the tutors to facilitate L2 writer comprehension. This may also be a factor in the simpler and more explicit directive forms that the tutors use with these students. Whether or not this interactive style is beneficial for the L2 writers remains to be seen.

Finally, there are two areas in which these findings may shed light on the development of SL pragmatic competence. First, given the somewhat different stances of the tutors with NE and SL writers, we may wish to question the validity of using NS speech events in developing target norms for SL learners. Do NE and SL writers participate in equivalent speech events, or are there important differences that impact norms for interaction? Do the norms change as a learner's proficiency increases? In most experimental studies of interlanguage pragmatics, there is an underlying assumption that the speech situation is constant; SL performance is measured against that of NSs in the same speech situations, an assumption that extends to assessment of pragmatic competence (e.g., Brown, 2001; Hudson, 2001). Yet, in writing center interaction at least, this assumption is only partially supported; indeed the input to L2 learners, suggested as a crucial factor in L2 pragmatic development (Bardovi-Harlig, 2001), may differ from the input in NE sessions. Second, the findings underscore the importance of learning not just rules for taking on specific roles in interaction, such as a graduate student in an advising session or client in a social service interview, but of learning how these roles can be actively negotiated in interaction. This presents a considerably more complex goal for the acquisition of SL pragmatic competence.

ACKNOWLEDGMENTS: This research was supported by a grant from the University of Illinois at Chicago Office of Vice Chancellor for Research. My thanks to Leane Dostaler for assistance in transcription and coding, and to the editors for their valuable suggestions.

REFERENCES

Agar, M. (1985). Institutional discourse. *Text, 5*, 147-168.

Aston, G. (1993). Notes on the interlanguage of comity. In G. Kasper & S. Blum-Kulka (Eds.), *Interlanguage pragmatics* (pp. 224-250). Oxford, England: Oxford University Press.

Aleksa, V., Bednarowicz, E., Smith, E., Brecke, C., & Huang, G. (2000). *Between a better grade and a meaningful conversation: Departures for writing interlocutors.* University of Illinois at Chicago Writing Center handbook.

Bardovi-Harlig, K. (2001). Evaluating the empirical evidence: Grounds for instruction in pragmatics. In G. Kasper & K. Rose (Eds.), *Pragmatics in language teaching* (pp. 13-32). Cambridge, England: Cambridge University Press.

Bardovi-Harlig, K., & Dörnyei, Z. (1998). Do language learners recognize pragmatic violations? Pragmatic versus grammatical awareness in instructed L2 learning. *TESOL Quarterly, 32*, 233-259.

Bardovi-Harlig, K., & Hartford, B. (1993a). The language of comembership. *Research on Language and Social Interaction, 26*, 227-257.

Bardovi-Harlig, K., & Hartford, B. (1993b). Learning the rules of academic talk: A longitudinal study of pragmatic development. *Studies in Second Language Acquisition, 15*, 279-304.

Bardovi-Harlig, K., & Hartford, B. (1991). Saying "no" in English: Native and nonnative rejections. *Pragmatics and Language Learning, 2*, 41-57.

Bardovi-Harlig, K., & Hartford, B. (1990). Congruence in native and nonnative conversations: Status balance in the academic advising session. *Language Learning, 40*, 467-500.

Bereiter, C., & Scardamalia, M. (1987). *The psychology of written composition.* Hillsdale, NJ: Lawrence Erlbaum Associates.

Blau, S., & Hall, J. (2002). Guilt-free tutoring: Rethinking how we tutor non-native-English-speaking students. *Writing Center Journal, 23*, 23-44.

Blau, S., Hall, J., & Strauss, T. (1998). Exploring the tutor–client conversation: A linguistic analysis. *Writing Center Journal, 19*, 19-48.

Blum-Kulka, S., House, J., & Kasper, G. (1989). *Cross-cultural pragmatics: Requests and apologies.* Norwood, NJ: Ablex.

Bouquet, E. (1999). 'Our little secret:' A history of writing centers, pre-to post-open admissions. *College Composition and Communication, 50*, 462-483.

62   *Williams*

Brooks, J. (1991). Minimalist tutoring: Making students do all the work. *Writing Lab Newsletter, 15,* 1-4.

Brown, J.D. (2001). Pragmatic tests: Different purposes, different tests. In G. Kasper & K. Rose (Eds.), *Pragmatics in language teaching* (pp. 301-325). Cambridge, England: Cambridge University Press.

Bruffee, K. (1984). Peer tutoring and the conversation of mankind. In G. Olsen (Ed.), *Writing centers: Theory and administration* (pp. 3-14). Evanston, IL: NCTE.

Cameron, R., & Williams, J. (1997). Senténce to ten cents: A case study of relevance and communicative success in nonnative-native speaker interactions in a medical setting. *Applied Linguistics, 18,* 415-445.

Capossela, T.-L. (1998). *The Harcourt Brace guide to peer tutoring.* Fort Worth: Harcourt Brace.

Clark, I. (2001). Perspectives on the directive/non-directive continuum in the writing center. *Writing Center Journal, 22,* 33-57.

Cumming, A., & So, S. (1996). Tutoring second language text revision: Does the approach to instruction and the language of communication make a difference? *Journal of Second Language Writing, 5,* 197-225.

Damon, W., & Phelps, E. (1989). Critical distinctions among three approaches to peer education. *International Journal of Educational Research, 58,* 9-19.

Donato, R. (1994). Collective scaffolding in second language acquisition. In J. Lantolf & G. Appel (Eds.), *Vygotskian approaches to second language research* (pp. 33-56). Norwood, NJ: Ablex.

Drew, P., & Heritage, J. (1992). Analyzing talk at work. In P. Drew & J. Heritage (Eds.), *Talk at work* (pp. 3-65). Cambridge, England: Cambridge University Press.

Dyehouse, J. (1999). Peer tutors and institutional authority. In L. Podis & J. Podis (Eds.), *Working with student writers* (pp. 53-57). New York: Peter Lang.

Erickson, F., & Schultz, J. (1982). *The counselor as gate-keeper.* New York: Academic Press.

Fiksdal, S. (1989). Framing uncomfortable moments in cross-cultural gatekeeping interviews. In S. Gass, C. Madden, D. Preston, & L. Selinker (Eds.), *Variation in second language acquisition: Discourse and pragmatics* (pp. 190-207). Clevedon, UK: Multilingual Matters.

Fisher, S., & Todd, D. (Eds.). (1983*). The social organization of doctor–patient communication.* Washington, D.C.: Center for Applied Linguistics.

Gadbow, K. (1992). Foreign students in the writing lab: Some ethical and practical considerations. *Writing Lab Newsletter, 17,* 1-5.

Gass, S., & Varonis, E. (1986). Sex differences in nonnative speaker–nonnative speaker interactions. In R. Day (Ed.), *Talking to learn* (pp. 327-351). Rowley, MA; Newbury House.

Gass, S., & Houck, N. (1999). *Interlanguage refusals: A cross-cultural study of Japanese-English.* Berlin: Mouton de Gruyter.

Gass, S., & Mackey, A. (2000). *Stimulated recall methodology in second language research.* Mahwah, NJ: Lawrence Erlbaum Associates.

Gillespie, P., Gillam, A., Brown, L.F., & Stay, B. (Eds.) (2002). *Writing center research: Extending the conversation.* Mahwah, NJ: Lawrence Erlbaum Associates.

Goldberg, J. (1990). Interrupting the discourse on interruptions. *Journal of Pragmatics, 14,* 883-903.

Harris, M. (1982). *Tutoring writing: A sourcebook for writing labs.* Glenview, IL: Scott Foresman.

Harris, M. (1995). Talking in the middle: Why writers need writing tutors. *College English, 57,* 27-42.

Harris, M. (1997). Cultural conflicts in the writing center: Expectations and assumptions of ESL students. In C. Severino, J. Guerra, & J. Butler (Eds.), *Writing in multicultural settings* (pp. 220-233). New York: Modern Language Association.

Harris, M., & Silva. T. (1993). Tutoring ESL students: Issues and options. *College Composition and Communication, 44,* 525-537.

He, A. (1993). Exploring modality in institutional interactions: Cases from academic counselling encounters. *Text, 13,* 503-528.

He, A. (1994). Withholding academic advice: Institutional context and discourse practice. *Discourse Processes, 18,* 297-316.

Hudson, T. (2001). Indicators for pragmatic tests: Some quantitative tools. In G. Kasper & K. Rose (Eds.), *Pragmatics in language teaching* (pp. 283-300). Cambridge, England: Cambridge University Press.

Kasper, G., & Rose, K. (1999). Pragmatics and SLA. In W. Grabe (Ed.), *Annual Review of Applied Linguistics, 19,* 81-104.

Kennedy, B. (1993). Non-native speakers as students in first-year composition classes with native speakers: Can writing tutors help? *Writing Center Journal, 13,* 27-38.

Kinkead, J., & Harris, J. (Eds.) (1993). *Writing centers in context.* Urbana, IL: NCTE.

Lantolf, J. (2000). Second language learning as a mediated process. *Language Teaching Abstracts,* 33, 79-96.

Lave, J., & Wenger. E. (1991). *Situated learning: Legitimate peripheral participation.* Cambridge, England: Cambridge University Press.

Makri-Tsilipakou, M. (1994). Interruption revisited: Affiliative vs. disaffiliative interruption. *Journal of Pragmatics, 21,* 401-426.

Mehan, H. (1985). The structure of classroom discourse. In T. van Dijk (Ed.), *Handbook of discourse analysis, Vol. 3* (pp. 120-132). London: Academic Press.

Moll, L. (1989). Teaching second language students: A Vygotskyan perspective. In D. Johnson & D. Roen (Eds.), *Richness in writing* (pp. 55-69). New York: Longman.

Moser, J. (1993). Crossed currents: ESL students and their peer tutors. *Research and Teaching in Developmental Education, 9,* 37-43.

Murata, K. (1994). Intrusive or co-operative? A cross-cultural study of interruption. *Journal of Pragmatics, 21,* 385-400.

Murphy, S., & Law, J. (Eds.). (1995). *Landmark essays on writing centers.* Mahwah, NJ: Lawrence Erlbaum Associates.

Murray, S. (1985). Towards a model of members' methods for recognizing interruptions. *Language in Society, 13,* 31-41.

Newkirk, T. (1995). The writing conference as performance. *Research in the Teaching of English, 29,* 193-215.

North, S. (1984). The idea of a writing center. *College English, 46,* 433-446.

Pathey-Chavez, G.G., & Ferris, D. (1997). Writing conferences and the weaving of multi-voiced texts in college composition. *Research in the Teaching of English, 31,* 51-90.

Powers, J. (1993). Rethinking writing center conferencing strategies for the ESL writer. *Writing Center Journal, 13,* 39-47.

Ritter, J. (2002). *Negotiating the center: An analysis of writing center tutorial interactions between ESL learners and native-English speaking writing center tutors.* Unpublished doctoral dissertation, Indiana University of Pennsylvania..

Rounds, P. (1987). Characterizing successful classroom discourse for NNS teaching assistant training. *TESOL Quarterly, 21,* 643-671.

Rudolph, D. (1994). Constructing an apprenticeship with discourse strategies: Professor–graduate student interactions. *Language in Society, 23,* 199-230.

Salsbury, T., & Bardovi-Harlig, K. (2000). Oppositional talk and the acquisition of modality in L2 English. In B. Swierzbin, F. Morris, M. Anderson, C. Klee, & E. Tarone (Eds.), *Social and cognitive factors in second language acquisition* (pp. 57-76). Somerville, MA: Cascadilla Press.

Sarangi, S., & Roberts, C. (Eds.). (1999). *Talk, work and institutional order.* Berlin: DeGruyter.

Sperling, M. (1991). Dialogues of deliberation: Conversation in the teacher–student writing conference. *Written Communication, 8,* 131-162.

Storch, N. (2002). Patterns of interaction in ESL pair work. *Language Learning, 52,* 119-158.

Swain, M., Brooks, L., & Tocalli-Beller, A. (2002). Peer–peer dialogue as a means of second language learning. *Annual Review of Applied Linguistics, 22,* 171-185.

Swain, M., & Lapkin, S. (1998). Interaction and second language learning: Two adolescent French immersion students working together. *Modern Language Journal, 83,* 320-338.

Tannen, D. (1984). *Conversational style: Analyzing talk among friends.* Norwood, NJ: Ablex.

Tannen, D. (1989). Interpreting interruption in conversation. *Chicago Linguistics Society Papers, 25,* 266-287.

Tannen, D., & Wallat, C. (1993). Interactive frames and knowledge schemas in interaction: Examples from a medical examination/interview. In D. Tannen (Ed.), *Framing in discourse* (pp. 57-78). Oxford, England: Oxford University Press.

Tarone, E., & Kuehn, K. (2000). Negotiating the social services oral intake interview. *TESOL Quarterly, 34*, 99-126.

Thonus, T. (2002). Tutor and student assessments of academic writing tutorials: What is "success?" *Assessing Writing, 8*, 110-134.

Thonus, T. (2001). Triangulation in the writing center: Tutor, tutee, and instructor perception of the tutor's role. *Writing Center Journal, 22*, 59-81.

Thonus, T. (1999a). Dominance in academic writing tutorials: Gender, language proficiency and the offering of suggestions. *Discourse and Society, 10*, 225-248.

Thonus, T. (1999b). How to communicate politely and be a tutor, too: NS–NNS interaction and writing center practice. *Text, 19,* 253-279.

Thonus, T. (1999c, March). *NS–NNS interaction in academic writing tutorials: Discourse analysis and its interpretations.* Paper presented at the annual conference of the American Association of Applied Linguistics, Stamford, CT.

Tyler, A. (1995). The coconstruction of cross-cultural miscommunication: Conflicts in perceptions, negotiation and enactment of participant roles and status. *Studies in Second Language Acquisition, 17*, 129-152.

Trimbur, J. (1987). 'Peer tutoring': A contradiction in terms? *Writing Center Journal, 7,* 21-28.

Ulichny, P., & Watson-Gegeo, K. (1989). Interactions and authority: The dominant interpretive framework in writing conferences. *Discourse Processes, 12*, 309-328.

van Gelderen, A. (1997). Elementary students' skills in revising. *Written Communication, 14*, 360-397.

Villamil, O., & De Guerrero, M. (1998). Assessing the impact of peer revision on L2 writing. *Applied Linguistics, 19*, 491-514.

West, C., & Zimmerman, D. (1985). Gender, language and discourse. In T. van Dijk (Ed.), *Handbook of discourse analysis, Vol.4* (pp. 103-124). London: Academic Press.

Williams, J. (in press). Tutoring and revision: Second language writers in the writing center. *Journal of Second Language Writing.*

Woken, M., & Swales, J. (1989). Expertise and authority in native-nonnative conversations: The need for a variable account. In S. Gass, C. Madden, D. Preston, & L. Selinker (Eds.), *Variation in second language acquisition, Vol.1* (pp. 211-222). Clevedon, UK: Multilingual Matters.

Wolfson, N. (1988). The bulge: A theory of speech behavior and social distance. In J. Fine (Ed.), *Social language discourse: A textbook of current research* (pp. 21-38). Norwood, NJ: Ablex.

Young, Virginia. *Politeness phenomena in the university writing conference.* Unpublished doctoral dissertation, University of Illinois at Chicago. 1992.

Zuengler, J., & Bent, B. (1991). Relative knowledge of content domain: An influence on native-nonnative conversations. *Applied Linguistics, 12,* 397-416.

APPENDIX

Transcription Conventions

T: tutor
W: writer
(.)   Each (.) represents a .5 second pause
—   speaker chaining/interruption; no pause between speakers
//   speaker overlap
< > unintelligible
( ) nonverbal action
ital relevant portion of interaction is italicized
[ ]   voice modulation (e.g., loud, softly)

3

Negotiating an Institutional Identity: Individual Differences in NS and NNS Teacher Directives

Lynda Yates
LaTrobe University

In cross-cultural and interlanguage pragmatics research on requests there has been a strong orientation toward understanding the commonalities in the way speakers from particular language backgrounds perform in different situations, that is, on intragroup similarities and intergroup differences in behavior (see, e.g., Blum-Kulka, 1982, 1985, 1987, 1989; Eslamirasekh, 1993; Fen, 1996; Fukushima, 1990; Ha, 1998; Huang, 1996; Kim, 1995; Koike, 1994; Kubota, 1996; Lee-Wong, 1993; Mir, 1995; Rose, 1990; Trosborg, 1995; Yu, 1999; Zhang, 1995). This has left out of focus the issue of individual variation. Moreover, the assumption is usually made that the gap between any group of nonnative speakers and the nativespeaker "control" or baseline data is that "the NS have an established pragmatic competence on which they can draw for the situation" (Bardovi-Harlig & Hartford, 1996, p. 172), and that this is relatively stable and uniform. Such approaches therefore obscure what we all know intuitively, as members of a speech community: that speakers vary in the ways in which they use language and project themselves as individuals in different situations. In this chapter, I draw on data collected in a school setting to explore the issue of individual variation among both native speakers and Chinese language background speakers of English as they negotiate their institutional identities as trainee secondary teachers in Australian classrooms.

A focus on the commonalities shared by speakers of a speech community can provide important insights into what Gumperz (1996, p. 402) calls "specific, taken-for-granted, knowledge of background information and verbal forms" that are shared by a community. However, this focus on the shared inevitably entails a simplification of the way language is used and underwrites the construction of broad generalizations in which variation between individuals is neglected. Culture-specific styles and norms can only represent in the broadest outline the true diversity to be found within a culture, and we should be wary of regarding any language and cultural group as a "monolithic unity" in which individual differences are obscured. As Shea (1994, p. 380) warned: "Culture is not an essentialist construct where members adopt similar values, maintain uniform beliefs, and have interpretive conventions."

Although cultural groups may differ in the way they behave and use language in any particular social situation or identity, there will nevertheless be differences between individuals in the way in which they behave linguistically (Hansen & Liu, 1997).

Social constructivist approaches to sociolinguistics have emphasized the active role played by an individual in the construction of their social identity in any situation. Drawing on the communicative resources shared by the community, speakers actively established their social identities, in part through their use of language (e.g., Gumperz, 1982). They can do this by choosing to express certain acts in certain ways, or adopting a particular "stance" or "socially recognized point of view or attitude" (Ochs, 1993, p. 288). The adoption of a particular stance may impact, for example, on how much certainty to display and how to do it, or how much and what kind of emotion to display in what kind of situation and so on. Although the means for such displays are not directly encoded in a language, they rely on interpretation through convention, and the projection of social identities therefore crucially depends on the existence of shared conventions, as well as a shared political and social history which associates the acts and stances used with the social identity intended (Ochs, 1993, p. 290).

However, although members of a speech community may draw on broadly shared conventions for the display of social identity, each individual will draw on these differently, in line with the way in which they wish to present themselves (see Goffman's [1956] notion of *demeanor*). Differences between ways in which individuals make use of these may relate to individual psychology, personal expression, relationship with particular groups, or the immediate interactive context (Gumperz, 1996, p. 376). Even within "the same gross social identity" (Ochs, 1993, p. 297), such as "parent," "student," "teacher," and so on, different speakers will construct their social identities in different ways. That is, although speakers may draw on the same conventions, speakers will use them variably to project different social identities, even within the same general social role, as they struggle to change what is normally expected from a social identity, or challenge their social identity over time. Moreover, individuals are not necessarily consistent across time or contexts; the same speakers may project themselves differently on different occasions and in different situations. Social identities are dynamic, and individuals belong to many different groupings in society; therefore, they have multiple identities or *subjectivities* which vary across situations and time as they enact a variety of roles (Weedon, 1987). People build multiple, compatible social identities that may be blended or even blurred. Thus, second language learners, like native speakers, find that "there are no simple social or linguistic formulae that spit out how to compose suitable identities for the occasion" (Ochs, 1993, p. 298).

Because we are socialized into particular ways of acting in social situations from an early age (e.g., Ochs, 1988, 1996), adults who arrive in a particular context in a new community may not be fully aware of what conventions, including what acts and what stances, are considered appropriate for the different social roles enacted in that context. Thus the negotiation of a social identity in a context is especially challenging for those who are interacting in a second language and operating in a social context with which they are familiar in general terms, but which is subtly different from that into which they were socialized as children. Adult immigrants to Australia from the Peoples' Republic of China may not therefore be familiar with the shared conventions that native speakers (NS) can draw on in constructing their identities as teachers in Australian English. They may have an incomplete awareness of the repertoire of forms that can be used to mitigate directives, and the exact force of these forms in interaction, or they may have incomplete or inaccurate sociopragmatic understandings of how much and what kinds of mitigation are appropriate in the context, and what kind of stances are familiar to the students. That is, they may be able to "perform particular acts and stances linguistically" (Ochs, 1993, p. 291) but may lack awareness of how these relate to particular social identities in a second culture.

Moreover, an adult nonnative speaker (NNS) of any language has already established identities which have found expression through interactions in a different language and culture. Although they may have spent many years in Australia, and act in many ways like other members of the Australian community, they may nevertheless hold values from their first culture (e.g., Busher, 1997), and may not feel comfortable adopting stances and expressing social identities that are unfamiliar. As Hinkel (1996) shows, interlanguage speakers may not accept aspects of the target culture, and thus may not want to be completely nativelike in their language use. They may therefore seek to diverge from the ways in which native speakers express themselves as a means of projecting their individual or group ethnic identity (e.g., Siegal, 1996). Indeed, if they are visibly ethnically different from the majority Anglo-background population, as most immigrants from the PRC are, they may not be ratified in any role in the same way a NS might be: Native speakerlike behavior may not be accepted from nonnative speakers, simply because they may look and sound different from NSs (Amin, 1997; Tang, 1997). In this study, I was originally motivated by the desire to see whether there were differences in the ways that Chinese background and Anglo-background trainee teachers mitigated their directives to students in the secondary classroom. This topic was of practical interest for me as a teacher-trainer, because of frequent reports of miscommunication difficulties experienced by Chinese background teachers in the Australian school system. These are frequently blamed on language difficulties, but may actually relate to difficulty in establishing rapport with learners and constructing a social identity as a teacher in an educational environment built on very different, and less hierarchical, cultural traditions of learning (see, e.g., Cortazzi & Jin, 1996; Hofstede, 1986, 1994; Scollon, 1999). Since directives are potentially face-threatening (Brown & Levinson, 1987), highly variable across cultures (e.g., Blum-Kulka, House, & Kasper, 1989; Huang, 1996; Yu, 1999), and reflective of social relationships, these were chosen as the focus of the analysis.

As the study progressed, however, I found that the rich, naturally occurring data collected in classrooms allowed the examination of both the ways in which language background appeared to influence the ways that the participants used mitigation, and the differences in use of mitigation among individuals from the same language background. This ability to examine both the differences and the commonalities has illuminated some of the different stances that teachers take as they attempt to negotiate their social identities as teachers in the classroom.

THE STUDY

The aim of the study was to investigate and compare the verbal mitigation of directives among two groups of speakers: one which had grown up and been educated in Australia, and the other in the People's Republic of China. In doing this, I wanted to explore the ways in which speakers pay symbolic attention to both speakers' negative face needs of nonimposition and positive face needs of approval and belonging (Brown & Levinson, 1987) because, with few exceptions (e.g., Scarcella & Brunak, 1981), most previous studies of interlanguage requests have focused on the more formal devices of politeness, and have not developed Brown and Levinson's essential insight. This neglect has been, in part, a function of the type of elicited data usually analyzed in such studies, since data which has been elicited through the use of a discourse completion task (DCT) or a role-play tends to be more formal and monitored (Hartford & Bardovi-Harlig, 1992; Lee-Wong, 1993; Rintell & Mitchell, 1989; Rose, 1992, 1994). Speakers are likely to feel they are being required to put on a performance for the researcher, and, where data are collected in written form, the very act of writing is likely to encourage more formal, "best" behavior, eliciting what speakers think they ought to do, rather than what they actually do. This favors the collection of devices associated with formal politeness, and disadvantages the collection of devices associated with address to positive face, such as the signaling of common group membership through the use of colloquial expressions (which are seldom written).

   The use of an institutional setting, therefore, offered a number of advantages. First, it allowed naturally occurring instances of language use in an authentic context rather than the metapragmatic judgments or simulated language used collected through elicitation techniques. Second, it represented a compromise between ethnographic approaches in which the contributions of all kinds of speakers are collected, and more controlled elicitation methods in which speaker and situational variables can be more carefully controlled. Thus the participants were all interacting in the same gross social identity in a similar context with broadly similar mid-term and long-term goals (to pass the practicum and to teach in a secondary school). Although the type of lesson they taught varied, there were similar phases to each class (setting up the activity, asking class questions, checking on individual work, directing practical activities, setting and returning homework, and so on). Moreover, a large number of directive tokens could be collected in ways that are replicable in future studies, but which also allowed a close examination of function in their interactive contexts. Each directive could therefore be examined for function on a number of levels.

Participants

For the study, 18 participants, nine Anglo-Australian background (AB) and nine Chinese background from the PRC (CB) were audio- and video-recorded teaching two lessons in an Australian secondary school as they undertook the practical teaching component of their initial teacher training qualification.[1] They were all graduates studying at various universities in Melbourne. The CB participants were aged between 25 and 39, while the AB participants were native speakers of Australian English, were slightly younger (between 21 and 28), and had all been educated in Australia. The CB were recruited for the study through the help of teaching practicum placement coordinators in the education departments of the major universities in Melbourne, who identified trainee teachers who met the criteria (i.e., who were born and raised in the PRC and who were teaching a subject other than Chinese). I included in the study the whole sample of trainee teachers who met these criteria and agreed to participate over a 2-year period. In general, most people I approached were sympathetic to the aims of the study, and agreed to participate, although life events (in one case a car crash!) forced some to withdraw. I identified the AB participants through my position in the education department at a Melbourne university (La Trobe)

Table 3.1. Summary of characteristics of Australian background and Chinese background participants

Characteristic	Australian Background		Chinese Background	
Age	Early to late 20s		Mid twenties to late thirties	
Country of Education	Australia		People's Republic of China (1 part-educated in Hong Kong, degree in Australia)	
Male	5		4	
Female	4		5	
Curriculum areas	Business	(1, yr 11)	Business	(1, yr 11)
	ESL	(2, young & yr 7)	ESL	(2, young & middle)
	Math	(2, yr 7, 11)	Math	(2, yr 8 & 9)
	Music	(1, yr 7/8)	Music	(1, yr 7)
	Science	(2, yr 11 & 11)	Science	(2, yr 10 & 11)
	Swimming	(1, yr 10)	Swimming	(1, yr 9)

Note: The school in which these sessions were recorded did not divide classes in ESL according to strict year level but had a young (7/8) and a middle class (9/10).

---

[1] In Australia, primary education runs from Kindergarten to Year 6, and secondary school from Year 7 to 12. The students were therefore between 11–18 years old.

and was able to match the CB for subject area and gender as far as possible (see Table 3.1).

Each participant was recorded in school teaching one of the two specialist subjects they were training to teach upon graduation. These ranged from swimming sports to math, and included business studies, science, and ESL, but not foreign languages (see Table 3.1). The students in these classes generally reflected the social and ethnic mix of the school community, except in ESL classes, where all students came from a non-English-speaking background. Again, I enlisted the aid of practicum placement coordinators throughout Melbourne in order to gain permission to record in schools. I needed permission from all regional school authorities, the ethics committee of my university, the participants themselves, their supervising teachers, and the parents of all the children in every class. In the latter case, permission was obtained through a signed consent form distributed as soon as the participant arrived at the school.

For each of the two lessons recorded, the participants wore a small portable cassette recorder with a lapel microphone which was switched on at the beginning of the class and left running until the end. Because most schools' scheduled classes to run for approximately 50 minutes, this enabled the majority of the lesson to be captured on a 45-minute tape. I also video-recorded each lesson and collected field notes so that the context of any directive could be clearly identified. After the recordings, I interviewed each participant about their experiences with the practicum. The classroom discourse recorded in this way was transcribed, and any directive given by the teacher identified.

Directives: Identification and Coding

Using Searle (1975) as a starting point, directives were broadly defined as attempts by the teacher to get a student to do something concrete in the future. No attempt was made to distinguish directive acts of different force (e.g., an order from a request), but certain kinds of pedagogical acts, such as general solicits, were not included in the analysis. Each directive was then coded for aspects of the context (e.g., whether they were made to a single person or the whole class) and for the mitigation devices used to soften it. Mitigation was coded in four major categories identified by Blum-Kulka et al. (1989): the strategy (level of directness) of the head act of the directive; syntactic modification of the strategy; lexical modification of the directive, and propositional modification (the use of additional moves to support the head act, called external mitigation in Blum-Kulka et al., 1989). The framework was expanded to include other devices identified in the data, and to include attention to both negative face concerns of nonimposition and positive face concerns for approval and belonging (Brown & Levinson, 1987; O'Driscoll, 1996).

To capture the ways in which positive face needs were addressed in mitigation, the coding framework included some specific devices which signaled warmth and approval (such as the use of praise or approval propositional moves to support the directive), or solidarity through the reduction of social distance (such as the use of humor or inclusive cultural references). The reduction of social distance was also tracked by assessing the extent to which the particular forms chosen by the participants reduced, maintained, or increased social distance. Thus more formal devices associated with formal politeness (such as *could you* and *please*) were considered to be more distancing than more colloquial forms such as the use of a solidary address term, such as *guys* or a vernacular term, as in the example in Table 3.2. A summary of the coding framework can be found in Appendices A and B, and examples of some of the ways in which social distance was reflected in the use of different devices is given in Table 3.2

In order to allow comparison with previous studies and some quantitative exploration of the data, the use of each category of mitigation and tokens of particular devices were counted and expressed as a percentage of the total number of directives used by an individual or a group. That is, the frequency with which particular types of mitigation were used was calculated both for language and gender groups (i.e., for AB females and males, and for CB females and males), as well as for individuals. This allowed the identification of both main trends in the data, and individual patterns of variation. The data were also explored qualitatively using the NUD*IST[2] program.

COMMONALITIES AND DIFFERENCES IN MITIGATING STYLE

As discussed earlier, an important overall finding of the study was that, although language background was important in explaining how the participants mitigated their directives, there were also considerable individual differences that appeared to relate, not only to gender and level of pragmatic sophistication in English, but also to differences in individual mitigating style, which reflected the way in which participants chose to project themselves as individuals and teachers in the classroom. These are discussed first in the next section, before discussion of the ways in which these styles differed and the extent to which they can be related to background discipline, life experience, and other factors.

Overall Trends for Language Background and Gender

The overall trends for both males and females from the two language backgrounds can be seen in Table 3.3, which presents the number of mitigated and unmitigated directives produced by each group. Because the number of participants in each language and gender grouping is small (three to five), group totals should only be considered a rough guide to patterns of use and interpreted in conjunction with the results for individuals discussed in the next section. Nevertheless, the frequencies shown in Table 3.3 suggest that both language background and gender influenced the mitigation of directives, since AB miti-

---

[2] An ethnographic data processing program developed by QSR.

Table 3.2. Examples of address to different types of face

Strategy	Syntactic mitigation
Distance-maintaining e.g., *you* + stem or *you will*: • *you copy it down* • *you are here. / you will start from here* Less distancing, e.g. 'going to' or 'I want': • *alright /so first we're going to listen now/ I want the boys all to move/ thata way/ ok*	More distancing: e.g. past tense: • *would you go and speak to Mr. X please (name)?* Less distancing, e.g., *going to* and defocalisers: • *you are going to have to stop distracting all the people around you* • *so, what I suggest you do/ is just read through it*

Lexical mitigation	Propositional mitigation
More distancing, e.g., politeness marker • *if you still talk you sit in there please, OK?* Less distancing, e.g., vernacular: • *grab a copy of that*	Warm but not solidary, e.g., approval moves, e.g., Praise • *ok that was good /come in here guys* Less distancing solidary rapport moves, e.g., personal/cultural reference: • *get off it (name) it's not a surfboard alright?*

gated more frequently than CB, and, within each language group, females mitigated more than males. The overall pattern of mitigation use follows the pattern AB females (72.7%) > AB males (64.8%) > CB females (58.2%) > CB males (54.8%).

The different groups also favored the use of different categories of mitigators. Table 3.4 shows the frequencies with which the groups of participants used the four categories of mitigation. In this table, the raw numbers of directives that contained a particular category of mitigation are reported as a percentage of the total number of directives given by that group. Reading across the second row, for example, we see that the four female AB participants produced a total of 631 directives, 208 or 33% of which used an indirect strategy. As the total number of directives produced varied widely between groups and individuals, percentages were used as the basis of comparison.

It is important to note that the categories of indirect strategies and syntactic, prepositional, and lexical mitigation (Tables 3.3 and 3.4) are not mutually exclusive. Any one directive can combine an indirect strategy and more than one mitigator. Reading across Table 3.4 in the first row we find that among the total number of directives produced by AB males, 24.5% exhibited indirect strategies, 9.7% used syntactic mitigation, 22.5% propositional mitigation, and 38.3% used lexical mitigation. As Table 3.3 shows, 35.2% of the directives had no mitigators. This shows the extent to which directives occur with multiple mitigators. In other words, some directives have no mitigators whereas other directives have more than one type.

Thus AB of both genders were less direct than CB males, and both AB groups used more syntactic and propositional mitigation than either CB group. Although there was less difference between CB and AB in the frequency with which the groups used lexical mitigation, as discussed in the following section, many CB tended to rely on the use of minimal tags or token agreements, while AB used a wider range of both minimizing and solidarity devices. Female AB tended to use most devices more frequently than their male counterparts. This was not always the case among CB, where level of pragmatic sophistication in English appeared to be a factor (see the section entitled *Variation Among the Chinese Background Speakers*).

Whereas overall comparisons with previous studies of Chinese background interlanguage speakers of English (Fen, 1996; Yu, 1999) are problematic because of differences in data collection and analysis (see Yates, 2000), these results nevertheless parallel those found for learners in Fen (1996) (the only study that investigated interlanguage speakers in high-power positions), and show some of the tendencies outlined for Chinese speakers of Mandarin suggested by Lee-Wong (1993). That is, Chinese background speakers in positions of relative authority mitigate less than do native speakers of English in similar roles: They are more direct, and use syntactic and propositional mitigation less frequently than native speakers of English, and rely more heavily on lexical mitigation.

Individual Variation

However, there was also considerable individual variation in the participants' use of mitigation which does not entirely fit within these patterns. Figure 3.1 shows individual participants ranked according to the frequency with which they used mitigation. Exact frequencies are shown in Appendix C.

Table 3.3. Mitigation of Directives by Language and Gender

Language/gender	Total indirect directives and/or directives with mitigation		Total directives without indirectness or mitigation		Total directives
	n	*% of tot*	*n*	*% of tot*	*n*
AB m	328	64.8	178	35.2	506
AB f	459	72.7	172	27.3	631
Tot AB	*787*	*69.2*	*305*	*30.8*	*1137*
CB m	241	54.8	199	45.2	440
CB f	399	58.2	287	41.8	686
Tot CB	*640*	*56.8*	*486*	*43.2*	*1126*

Table 3.4. Mitigation of Directives by Language and Gender

Language/ gender	Total indirect strategies		Directives with syntactic mitigation		Directives with propositional mitigation		Directives with lexical mitigation		Total directives
	n	*% of tot*	*n*	*% of tot*	*n*	*% of tot*	*n*	*% of tot*	*n*
AB m	124	24.5	49	9.7	114	22.5	194	38.3	506
AB f	208	33.0	98	15.5	173	27.4	295	46.8	631
Tot AB	*332*	*29.2*	*147*	*12.9*	*287*	*25.2*	*489*	*43.0*	*1137*
CB m	79	18.0	24	5.5	65	14.8	173	39.3	440
CB f	134	19.5	24	3.5	120	17.5	253	36.9	686
Tot CB	*213*	*18.9*	*48*	*4.3*	*185*	*16.4*	*426*	*37.8*	*1126*

Each participant is identified by two initial letters that indicate whether they are Anglo-Australian (*A*) or Chinese background (*C*), female (*f*), or male (*m*), followed by a number that identifies them uniquely (as in *Af1* or *Cm1*). A mitigation index was calculated for each individual participant by adding together the number of directives that contained lexical mitigation, propositional mitigation, syntactic mitigation, and indirect strategies and dividing the sum by the total number of directives to give an overall mitigation index. Because an individual directive can contain a mitigator from more than one category of mitigation (and possibly from all four), the total index may amount to more than 1.0. The results for individuals are presented in the order of this ranking, from the participant who had the highest mitigation index, *Af1* with a total of 1.69 (mitigator categories per directive) to the lowest mitigator, *Cm4* with an index of only .42 (fewer than one mitigator category for every two directives). From these results, it can be seen that individuals varied considerably in the frequency with which they used mitigated directives in general, and also in their use of the different categories of mitigation. Thus, for example, although participants *Cf3* and *Am3* had similar mitigation indices overall (.86 and .85 respectively), they tended to use different categories more frequently: *Cf3* tended to use more indirect strategies and less syntactic mitigation, whereas *Am3* used lexical mitigation, particularly vernacular, more frequently, but was generally more direct in the strategy he used in the head act.

From Figure 3.1 it is clear that, although language background and gender were important predictors of how frequently participants used mitigation with their directives, individuals varied in relation to the general tendencies for their language and gender peers. Thus AB females, as might be anticipated from the overall results presented in the previous section, generally mitigated more frequently than the other participants. They provided the two highest users of mitigation, *Af1*, and *Af2*, who had mitigation indices of 1.69 and 1.26 respectively. However, two of the four AB females, *Af3* and *Af4*, mitigated less

Figure 3.1. Individual Variation in Frequency of Mitigation

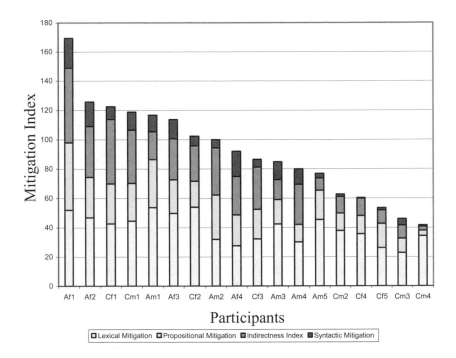

frequently, and had somewhat lower indices of 1.14 and .92, respectively. AB males generally mitigated slightly less frequently than the females, with indices between 1.17 and .77. Although, in accordance with the overall trends discussed in the previous section, CB participants in general mitigated infrequently (five of them exhibiting low indices ranging from only .63 to .42), two CB participants, *Cf1* and *Cm1,* nevertheless ranked third and fourth overall in the frequency with which they used mitigation, with mitigation indices of 1.22, and 1.19 respectively.

It is clear, therefore, that although background and gender were important in understanding how frequently a participant mitigated, individuals within the same language and gender group varied considerably. This variation was also evident in the types of devices that participants used, as becomes more evident in the following section where individual mitigating style is discussed.

Mitigating Style

Both AB and CB trainee teachers varied considerably, not only in how frequently each used a particular category of mitigation or device, but also in the type of device they chose to use and the "teacher" social identity they were projecting through their choices. However, in one respect all CB were similar

Table 3.5. Individual Styles and Factors

	Style	Features	Factors
Af l, 2, 3	*Friendly, solidary, non-impositive*	Low-distance, highly mitigated style	Female, young, projecting a solidary identity
Am1	*Matey. Academic*	Medium mitigation style with low-medium distance	Male-influenced discipline, (engineering), young, solidary
Am2	*Matey, non-impositive*	Medium mitigation, but low distance. Lower lexical	Young, less gendered discipline (drama)
Am5	*Super-matey, 'sports'*	Low frequency of mitigation, plus low distance. Relatively direct, high	Solidary, male-oriented discipline (sport)
Af4	*Authoritative, but non-impositive. Mildly solidary. Signals separateness.*	Medium mitigation style with medium distance. Relatively indirect, high syntax	Older/experienced, content-focused, tertiary-oriented. Female
Am3		As for Af4, but overall less indirectness and syntactic, more propositional and lexical. Male characteristics.	Confident, tertiary-oriented. Male.
Am4	*Vacillating, authoritative*	Vacillation between distanced and solidary	Young, confused about teaching identity
Cf1 **Cm1**	*Warm, friendly but non-solidary, non-impositive. Emphasises separateness.*	Highly-mitigated, but *minimization* more target-like than address to *social distance*	Pragmatic sophistication in English, inexperience of role, desire to fit in. Sought out English-speaking room-mates.
Cf2	*Warm, non-impositive, separate, a little solidary*	Highly-mitigated, *minimisation* more target-like than address to *social distance*, but used some more non-distancing devices than other CB	Pragmatic sophistication in addressing negative face needs, desire to fit in, some experience of role. Sought out English-speaking room-mates
Cf3	*Warm, distant and limited*	Indirect and relatively frequent syntax compared to other CB, but little flexibility or solidarity	Partial pragmatic sophistication. Less intense experience of native speakers.
Cf4 **Cf5** **Cm2** **Cm3** **Cm4**	*Impositive and very distant, sometimes warm*	Non-target-like address to all dimensions. Frequent features indicating language proficiency difficulties	Lower pragmatic sophistication in English, limited understanding of teacher role in Australia, less intense experience of native speakers, language proficiency issues

and differed from AB: They tended to use a mitigating style that was less solidary. That is, AB participants regularly addressed positive face needs of belonging and inclusion, by choosing forms that reduced, or at least did not increase, social distance. None of the CB used such devices to the same degree although they used formal politeness markers such as *please* more frequently. They did not, therefore, seem to reduce social distance to adopt the more "matey" stance taken by the AB teachers. This can be seen in Table 3.5 which summarizes the different styles used by the participants. In addition, among the CB, awareness of the types of usage of mitigating devices appeared to be a factor. The mitigating styles adopted by the AB and the CB participants are explored in greater detail in the following two sections.

VARIATION AMONG THE AUSTRALIAN BACKGROUND PARTICIPANTS

In addition to the considerable differences between AB individuals in the frequency with which they used the categories of mitigation, there were also differences in the forms and devices they used, and in particular in the degree of social distance they projected vis-à-vis their interlocutors through their choice of mitigating device. These differences seem to have been motivated, by gender, discipline background, and context, and also by other, more individual factors related to the way in which the participants each negotiated their identities as teachers. Those who mitigated more frequently tended also to use distance-reducing devices more frequently, and distance-maintaining devices less frequently, than those AB participants who mitigated less, as can be seen by their more frequent use of all categories of mitigation. Table 3.6 summarizes the use of the four categories of mitigation by the Australian background participants, together with an assessment of the degree of distance they projected based on the forms and types of devices they used.

As shown in Table 3.6, those AB who used the most mitigation, *Af2*, *Af1*, *Af3*, and *Am1*, also tended to adopt a lower distance approach to mitigation than did *Af4*, *Am4,* and *Am3*. Males *Am2* and *Am5* were exceptions to this tendency. This difference in the projection of social distance could be seen in all four categories of mitigation, that is, in their choice of strategy, in their syntactic modifications, lexical choice, and the propositional support they gave their directives, although some participants tended to be more distanced in their approach in one category of mitigation than in others. *Af1*, *Af2,* and *Am1* were consistently low distance in their approach to all categories. *Af3* adopted a lower distance approach in her use of syntactic, propositional and lexical mitigation, but not in her use of substrategies. Context may have been important here, since she was teaching a lively class so that a relatively high percentage of her directives related to discipline issues in response to perceived misbehavior. This seems to have encouraged her to adopt greater distance in her choice of strategy, as in the following examples. In Example (1), she chooses a more distancing conventionally polite formula 'would you' to increase social distance as she

Table 3.6. Overall Use of the Categories of Mitigation by the Australian Background Participants

Participants	Indirectness strategies	Syntactic mitigation	Propositional mitigation	Lexical mitigation	Distance
Am1	√	√	+	+	Low
Am3	√	+	√	√	High
Am4	√	+	−	−	High
Am5	−	−	√	+	Sports
Am2	+	√	+	−	Low
Af2	+	+	+	+	Low
Af1	+	+	+	+	Low
Af3	+	+	√	+	Low
Af4	√	+	√	−	High

Note. + = frequent use; √ = moderate use; − = low use (relative to all 18 participants, including CB).

asserts her authority, while in Example (2), she reinforces the formal politeness of 'would you' with the formal and distancing on-record marker 'please':

(1) (*Af3*)

   Would you boys stop being silly because you were working so well.

(2) (*Af3*)

   Would you go and speak to Mr. Smith[3] please Ryan?

Thus three of the four AB females (*Af1, Af2, Af3*), used mitigation frequently and reduced social distance through their choices of mitigation. They did this by using fewer distancing strategies, modifying their directives with low distance syntactic mitigation, such as deflectors, as in Example (3), or heavy use of positive politeness hedges as in Example (4) taken from a business class with Year 11 students. All three were relatively young (early 20s) and seemed to be projecting a friendly, solidary persona, in which directives were softened by appeal to in-group membership and reduced social distance.

(3) Solidary female (*Af3*)

   So, *what I suggest you do*/ is just read through it,

---

[3] All names have been changed.

(4)   Solidary female (*Af1*)

> OK. /Now *like* beside that /I'm sorry I've (there's not) not much room on the board /you can put something like/ 'if the store has a run down look and stock looks like shop worn '/[..] *that sort of thing*

Female participant *Af4* used mitigation with her directives slightly less frequently than her female peers, as she used fewer lexical devices (e.g., *just* or *I think*) and maintained more social distance than the other three. Unlike the other three, for example, she did not use a single positive politeness hedge (e.g., *like*, *sort of*), and used vernacular and personalization (e.g., *for me*) less frequently. She did, however, make relatively high use of syntactic mitigation using modals and conditionals, which tended to be a little more distancing, as in Example (5) and Example (6), and used more distancing lexical mitigation, such as *please* more frequently, as in Example (7).

(5)   Authoritative female (*Af4*)

> Year 11, *would you like* to take a five minute break now?

(6)   Authoritative female (*Af4*)

> Now, *if you can* get into groups of two,

(7)   Authoritative female (*Af4*)

> Can you two share a text book between you, *please*

Her rather more formal mitigating style may be, in part, related to regional differences in that *Af4* had grown up in a country town, whereas the other three had grown up in Melbourne. It may also reflect the fact that she had had experience of tertiary teaching, while the other three had not, and that she was also a little older. Although the exact influences on her mitigating style remain unclear, it seems that she positioned herself in a more authoritative position in relation to her students through her less solidary approach to mitigation.

Individual variation was even more evident among the AB males, and this may reflect the influence of changing gender roles and perceptions of manhood as Anglo-Australian culture absorbs the impact of feminism and the renegotiation of gender roles in the postindustrial era. While all AB males mitigated their directives less than the three high-mitigating females, as shown in Table 3.6, two males, *Am1* and *Am2*, adopted a relatively high-mitigating and low-distance approach to mitigation. This low distance style projected a *matey* rapport through frequent use of propositional mitigation, and the reduction of social distance through choice of strategy and lexis. The directive in Example (8) given by *Am1* starts with "yeah," and so signals alignment. It also projects authority, in that he clearly states what he wants done by using a direct "I want" strategy, but this is modified syntactically to become the softer "I'd like." He adds a reason, so that the students know why he is directing them in this way, and addresses them using the vernacular "guys" to emphasize solidarity rather than social distance.

(8) Matey, academic (*Am1*)

> Yeah. I'd like it in your own words 'cause that way I can see whether you guys know what you're doing.

The style used by *Am2* was less direct than that used by *Am1* (as in Example 9), and he used lexical mitigation much less frequently. He seemed to be adopting a style that was masculine and matey, but also relatively nonimpositive and inclusive. Although they both used support moves frequently to justify or contextualize their directives, *Am1* tended to provide reasons, whereas *Am2* tended to use preparators and sequence moves (which let students know what was happening next, as in Example 10). In addition, like the three high-mitigating females, he used positive politeness hedges and personalization in an apparent attempt to signal solidarity.

(9) Matey, nonimpositive (*Am2*)

> George, *do you want to* give *me* some homework on Monday?

(10) Matey, nonimpositive (*Am2*)

> and if you want to finish your report for homework 10 and give it to me, *I'll go through it and correct it for you OK?*

Background discipline and context may have influenced the type of classroom persona that each wanted to project. Participant *Am1* trained in engineering, a traditionally male-dominated profession, in which all-male discourse is common. Inasmuch as interlocutor gender is an important influence on the use of politeness phenomena (Holmes, 1995), it is likely that norms of interaction within this profession are more traditionally masculine, and this may underpin *Am1's* use of directness and solidarity. Participant *Am2*, on the other hand, trained in media studies, which is a more "feminized" discipline, traditionally more tolerant of different ways of expressing gender, and this may have influenced his tendency to use indirect strategies. His lower use of vernacular, however, may also have been a reflection of the modifications made by teachers who are teaching learners from other language backgrounds (i.e., "foreigner talk"; Ferguson, 1975).

Two other male participants, *Am3* and *Am4*, adopted a more distanced approach and used mitigation less frequently. These two not only mitigated overall less frequently (see Figure 3.1), but also made relatively high use of various distance-maintaining devices (e.g., *please* and past tense syntactic mitigation) and relatively low use of distance-reducing devices (such as positive politeness hedges and propositional mitigation). Although both appeared to be projecting distance in order to assert their authority, they seem to have done this for different reasons. Participant *Am4* seems to have projected distance reactively, in response to discipline difficulties. Unlike *Af3*, however, his irritation showed and was noticed by the students. As is evident from the classroom transcripts of his lessons and from his own reports in the postrecording interviews, he was not always in control of the class and seemed to waver in his approach to the students, at times appearing to want to establish a good rapport with them and at others appearing to emphasise the power differences in an aggressive way. At one point, one of the students inquires of him, "You don't like this class, do you, Sir?" In Example (11), he uses a conventionally polite form ("could you") to request a book for some students who were not well-prepared for the lesson. He also refers to the students for whom the book is destined as "clowns," thus apparently colluding with the girls and signaling separateness from the boys.

(11) Vacillating *(Am4)*

> *Could one of you* girls lend these two *clowns* in the front row a book? They'll look after it. *Thanks*

On occasion, he switched from a more direct style to a more conventionally polite and distancing style in response to noncompliance. In Example (12), he is attempting to get his students to come into the classroom. He starts with a direct head act, reinforces this with an elliptical directive and finally resorts to formal, conventional politeness as he signals his displeasure at their unsatisfactory behavior and makes them go back outside to repeat the requested action.

(12) Repetition *(Am4)*

> So *come in* quietly.
> Quietly Year seven.
> *Excuse me* Year seven *could you* go back outside and line up *please.*

Both *Am4* and *Am3* used high amounts of vernacular, however, which reflects the fact that they used both formality and informality as part of a mitigating style that both distanced and signaled solidarity. Participant *Am3*, however, used the projection of distance proactively. In a similar way to *Af4*, he appeared to project a certain amount of distance, deliberately in order to maintain authority (i.e., in the absence of any discipline difficulties). In Example (13), *Am3* uses an Australian masculine diminutive ending in -*o*, thus signaling solidarity, with a conventionally polite request with *please*.

(13) *(Am3)*

> *Danno, can you* put that chair down next to you *please?*

The fifth AB male, *Am5,* who was recorded teaching swimming classes, adopted a style that was very direct and very matey (Example 14). His use of devices of nonimposition (e.g., indirect strategies) and distancing syntactic mitigation was very low, but he made frequent use of lexical mitigation, particularly vernacular, and of propositional mitigation, including humor and personal/ cultural references, which were sometimes bantering and apparently abusive. He thus drew heavily on solidarity devices and low-distance forms. This style seems to have drawn on the discourse of sporting events, particularly male sporting events in Australia. Kuiper (1991) noted similar tendencies in sporting events in New Zealand, and Deby (2003) in ice hockey commentaries in Canada. Deby (2003) suggests that such language use relates to displays of the ability to both dole out and withstand psychological as well as physical intimidation, a sort of verbal correlate of actual sporting prowess. The fact that *Am5* was recorded in a swimming class in an all-male school seems to have encouraged the use of this kind of particularly "masculine" style of mitigation. Note the use of a direct strategy and the solidary term of address, "mate" in Example (14).

(14) (*Am5*)

Get out of the pool *mate,*/your nose is all bloody

Thus, although there were commonalities in the way AB mitigated their directives, each drew on these in often subtly different ways to project their social identity. Each was constructing himself or herself as a male or female, as a teacher and as an individual in the classroom context where their previous experience was as a student rather than as the authority figure, and each did this differently in relation to what may be considered customary in Australia for their gender. Such insights remind us that variables such as language background and gender are influential but not deterministic. Rather, they should be seen as dynamic influences which are themselves in a state of constant change. Similar variation might also therefore be expected among the CB. However, as noted earlier, the picture here is further complicated by issues related to grammatical, pragmalinguistic and sociopragmatic proficiency in English and in familiarity with the *gross social identity* of being a teacher in an Australian school.

VARIATION AMONG THE CHINESE BACKGROUND PARTICIPANTS

Like the AB participants, the ways in which the CB mitigated their directives were also influenced by the type of identity they wished to project in the classroom. However, they not only had been socialized into a culture drawing on different views of personhood, gender, and social relations, but were also constrained in the ways in which they could relate to target culture norms by their linguistic and pragmalinguistic competence in English. Several of them seemed to have a less well-developed repertoire of mitigating devices at their disposal, as well as a potentially different understanding of the force these may have in an Australian classroom. Thus one factor that seems to be important in understanding is the variation among the CB is their *level of pragmatic sophistication in English*, which I characterize here in terms of the size of their repertoire of mitigating devices and the way in which it was used.

As shown in Figure 3.1 and Table 3.7, the CB varied widely in how frequently they used mitigation, from the three highest users of mitigation, *Cf1, Cm1,* and *Cf2* (with mitigation indices of 1.22, 1.19 and 1.02, respectively), to the low use of mitigation by *Cm2, Cf4, Cf5, Cm4,* and *Cm3,* with indices of between 62.8 and 41.7. Participant *Cf3* seemed to fall between the two groups. The former group appeared to be more pragmatically sophisticated in English than their peers. They mitigated more frequently, used more indirect strategies, propositional support moves, and syntactic and lexical mitigation than their peers. They offered more options (through, e.g., using an interrogative rather than an imperative form) and used devices which minimised the imposition of the request (by, e.g., downtoning or underplaying the request with devices such as *just* or *for a minute*). Their patterns of mitigation converged more closely on those of the AB. However, while they did reduce social distance more than their CB peers, they did not do this as frequently as did AB. These trends were evident in their use of all four categories of mitigation. As shown in Figure 3.1 and Table 3.7, however, they also differed from each other in some respects in their mitigating style.

As shown in Figure 3.1, *Cm1* mitigated a much higher percentage of his requests than any other CB male. In this, he was closer to the general pattern for the younger AB females than to that for the AB males. Although he mitigated his directives with roughly the same frequency as *Am1*, his style differed in that he used indirect strategies far more frequently (ranking second in his use of

Table 3.7. Overall Use of the Categories of Mitigation by the Chinese Background Participants

Participants	Indirectness	Syntactic mitigation	Propositional mitigation	Lexical mitigation	Solidarity
Cm1	+	+	+	√	√
Cm3	−	−	−	−	−
Cm2	−	−	−	√	−
Cm4	−	−	−	√	−
Cf2	√	√	√	+	√
Cf1	+	√	+	√	√
Cf5	−	−	−	√	−
Cf4	−	−	−	−	−
Cf3	√	√	√	−	−

Note. + = frequent use; √ = moderate use; — = low use (relative to all eighteen participants, including CB).

indirectness compared to 12th for *Am1*). This was because he made frequent use of the relatively distancing conventionally indirect strategies, "can you" and fewer of the directives phrased as "I want" or "you have to" which were favored by *Am1*. He did not use the high levels of vernacular and personalization characteristic of *Am1* (Example 15), but used distancing forms such as "please" frequently (whereas *Am1* did not use "please" once!) and addressed his student as "kids" as in Example (16), rather than the more solidary form "guys" used by *Am1*. Unlike *Am1*, he was therefore quite distancing in his mitigating style.

(15) *(Am1)*

> I'd do it with that one I reckon/ 'cause some of these calorimeters I think are a bit stuffed[4]

(16) *(Cm1)*

> That's too much noise, *kids*, keep it down *please*

He had been in Australia for 6 years, and seems to have made a very concerted effort to gain as much exposure to Australians and English usage as possible. He had deliberately moved into shared accommodation with Australians, and had worked in the retail industry where he used English daily. From his general use of language, these strategies seem to have paid off in that he was largely accurate and commanded a wide range of devices. Although he seems to have understood enough about interpersonal pragmatics in the Australian community to realize that requests, even to those in lower social positions, are frequently mitigated, he perhaps did not have sufficient familiarity with how to do this as a male in a position of authority. Whereas *Am1* mitigated frequently, he was able to establish his authority clearly through the use of relatively direct directives, but mitigate their impact through a reduction of social distance, and this seemed to be important in the way that at least some of the AB males projected their identity as teachers. Perhaps because he was not quite able to establish his credentials as a teacher, *Cm1* was the only participant who failed the teaching practicum on which he was recorded. Moreover, it was only when he viewed the video recordings of his classes that he understood why he had failed![5]

Female *Cf1*, like *Cm1*, mitigated very frequently, was relatively indirect in her strategy use and supported her directives with additional propositions, as in Example (17). She used lexical devices less frequently, although, like the other high-mitigating female CB, *Cf2*, and the AB females, she used hedges more frequently. She was often less accurate in her use of grammar, as can be seen in Example (18). Her overall style was warm and friendly rather than solidary,

---

[4] Which could be glossed as "Use that one because some of these calorimeters are not working properly."
[5] He subsequently undertook a further practicum placement which he passed.

which is to say she communicated warmth and approval, but she did not use displays which actively reduced social distance to signal solidarity. For example, like *Cf2,* she used very little vernacular and no personalization at all. She used a restricted range of devices, albeit with a frequency that was often similar to that of her AB counterparts.

(17) *(Cf1)*

> Rosie, did see your homework I correct for you? I just gave to you a corrected homework, could you correct them? And then I can tell you understand

(18) *(Cf1)*

> or you maybe you are not all the same problem you want to work indiv individually and you can

Overall, female *Cf2* was far more accurate in her use of English generally, and she used a wider range of mitigating devices. Her style was also a little less distancing than that of *Cm1* and *Cf1*, as she very occasionally used less distancing syntactic devices (such as the future as in "you're gonna do....") which no other CB did. Like AB in general, when she used a direct strategy it was often in the form of "I want" rather than an imperative. Both *Cf1* and *Cf2* had lived with and had partners who were native speakers of English, and had worked with young native speakers, *Cf1* as a nanny, and *Cf2* as a technical assistant in a school. It seems that these experiences had enabled them to have a closer appreciation of how directives are mitigated, although *Cf2's* greater overall linguistic proficiency allowed her to use a wider range of devices than *Cf1*.

Participants *Cf5, Cf4, Cm3, Cm2,* and *Cm4* appeared to be pragmatically less sophisticated in English, since they relied more heavily on minimal lexical devices such as *please,* the downtoner *just,* agreement (e.g., *yeah*) and token tags. They tended to use direct strategies, particularly the imperative, as in Examples (19) and (20) and *"you assert"* (*you* plus a stem form), as in Example (21), more frequently. Where they did use indirect strategies, these tended to be formulaic conventional requests (e.g., "can you") rather than the apparently advisory strategy (e.g., "you can" or "you should") that AB participants used more frequently. They made very little use of syntactic mitigation, and when they did it was mostly in formulaic uses of the past tense, and their use of propositional mitigation was also generally lower. They, therefore, exhibited mitigation behavior that more closely reflected that described in the literature on the realization of directives in Chinese (Fen, 1996; Huang, 1996; Lee-Wong, 1993, 1994; Yu, 1999). These findings suggest that they may have transferred from their first language a tendency to rely on economical lexical means of mitigation (Lee-Wong, 1993) or hierarchical understandings of the teacher–student relationship which licence the routine use of bald directives to students.

(19) *(Cf5)*

Take a your note book out.

(20) *(Cm4)*

Ah boys boys () take em (xx)

(21) *(Cf4)*

it your homework, you exercise now.

However, there were still some observable differences in their styles. Participant *Cm3* appeared to be very limited by his linguistic proficiency, perhaps because he had only been in Australia for 3 years. He used only a limited range of mitigating devices and relied on a few more salient formulaic politeness formulae which tended to be more distancing, such as *could you* (Example 22). This type of address to negative face is all the more distancing because it takes place in a male sporting environment. As we saw earlier, his AB counterpart (Am5) who was also recorded teaching a water sports class, had a style which was direct like that of *Cm3*, but highly solidary. *Am5* used mostly direct strategies, but they were mitigated with vernacular, inclusive address terms, personal references, and even swearing, as in Example (23).

(22) *(Cm3)*

Now first training because the here not in deep enough () could you please move to the deep side (students swim to deep end)

(23) *(Am5)*

T: What are you doing?
St: xx
T: Don't, Alan, that is bloody stupid, don't do it. Alright? Particularly if someone's coming down. () You of all people should know better

Male *Cm2* used very many direct strategies, and displayed very little grasp of syntactic mitigation. It appears from other aspects of his teaching discourse not analyzed here that he was trying to project a warm teacherly identity. His heavy use of "please" was somewhat distancing, although it illustrates some understanding of the need to mitigate requests to students. Females *Cf4* and *Cf5* also projected a distanced identity. Their directives were often short and direct. Participant *Cf4* often projected irritation and impatience, and appeared intolerant of the off-task activities of the young learners in her class, which she sometimes attempted to deal with by using directives with threats, as in Example (24). It is interesting to note, too, that this extract shows that she was able to manipulate a conditional construction, although she never used it as a mitigating device, as did AB, as in Example (25). This suggests she was either unaware of the pragmalinguistic function of the conditional, or of its relatively frequent use in directives by teachers.

(24) (*Cf4*)

> (XX taps watch) If you don't want to go home . . . if you don't want to exercise, if you keep talking you see me after lunch. ok, (=start now)

(25) (A*f4*)

> Now, if you turn to page 147 in the text,

In contrast to the apparently irritated style of *Cf4*, *Cf5's* somewhat bald manner of delivering directives (as in Example 19, "Take your notebook out") seemed to be more closely associated with a deliberate desire to project a teacherly identity from a position of superiority and distance. Support for this view came from discourse overheard after the recording devices had been switched off. It was the last class of her teaching practicum, and once she was assured that she had "passed" she seemed to relax and engaged in social exchanges with the students sitting in the front rows.

Thus the Chinese background teachers differed in the use they made of mitigation for a variety of reasons. In part, this variation may have been due to the fact that they were at different levels of language proficiency, and this may have influenced their ability to use certain devices. In addition, though, they also seemed to be at different levels of awareness of how classroom directives might be formulated and of the impact that different directive styles might have on interlocutors. Although the focus of this analysis was on the teachers' use of language rather than on students' responses, there were some indications in the data that the students reacted unfavorably to some aspects of mitigating style used by CB. Thus, after a rather abrupt directive by *Cf5* ("notebook out"), one female student uttered under her breath "Yes, Sir!", although *Cf5* either did not notice the comment or did not understand its force. Similarly, *Cf3* farewelled her class using the address term "boys and girls". After the recording equipment had been turned off, one of the students in the class said to another *sotto voce*, "We're not boys and girls, we're guys." This seemed to indicate some resentment among the students that they were being constructed as children rather than as apparent equals. Again, *Cf3* appeared unaware of the impact of her use of this address term.

MAKING SENSE OF DIVERSITY

As Ochs (1993) noted,

> communities often differ in which acts and stances are preferred and prevalent cultural resources for building particular identities. In one community, a stance

or act may be widely used to construct some social identity, whereas in another that stance or act is rarely drawn on to construct that identity. (p. 300)

Thus cross-cultural comparisons may be usefully made of the conventions relating to how different acts and stances are performed and identified, and how they are related to particular social identities. The overall trends in mitigation highlighted in this study suggest that the adoption of a solidary stance might be an important aspect of some teachers' social identity in the classroom, and that this may be either unfamiliar or difficult for those raised and educated in a Chinese learning culture.

However, as I have shown, individuals vary in the way in which they project themselves through language use, in this case, in how they mitigate directives in the social identity of (trainee) teacher. The variation found here is a useful reminder that all speakers of a language, both native and nonnative, are actively engaged in projecting themselves as individuals in relation to cultural norms with such resources as they have at their disposal. Although the identification and discussion of cultural norms is something of a commonplace in cross-cultural communication, they are, at best, a shorthand for what is acceptable to an important section of the community, at worst, a crude generalization or stereotype of that community. Speakers in any community command a repertoire of speech styles, and the selections they make from these arise not only from particular strategic considerations or from a desire to behave in normative ways, but are also constrained by the nature of speakers' experience of what is normative, and how they wish to project themselves in any context. That is, speaker' uses of politeness phenomena also say something about them as an individual since individuals vary in the experience they have of the norms of a community and also in the extent to which they want to project themselves normatively or creatively with respect to any norms of which they are aware. Thus the diversity found among individuals can relate to a number of background and personality variables, as well as to factors of specific context, and is evident in both native speakers and nonnative speakers of a language. In the latter case, of course, the issue is complicated by different levels of awareness or uptake of pragmatic aspects of language use (e.g., Norton, 2000; Schmidt, 2001).

What implications are there, then, for advanced language learners seeking to construct their social identities in a new language and culture? Although "optimal convergence" (Giles, Coupland, & Coupland, 1991) has been argued as an appropriate goal for interlanguage learners, we can assume neither that this should be identical to native speaker patterns of use, nor that these patterns are or can be uniform. Indeed, the data examined here demonstrate that they are not. Moreover, from an interlocutor's perspective, it may be that there is a certain threshold of tolerance for certain amounts of convergence, but that beyond a certain point, a speaker's attempts to converge too closely on a native speaker performance may be perceived as patronizing (Giles, Coupland, & Coupland, 1991, p. 79). In the words of my teenage son, who was a student at one of the schools where data was collected, a speaker who passes beyond this threshold may be dismissed as a "try hard." Because they are NOT native speakers, Chinese background trainee teachers may not be accepted by their students if they construct teaching identities that are too obviously "native speakerlike." For example, they may have difficulty addressing a student as "mate" or employing frequent colloquialisms to reduce social distance. The challenge for them is to project an identity that is both acceptable to their interlocutors and to themselves as individuals.

Viewed from an applied perspective, the findings of this study suggest that any instruction in the use of mitigation, or any other aspect of language use, needs to tackle a range of issues. First, we need to ensure that instruction programs take into account and make available for examination sociopragmatic issues of what is valued in communication and communicative style, how roles are perceived and played out in different communities, what interlocutor expectations of particular role-relationships might be, and so on in any context. In this way learners can come to understand more about expectations both within their new community and in the communities into which they were socialized as youngsters. Second, there needs to be a focus on the pragmalinguistic devices available for use and their force in context, so that learners can increase their awareness of the different devices available and how they function. Third, as we have seen, individuals make differential use of the repertoires of devices at their disposal, and exploration of this individual variation can be useful, not only in demonstrating the range of behaviours found in native speaker performance, but also in illustrating the creative ways in which individuals can draw upon their linguistic resources to project a social identity that accurately reflects their intentions.

REFERENCES

Amin, N. (1997). Race and the identity of the nonnative ESL teacher. *TESOL Quarterly, 31*, 580-582.

Bardovi-Harlig, K., & Hartford, B. S. (1996). Input in an institutional setting. *Studies in Second Language Acquisition, 18*, 171-188.

Blum-Kulka, S. (1982). Learning how to say what you mean in a second language: A study of speech act performance of learners of Hebrew as a second language. *Applied Linguistics, 3*, 29-59.

Blum-Kulka, S. (1985). Modifiers as indicating devices: The case of requests. *Theoretical Linguistics, 12*, 2-3.

Blum-Kulka, S. (1987). Indirectness and politeness in requests: Same or different? *Journal of Pragmatics, 11*, 131-146.

Blum-Kulka, S. (1989). Playing it safe: The role of conventionality in indirectness. In S. Blum-Kulka, J. House, & G. Kasper (Eds.), *Cross-cultural pragmatics: Requests and apologies.* Norwood, NJ: Ablex.

Blum-Kulka, S., House, J., & Kasper, G. (Eds.). (1989). *Cross-cultural pragmatics: Requests and apologies* (Vol. XXXI). Norwood, NJ: Ablex.

Brown, P., & Levinson, S. (1987). *Politeness: Some universals in language usage.* Cambridge, England: Cambridge University Press.

Busher, S. (1997). Language and cultural identity: A study of Hmong students at the postsecondary level. *TESOL Quarterly, 31*, 593-602.

Cortazzi, M., & Jin, L. (1996). Cultures of learning: Language classrooms in China. In H. Coleman (Ed.), *Society and the language classroom*. Cambridge, England: Cambridge University Press.

Deby, J. (2003). *Masculinity and the place of physical aggression in the structure of Canadian televised ice-hockey commentary*. Paper presented at the Eighth International Pragmatics Conference, Toronto, Canada.

Eslamirasekh, Z. (1993). A cross-cultural comparison of the requestive speech act realisation patterns in Persian and American English. *Pragmatics and Language Learning, 4*, 85-103.

Fen, H. L. (1996). *Requests and apologies: A study in cross-cultural pragmatics of native Chinese speakers, ESL Chinese speakers and native Australian English speakers*. La Trobe University, Melbourne, Australia.

Ferguson, C. (1975). Towards a characterisation of English foreigner talk. *Anthropological Linguistics, 17*, 1-14.

Fukushima, S. (1990). Offers and requests: Performance by Japanese learners of English. *World Englishes, 9*, 317-325.

Giles, H., Coupland, J., & Coupland, N. (Eds.). (1991). *Contexts of accommodation*. Cambridge, England: Cambridge University Press.

Goffman, E. (1956). The nature of deference and demeanour. *American Anthropologist, 58*, 473-502.

Gumperz, J. J. (1982). *Discourse strategies*. Cambridge, England: Cambridge University Press.

Gumperz, J. J. (1996). The linguistic and cultural relativity of conversational inference. In J. J. Gumperz & S. C. Levinson (Eds.), *Rethinking linguistic relativity*. Cambridge, England: Cambridge University Press.

Ha, C. T. (1998). *Requests by Australian native speakers of English and Vietnamese learners of English: A cross-cultural communication study in pragmalinguistics*. La Trobe University, Melbourne, Australia.

Hansen, J. G., & Liu, J. L. (1997). Social identity and language: Theoretical and methodological issues. *TESOL Quarterly, 31*, 567-576.

Hartford, B., & Bardovi-Harlig, K. (1992). Experimental and observational data in the study of interlanguage pragmatics. In L. Bouton & Y. Kachru (Eds.), *Pragmatics and language learning: Monograph series Volume 4*, University of Illinois at Urbana-Champaign.

Hinkel, E. (1996). When in Rome: Evaluations of L2 pragmalinguistic behaviors. *Journal of Pragmatics, 26*, 51-70.

Hofstede, G. (1986). Cultural differences in teaching and learning. *International Journal of Intercultural Relations, 10*, 301-320.

Hofstede, G. (1994). *Cultures and organisations*. London: Harper Collins.

Holmes, J. (1995). *Women, men and politeness*. Harlow: Longman.

Huang, M.-C. (1996). *Achieving cross-cultural equivalence in a study of American and Taiwanese requests*. Unpublished doctoral thesis, University of Illinois, Urbana-Champaign.

Kim, J. (1995). "Could You Calm Down More?": Requests and Korean ESL learners. *Working Papers in Educational Linguistics, 11*, 67-82.

Koike, D.-A. (1994). Negation in Spanish and English suggestions and requests: Mitigating effects? *Journal of Pragmatics, 21*, 513-526.

Kubota, M. (1996). Acquaintance or fiancee: Pragmatic differences in requests between Japanese and Americans. *Working Papers in Educational Linguistics, 12*, 23-38.

Kuiper, K. (1991). Sporting formulae in New Zealand English: Two models of male solidarity. In J. Cheshire (Ed.), *English around the world: sociolinguistic perspectives*. Cambridge, England: Cambridge University Press.

Lee-Wong, S. M. (1993). *Requesting in Putonghua: Politeness, culture and forms*. Unpublished doctoral thesis, Monash University, Melbourne.

Lee-Wong, S. M. (1994). Qing/please – a polite or requestive marker?: Observations from Chinese. *Multilingua, 13*, 343-360.

Mir, M. (1995). The perception of social context in request performance. In L. F. Bouton (Ed.), *Pragmatics and language learning, Monograph series Volume 6*, University of Illinois at Urbana-Champaign.

Norton, B. (2000). *Identity and language learning: Gender, ethnicity and educational change.* Harlow, England: Longman.

Ochs, E. (1988). *Culture and language development: Language acquisition and language socialization in a Samoan village.* Cambridge, England: Cambridge University Press.

Ochs, E. (1993). Constructing social identity: A language socialization perspective. *Research on Language and Social Interaction, 26,* 287-306.

Ochs, E. (1996). Linguistic resources for socializing humanity. In J. J. Gumperz & S. Levinson (Eds.), *Rethinking linguistic relativity.* Cambridge, England: Cambridge University Press.

O'Driscoll, J. (1996). About face: A defence and elaboration of universal dualism. *Journal of Pragmatics, 25,* 1-32.

Rintell, E. M., & Mitchell, C. J. (1989). Studying requests and apologies: An inquiry into method. In S. Blum-Kulka, J. House, & G. Kasper (Eds.), *Cross-cultural pragmatics: Requests and apologies* (Vol. XXXI). Norwood, NJ.: Ablex.

Rose, K. R. (1990). Cross-cultural pragmatics: Requests and apologies. *Issues and Developments in English and Applied Linguistics, 5,* 107-115.

Rose, K. R. (1992). Speech acts and questionnaires: The effect of hearer response. *Journal of Pragmatics, 17,* 49-62.

Rose, K. R. (1994). On the validity of the discourse completion tests in nonwestern contexts. *Applied Linguistics, 15,* 1-14.

Scarcella, R., & Brunak, J. (1981). On speaking politely in a second language. *International Journal of the Sociology of Language, 27,* 59-75.

Schmidt, R. (2001). Attention. In P. Robinson (Ed.), *Cognition and second language instruction.* New York: Cambridge University Press.

Scollon, S. (1999). Not to waste words or students: Confucian and Socratic discourse in the tertiary classroom. In E. Hinkel (Ed.), *Culture in second language teaching and learning.* Cambridge, England: Cambridge University Press.

Searle, J. R. (1975). Indirect speech acts. In P. Cole & J. L. Morgan (Eds.), *Syntax and Semantics 3: Speech Acts* (pp. 59-82). New York: Academic Press.

Shea, D. (1994). Perspective and production: Structuring conversational participation across cultural borders. *International Pragmatics Association, 4,* 357-389.

Siegal, M. (1996). The role of learner subjectivity in second language sociolinguistic competency: Western women learning Japanese. *Applied Linguistics, 17,* 356-382.

Tang, C. (1997). The identity of the nonnative ESL teacher: On the power and status of nonnative ESL teachers. *TESOL Quarterly, 31,* 577-579.

Trosborg, A. (1995). *Interlanguage pragmatics: Requests, complaints and apologies.* Berlin: Mouton de Gruyter.

Weedon, C. (1987). *Feminist practice and poststructuralist theory.* Oxford, England: Blackwell.

Yates, L. (2000). *"Ciao, guys!": Mitigation addressing positive and negative face concerns in the directives of native-speaker and Chinese background speakers of Australian English.* Unpublished doctoral thesis, La Trobe University, Melbourne.

Yu, M.-C. (1999). Universalistic and culture-specific perspectives on variation in the acquisition of pragmatic competence in a second language. *Pragmatics, 9,* 281-312.

Zhang, Y. (1995). Strategies in Chinese requesting. In G. Kasper (Ed.), *Pragmatics of Chinese as native and target language.* Hawai'i: University of Hawai'i Press.

APPENDIX A
Summary of Strategy Coding Framework

STRATEGY

Substrategy	Social distance	Examples
1. Nonexplicit negotiable strategy		
State non-conventional	Mixed	*Now everybody is waiting for you.* (=hurry up) (*Cf2*)
Question non-conventional	No?	OK, /*who's our reporter in the back group?* / John? (*Af2*)
State conventional	Mixed	*so now's the chance to get it down.* (*Af1*)
Question conventional	Mixed	*OK,/ are you copying this down?* (*Cm1*)
2. Apparently negotiable strategy		
Permission	Yes	alright /*can I have your attention* this way (*Am5*)
Suggestory formulae	Depends	*why don't you just write down* somewhere/ (*Cm1*)
Question ability	Yes	(name) /*can you* please get it out? (*Af3*)
Willingness question	No	a) *so do you want to* start, (*Cf1*)
	Yes	b) (name)/ *would you* please sit down? (*Cm2*)
3. Apparently advisory strategy		
Willing state	No	*you want to write it down* too Natalie (*Am1*)
Ability state	No	*you can copy this down* into your books .. (*Af1*)
Suggest state	Mixed	*I think it's best/ now, /we just get stuck into the prac* (*Am1*)
Advise state	Mixed	*all eyes should be on books* (*Am4*)
4. Apparently assertive strategy		
Wants/Needs	No	Now/ *I want the boys* all to move /thata way /okay (*Cm3*)
Obligation	No	*You'll have to move that car* (Blum-Kulka, Kasper & House, 1989, p. 279)
Predictive	No	alright /so first *we're going to* listen (*Af2*)
Teacher assert	Depends	*now this is homework,/ yeah* (*Cm2*)
Elliptical	Depends	*back crawl* /not breast stroke (*Am5*)
Imperative	Mixed	*Clean up* that mess (Blum-Kulka, Kasper & House (1989)
You assert (*+ stem or will*)	Yes	a) *you go on* with your work (Holmes, 1983:99)
	yes	b) you are here. / *you will start* from here (m) (*Cm21*:7)

APPENDIX B
Summary of Mitigation Coding Framework

SYNTACTIC MITIGATION

Syntactic device		Social distance	Example
Unrealisers	Past tense	Mostly	*Could* you hand me the paper please? (Trosborg, 1995, p. 210)
	Conditionals full/suppressed	Depends on use	now, *if you can get into groups of two*, (*Af4*)
	Modals	Depends	all right /*may I* have your attention please (*Cf5*)
Deflectors	Future going to/will	No	you *are going to* have to stop distracting all the people around you (*Af3*)
	Defocalisers pseudo-clefting	No	a) so, *what I suggest you do/ is* just read through it, (*Af3*)
	Continuous	No	*treading* water guys,/ not floating, (*Am5*)

PROPOSITIONAL MITIGATION

1. Nonimpositive propositional mitigation

	Example
Reason	*I missed class yesterday.* Could I borrow your notes? (Blum-Kulka et al., 1989)
Preparator	OK, / *Got everything?* FS: No T: Just hurry up. / Chop chop (*Cm1*)
Conditions	*now* what I'd like you to do is /just heat that up /*we've got thermometers here*, (*Am1*)
Sequence	try it again with the fifty /and *I'll see if I can find another calorimeter* (*Am1*)
Examples	and you work out what's the answer to this one /*for example,/ what's that fraction*? (*Af3*)
Underplay	i) *Look I'm sorry/, I don't wanna have to keep going on/ at your back /but* /but otherwise I'm going to have to move you/ OK? (m) (*Af11*:12) ii) and (name)/ you can report *if you like*, (=be reporter in your group) (m) (*Af21*:7)

APPENDIX B (continued)

---

2. Positive propositional mitigation

Encouragement	*Ok that was good* /Come in here guys (*Am5*) OK,/well,/ just go on with chapter nine/ *don't worry about it. OK.* (*Af3*)
Personal or cultural reference	get off it (name) /*it's not a surfboard* alright? (*Am5*)
Humour	how have we gone three B./ Finished? T: *You lucky girl.* / T: come on. (*Af1*)

LEXICAL MITIGATION DEVICES

1. Please

Requestive politeness marker, *Please*	Hand me the paper, *please* (Trosborg, 1995, p. 212)

2. Minimising negative devices

(i) Downtoner (*just*) (ii)Understater	i) and ii)*just* oh sorry () can everyone just () listen *for a minute.* (*Am1*)
Epistemic uncertainty /undermining hedge	Let's *maybe* look at this one *I think* (*Af2*)

3. Warmth and approval positive devices

Agreement	i) *yes,* /write this down. (*Cm4*)
Token tag	Clean up the kitchen, *okay*? (Blum-Kulka, Kasper, & House, 1989, p. 285) so now /you/ you look at it this yourself /*you understand*? (*Cf1*)

APPENDIX C

Use of the Four Categories of Mitigation by Individual Participants

Participant	Indirect strategies/total directives	Syntactic mitigation/total directives	Lexical mitigation/total directives	Propositional mitigation/total directives	Mitigation index
Af1	.510	.204	.520	.459	**1.69**
Af2	.346	.167	.468	.276	**1.26**
Cf1	.438	.087	.427	.272	**1.22**
Cm1	.361	.123	.445	.258	**1.19**
Am1	.189	.114	.538	.326	**1.17**
Af3	.279	.130	.498	.229	**1.14**
Cf2	.241	.065	.540	.177	**1.02**
Am2	.320	.056	.320	.304	**1.00**
Af4	.262	.171	.276	.211	**.92**
Cf3	.282	.051	.322	.203	**.86**
Am3	.136	.121	.424	.167	**.85**
Am4	.274	.104	.301	.120	**.80**
Am5	.084	.031	.454	.200	**.77**
Cm2	.113	.017	.379	.119	**.63**
Cf4	.119	.005	.356	.124	**.60**
Cf5	.092	.015	.262	.165	**.53**
Cm3	.091	.044	.228	.097	**.46**
Cm4	.028	.009	.343	.037	**.42**

4

Before, During, and After the Event: Getting the Job (or Not) in an Employment Interview

Julie Kerekes
California State University, Los Angeles

Advances in sociolinguistic investigations of intercultural gatekeeping encounters have evolved from those which attribute miscommunication and the resulting failure of such encounters to cultural mismatches (e.g., Akinnaso & Ajirotutu, 1982; Gumperz, 1982, 1992), to a more complex recognition that there is indeed no one-to-one correspondence between cultures and communicative styles. More recently, scholars have suggested that shared discourse styles (Gee, 1996) and an establishment of rapport through co-membership (Erickson & Shultz, 1982) contribute to a matching of communi-cative styles. It is these matches, they claim, rather than the more simplistic view, which, similar to previous claims about cultural matches, can lead to smooth verbal interactions. Moreover, further consideration has led scholars such as Shea (1994) and Meeuwis and Sarangi (1994) to recognize the role that pretext—the greater context of an interaction, including structural parameters, power dynamics, dominance, and prejudice—plays in influencing the potential for a successful gatekeeping encounter.[1] A number of similar studies have also indicated that one main determiner in the outcome of a gatekeeping encounter is the establishment (or lack thereof) of a trusting relationship between the inter-locutors involved in that gatekeeping encounter (Gumperz, 1992; Kerekes, 2003); that is, the relationship between the person being judged and the judging authority figure whose legitimate, institutionalized role enables her or him to make a decision which will effect the future of the person she or he judges. Although scholarly perspectives on gatekeeping encounters have thus widened to include factors not evident merely in the verbal interactions themselves, the focus of most sociolinguistic studies on this topic still lies primarily on the verbal actions which occur during the gatekeeping encounter, and/or nonverbal factors immediately and directly affecting those verbal actions. It is the aim of this chapter to consider, therefore, to what degree factors outside of the gatekeeping encounter itself—even those that do not overtly or directly come into play during the gatekeeping encounter—affect its outcome.

---

[1] For the purposes of this discussion, I have adopted Schiffrin's (1994) definition of gatekeeping encounters: "asymmetric speech situations during which a person who represents a social institu-tion seeks to gain information about the lives, beliefs, and practices of people outside of that institu-tion in order to warrant the granting of an institutional privilege" (p. 147).

The data source for this chapter is a set of job interview transcripts and related data collected at a San Francisco Bay Area branch of an employment agency which I will call FastEmp.[2] Forty-eight job candidates and four staffing supervisors (who interviewed them) participated in this study, by allowing their interviews to be observed and audio- and video-recorded, and by partaking in follow-up and debriefing interviews with the researcher after they had completed their job interviews.

THE INSTITUTION

Although a candidate's qualifications are purportedly evaluated by means of the job interview and the documents accompanying the interview (résumés, job applications, test scores), in reality the staffing supervisor's assessment of the job candidate derives from a complex web of information obtained outside and inside the interview, including before, during and after the interview. Therefore, on a more macro level, in this chapter assessments are made on the staffing supervisor's—and her institution's—stereotypes of expected behavior on the parts of particular subgroups of job candidates. It is necessary, therefore, to consider the greater context in which these interviews occur.

Employment Agencies and the Job Market

Employment agencies play an indispensable role in the American economy and work culture not only because of the high revenues they bring in—in 1998 alone, they brought in $72 billion—but also because of the unique purposes they serve.[3] When an employer has a sudden need to increase the workforce, does not have the time or resources to employ a new worker directly, or otherwise does not want to take on the responsibilities of permanently hiring a new employee, the employer seeks assistance through such employment agencies (i.e., the staffing industry). When an individual seeks immediate employment, has commitments which leave her or him unable to go through the (often lengthy) process of applying for permanent work, or is otherwise unable to obtain a permanent job, she or he can apply for a job through an employment agency and, often, begin working the same day. In general, employment agencies serve as the inter-mediate agent in a transaction between a client company and a potential worker (a job candidate).

Client companies use staffing services in situations of temporary skill shortages, seasonal workloads, employee absences, and special assignments or projects. They place their order with an employment agency, specifying the qualifications they seek in a job candidate; it is then the job of the employment agency to find a candidate who meets these requirements. At the same time,

---

[2] This chapter draws from a larger study discussed in Kerekes, (2001, 2003a, 2003b).
[3] In addition to the sources cited in this section, employment agency statistics discussed in this chapter were obtained from sources listed in footnote 6.

individuals regularly seek jobs through employment agencies by presenting their skill sets, stating their job requirements (in an interview), and applying for a match through the employment agency.

Not only does the staffing industry have an impact on the efficacy and success of a variety of businesses and other organizations, it also touches an impressively diverse range of the U.S. population, serving every socioeconomic class. Companies ranking highest in the Fortune 500 all the way down to one-person businesses, as well as organizations in the nonprofit sector, rely on employment agencies to provide temporary work services. Whereas many temporary positions require highly educated and technically skilled candidates, others require skills not learned in the classroom, and often performed by workers with very little formal education or training. Temporary workers represent the whole spectrum of educational backgrounds, from those with less than a high school education to others with multiple advanced degrees. They represent a range from young, novice workers seeking work experience to upgrade their résumés, to veteran workers with extensive and varied professional experience. They represent the United States' myriad ethnicities, classes, and sociolinguistic backgrounds.

Given their crucial role in the U.S. employment industry, accurately assessing their job candidates and making correspondingly successful job placements are, therefore, crucial matters taken seriously by employment agencies. Employment agency staff undergo extensive training—the most important parts of which address the job interviews they conduct—to improve their hiring practices, with the aim of making successful matches between client companies and job candidates.

FastEmp

FastEmp is a national employment agency with approximately 200 branches across the United States. Silicon Valley's South Bay branch of FastEmp (henceforth referred to as "FastEmp"), the site of this study, serves job candidates who represent diverse career interests and a wide range of language and educational backgrounds. The majority of nonnative speaker (NNS) job candidates undergo FastEmp placement procedures in English, but some are assisted by bilingual interpreters (these are usually family members or friends who accompany the candidates to their appointments at FastEmp).

The FastEmp staff are aware of the preponderance of culturally and linguistically diverse job candidates at this branch, as well as of FastEmp's reliance on the NNS segment of the population to fill many of their positions, especially those in the light industrial sector. For this reason, they are generally enthusiastic about doing what they can to improve the compatibility of their hiring procedures with the needs of their NNS job applicants. Regional supervisors of FastEmp have made a call for innovative developments to better meet the needs of their linguistically diverse clientele. In contrast to their clientele, the South Bay FastEmp staff is much more socioeconomically homogeneous: European-American women born in the United States, native speakers of English, and self-described as middle class, with two or more years of higher education.

THE JOB INTERVIEW

It is through the job interview that the staffing supervisor assesses the candidate's qualifications for work opportunities with FastEmp. Qualifications include but are by no means limited to the actual job skills a candidate possesses and is able to exhibit. In addition, and of great importance to the staffing supervisor, is her evaluation of how well the candidate communicates, and what kind of impression she feels this candidate would make on potential clients in various job settings. She assesses these qualities on the basis of her perception of the job candidate's flexibility, ability to learn quickly, and trustworthiness. Finally, from the staffing supervisor's perspective, the job interview is her opportunity to make the possibility of employment at FastEmp attractive to the candidate, especially if she has a positive impression of the candidate. For the job candidate, the interview is also potentially a time to determine what the work options are and to assess whether they are worth taking.

Components of the Job Interview

The interview is generally comprised of a fairly routinized question and answer sequence, structured to include the following components: introductions, work preferences, work qualifications, wrap-up. In addition to basing her assessment of the job candidate on the verbal answers supplied by the candidate, the staffing supervisor refers to the candidate's completed application form and/or résumé, test scores, and conversations she may have had with the candidate's professional references.

Introductions. After a brief greeting, the staffing supervisor goes through a short series of rote questions, verifying the job candidate's address, phone number, and other information the candidate has supplied on the written application. She asks the job candidate how she or he found out about FastEmp's service and whether her or his attention was drawn to a particular advertisement or current job description. While on the surface purely practical—FastEmp must have accurate contact information for the job candidates in order to eventually place them on assignments and pay them—these questions also give the staffing supervisor her first impression of the candidate's social and literacy skills (What does her/his written application look like? Is her/his writing legible? Are there spelling errors? Have the printed questions been correctly interpreted?). The following excerpt from an interview between Erin (staffing supervisor) and Frank, a Spanish L1 light industrial candidate, exemplifies the introduction segment (lines 1–28). Frank is interested in a specific job order that has been placed with FastEmp, to do temporary warehouse work at a company called Eagle:[4]

(1)   Erin and Frank (L1 Spanish-speaker, light industrial candidate)

```
 1    Erin     Now you were referred by... who is it that you knew
 2             at xx in um, at Ea[gle?]
 3    Frank               [Uh, ]Ernesto.
 4    Erin     Ernesto, okay (3.0)  great, um, and you've already
 5             spoken with Oscar, is that correct?
 6    Frank    Yeah.
 7    Erin     Okay (3.0) terrific. What we're gonna do is we're
 8             gonna confirm the information on your application,
 9             and um talk a little bit about what it is um ideally
10             that you're looking for 'n specifically about Eagle
11             since you're here for=
12    Frank    =Oh.=
13    Erin     =the Eagle position.
14    Frank    Yes.
15    Erin     Um, talk a little bit about the references that I
16             can call, and then we'll go from there.
17    Frank    Oh.
18    Erin     Um ... you're at three twenty-one third lane?
19    Frank    Yeah.
20    Erin     Is that correct in South San Francisco.
21    Frank    Mhm
22    Erin     And at this home phone number, six five four four
23             one two eight, is there an answering machine at that
24             number?
25    Frank    Yes.
26    Erin     Okay. (2.0) And this other number, what kind of..
27             [contact is]
28    Frank    [Uh, that's]  .. my dad's house.
29    Erin     Okay. Great. Um. And what are you looking for
30             hourly?
31    Frank    Hourly, it doesn't really matter, whatever, e[ight.]
32    Erin                                                 [Okay.]
33             Eight plus okay. Um Eagle typically starts at nine
34             plus,=
35    Frank    =oh=
36    Erin     =so I'll just put that on there, if you don't mind.
37    Frank    Yeah.
38    Erin     Um,   and you're looking for part-time?
39             [Are] you look[ing] for evenings or [or full time?]
40    Frank    [uh]          [or]               [full time]
41             yeah.
42    Erin     Okay. What hours are you looking to work, ideally?
43    Frank    Um, just basically prob'ly from .. seven to when I
44             can I mean night, midnight.
45    Erin     Seven p.m.?
46    Frank         Yes. [xx]
47    Erin             [Okay]...to midnight-ish. Okay. Um, an:d
48             {((reading his application)) looking for [or] fast paced
49             environment}, you'll get that at Eagle. Um, your
50             high school diploma, you have not
51                            re[ceived it?]
52    Frank    {((shakes head)) [No.]}
53    Erin     {((writing))Okay}. (2.0) Mkay. So what brings you to
54             Eagle?
```

---

[4] This and all other company and employee/employer names are pseudonyms.

Work Preferences. In the work preferences component of the interview, the staffing supervisor ascertains details from the candidates about time, location, and other constraints the candidates may have on types of work they are willing to do. She asks the job candidates how far they are willing to travel, their expected salary, whether they seek temporary or permanent work, and when they are available to begin work. This series of short-answer questions provides the candidates with opportunities to show the staffing supervisor how flexible or inflexible they are regarding the range of assignments they are willing to take. During this time it also becomes apparent to the staffing supervisor how familiar the candidate is with the institutional job placement procedure: Do they have ready answers to her routine questions, exhibiting a knowledge of how employment agencies function? Do they understand what sorts of answers are expected of them? Finally, how clearly can they answer the staffing supervisor's more open-ended question, "What is it ideally that you're looking for?" An example of the work preferences segment of the job interview can be found in Frank and Erin's interview (Example 1), lines 29–54. In this segment Erin asks Frank a series of questions including "What are you looking for hourly?" (line 29), "You're looking for part-time?" (line 38), "What hours are you looking to work, ideally?" (line 42). She also helps him fit his answer about hours more closely to what is expected at the company he is interested in (lines 32–37).

Work Qualifications. Discussion of what type of work the job candidate seeks generally segues into the third component of the interview, in which the candidate's work qualifications are discussed. In this section, the staffing supervisor verifies the job candidate's employment history, related experience, and educational background. The framework for this discussion is a chronological account of the candidate's work history, using jobs listed on the application and/or résumé as cues. There is great variation as to which details are attended to, however, depending on the staffing supervisor's impression of the candidate thus far. While this component may include detailed description of actual work done and skills learned, it may also focus solely on precise dates and locations of previous assignments. It is in this part of the interview that a certain level of trust or distrust manifests itself between the interlocutors. The extent to which the staffing supervisor questions the job candidate about exact dates and locations of previous jobs hinges on whether she finds the job candidate credible on the basis of what she has seen up to this point. The theme of trustworthiness is associated with the potential which this candidate may have to complete a job assignment successfully (see Kerekes, 2001, 2003a, 2003b). In Example 2, we see part of the work qualifications segment of a job interview between Carol, a staffing supervisor, and Lisa, a native-speaking African American candidate for light industrial work.

(2) Carol and Lisa (NS, light industrial candidate)

```
 1   Carol     An:d you're currently working at Norin
 2             Product[s?]
 3   Lisa           [Mhm.]         [Yes.]
 4   Carol                         [Doing assembly] work?
 5   Lisa      Yes.
 6   Carol     Okay um:, and you've been there since February?
 7   Lisa      Mhm.
 8   Carol     Kay. Building a variety of cabinet coolers for
 9             customers.
10   Lisa      Cabinet coolers um they cool electrical systems in
11             .. in machinery.. from big heavy duty fans, to, it's
12             just a a coolant system.
13   Carol     Do you enjoy that kind of work?
14   Lisa      No [((laughs))].
15   Carol        [No. Okay.]   Okay. I can understand that I get
16             a lot of people that find um assembly work a little
17             tedious?=
18   Lisa      =The assembly is fine because I'm I'm mainly used to
19             doing medical assembly, technical assembly, the
20             electronic assembly, (·hhh) and this is just I
21             *thought* it was gonna be all right but when they
22             hired me (·hhh) they hired me to do testing and I'm
23             not doing testing  I'm doing everything I'm cleaning
24             floors I'm doing everything else *but* testing.=
25   Carol     =Okay. (5) So what is it that you *do* enjoy doing
26             Lisa
27   Lisa      (·hhh) Um, I I like the assembly aspect because I
28             like the speed of it sometimes their speed um, the
29             technical aspect of it. You have to be very
30             pre*cise*, uh very detail *oriented* (3) very
31             flexible ((laughs))
32   Carol     (3) Great. Is there anything you just really don't
33             want to do?=
34   Lisa      =Telemarketing ((laughs)).
35   Carol     That's good for us to know. We will- we'd docu-
36             document that in our system,=
37   Lisa      =Oh, o[kay].
38   Carol           [and then] that way we would never call you
39             for that [type] of position.
40   Lisa                [Okay.]                Right.
41   Carol     What would a former employer tell me about your work
42             performance?
43   Lisa      Um that I'm that I'm very reliable, that I show up,
44             {((laughing)) on time}. A::nd uh that even though I
45             have a bike um I always make arrangements if
46             there's if I hear that there's we're gonna have
47             really bad weather I always try to make arrangements
48             way in advance to let them know that I'm gonna be
49             late if I'm gonna be late.
50   Carol     Ever had any attendance issues on any of your jobs?=
51   Lisa      =Never. The only time I'm ever out is if I'm sick.
52   Carol     And what are your long term goals?
53   Lisa      Long term goals I'd love to find a company that I
54             can stay with and grow with and stay with for ..
55             many years and move up in the company.
```

Wrap-up. The wrap-up component consists primarily of a monologue on the part of the staffing supervisor, who explains in varying amounts of detail what the next steps are for the job candidate (depending on her or his potential to be placed on an assignment). She may have the candidate fill out legal forms, and walk the candidate through an orientation packet with information about company policies. In addition, if there is currently an open position the staffing supervisor feels the candidate may be able to take, she describes it to her or him.[5]

Upon completing the interview, the staffing supervisor makes an assessment of the candidate and has a fairly clear idea as to whether or not the candidate is hirable. In many cases, the staffing supervisor has not yet finished checking the job candidate's references, however; these may result in her changing her assessment of the job candidate.

THE PARTICIPANTS

Job Candidates

The 48 job candidates in this study are equally distributed across gender (24 females and 24 males) and job type (24 light industrial and 24 clerical candidates). The job candidates are also equally distributed according to their native language status (24 NSs and 24 NNSs). NSs self-identified as such, were raised speaking English, and named English as the language in which they felt most proficient. NNSs were raised speaking a language other than English and self-identified as nonnative speakers.[6] Four of the 48 job candidates self-identify as bilingual. Of these, two consider their native language to be English and are widely recognized as native speakers of English; the other two speak English with phonological features of Spanish and are seen by their interlocutors (i.e., the staffing supervisors in this study) as NNSs.

All of the NNSs in this study, as well as 11 of the NSs, are people of color, self-identified as well as determined on the basis of appearance. In terms of the five races recognized by the U.S. Census Bureau,[7] with the addition of "Latino" as a race, 13 of the NNS participants are Asians, 9 of the NNSs are Latino, and 2 of the NNSs are Pacific Islanders. In total, of the 48 participants (including

---

[5] The staffing supervisors requested that this segment of the job interview not be recorded for this research project, in order to protect the privacy of the candidates, who often filled out legal forms during this concluding part of the interview.

[6] In total, participants represent eleven native languages: Cantonese, English, Hindi, Japanese, Mandarin, Samoan, Spanish, Tagalog, Tongan, Urdu, and Vietnamese.

[7] The U.S. Census Bureau designated the following as race categories in the 2000 Census: White; Black or African American; American Indian and Alaska Native; Asian; Native Hawaiian and Other Pacific Islander; and "Some other race." The question of Hispanic (Spanish/Hispanic/Latino) origin is asked separately in the 2000 Census.

Table 4.1. Job Candidates by Gender, Job Type, Native Language, and Race

Job type	Gender			
	Female		Male	
	Language status	Background	Language status	Background
Light industrial	NNS	5 (2A,2L,1P)	NNS	9 (4A, 5L)
(total 24)	NS	5 (3B, 2W)	NS	5 (3B, 1L, 1W)
Clerical	NNS	5 (3A, 2L)	NNS	5 (4A, 1P)
(total 24)	NS	9 (3B, 1L, 5W)	NS	5 (5W)
Total	*24 Females*		*24 Males*	

Note. A = Asian; B = Black/African American; L = Latino; P = Pacific Islander; W = White/European American

NSs and NNSs), 13 (27%) are Asians, 9 (19%) are Black, 11 (23%) are Latino, 2 (4%) are Pacific Islanders, and 13 (27%) are white.

The racial distribution across job type for male participants is not equal, but rather a realistic representation of the general distribution of such jobs among FastEmp employees: All of the NS male clerical candidates are white, while 4 out of 5 of the NS male light industrial candidates are Black or Latino. Among the female candidates, the racial distribution represents a closer balance across job type, again realistic for FastEmp's general patterns of job distribution. These numbers are summarized in Table 4.1.

The job candidates' ages range from 18 to mid-60s, with more than two thirds of them in their 20s to 40s. Educational backgrounds (highest grade completed) range from not finishing high school to completing a master's degree or medical degree, or currently working on a Ph.D. The majority of the job candidates have completed some post-high school course work but have not obtained a higher degree. Many of these candidates have taken vocational classes (e.g., electronics, welding). Figure 4.1 shows the distribution of educational backgrounds of the job candidates, with a general trend toward the left half of the graph for light industrial candidates, that is, candidates whose highest completed level of education is high school or just a few classes (but no degree) beyond high school, and toward the right half of the graph for clerical candidates. All clerical candidates have graduated from high school, and more of them have taken college classes or received higher degrees than of their light industrial counterparts.

Staffing Supervisors

Three full-time staffing supervisors, Amy, Carol, and Erin—NS White, self-proclaimed middle class women between the ages of 25 and 30—were

Figure 4.1. Job Candidates' Educational Backgrounds

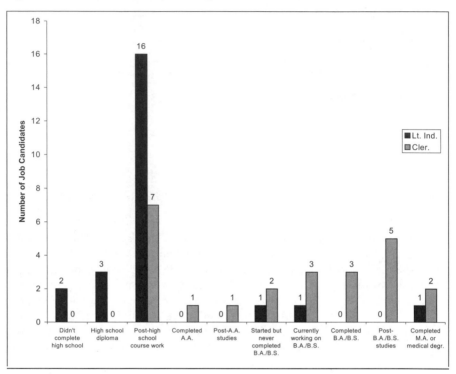

employed at FastEmp during the data collection phase of this study (but not all concurrently, due to a high turnover rate). The fourth, Renata, was "borrowed" from a different Bay Area branch of FastEmp on a few occasions, to help out on the days they were understaffed. Also female and in her late 20s, Renata is of Latin American descent and a native speaker of English; she conducted one job interview which is used in this study.

DATA SOURCES

Over a 14-month period, a combination of seven data sources was used to investigate when and why a job candidate succeeded or failed to be eligible for work with FastEmp; each source contributed different kinds of information, and also, together, provided a means of triangulation (Denzin & Lincoln, 1994). They included the following sources, each described below:

1. Introductory interviews with FastEmp staff.
2. Job interviews for prospective employees.
3. Follow-up interviews with job candidates.
4. Debriefing interviews with FastEmp staffing supervisors.

5. Final interviews with staffing supervisors.
6. Site documents.
7. Field notes.

Introductory interviews with FastEmp staff were conducted at the beginning of the study, in order to get acquainted with them and their institution. The questions I asked served to determine the typicality of the South Bay branch of FastEmp, in relation to other FastEmp offices, as well as in relation to other employment agencies. My questions focused on: (a) the procedures routinely carried out at FastEmp; (b) the job placement process as it affects both the staffing supervisors and the job candidates; (c) the degree to which staffing supervisors are aware of issues involving intercultural communication with job candidates and/or clients of diverse cultural/linguistic backgrounds; and (d) identification of characteristics of prototypical job candidates and clients. Further questions addressed the staffing supervisors' philosophies and perspectives on the job interviewing process; how they find quality candidates and what constitutes a quality candidate; and their attitudes about candidates' skills, their language use, and their L2 abilities (where relevant).

Forty-seven job interviews were observed, recorded (audio- and video-taped), and transcribed. They were analyzed, using an interactional sociolinguist-tic approach, to illustrate how successful and failed job interviews were coconstructed.

Thirty-seven follow-up interviews with job candidates were conducted after the candidates had completed their job interviews and all other FastEmp-related business (i.e., filling out papers and receiving instructions). These semi-structured interviews were designed to determine the job candidates' perceptions of the interactions that had taken place during the job interview; to compare their intrepretations to those of the staffing supervisors; to learn about their expectations of job placement possibilities and attitudes toward looking for work and to learn about their linguistic and educational backgrounds as well as their knowledge of the employment agency interviewing protocol. Of particular importance were questions focusing on the candidates' awareness of what they thought their strengths were, how they tried to "sell" themselves in the interview, and what qualities they thought the interviewer was looking for.

Forty-two debriefing interviews with staffing supervisors were held immediately after they finished interviewing the job candidates. These were designed to discern their overall impressions, including their assessment of the job candidates' skills, qualifications, language use, and interviewing competence (as manifested in this particular job interview).

Final interviews with staffing supervisors were conducted at the conclusion of the study. As the data collection progressed, the FastEmp staff became increasingly familiar with my research and the sorts of questions I was interested in investigating. On occasion, they volunteered tidbits they thought would help me, such as intercultural encounters they had had, their experiences being video-taped in job interviews, and information about individual clients and job candidates. My final interviews with them were therefore designed to allow them to elaborate on their thoughts and stories. They talked about their current positions, future career plans, and FastEmp's role in their professional aspirations. I repeated or rephrased some of the questions I had originally asked in the introductory interviews, and also obtained updated information regarding the current status of each job candidate who participated in the study. The staffing supervisors revealed that some job candidates who had had excellent job interviews had since been disqualified for future FastEmp assignments for various reasons ranging from perceived attitude problems to failing to perform required assignments satisfactorily.

Various site documents were gathered containing information about the job candidates' work and educational history as well as other socioeconomic information. Sources included the candidates' job applications, résumés, placement test scores, and notes taken by staffing supervisors during the job interviews. Other site documents provided information about FastEmp policies and professional goals and FastEmp's institutional culture. These included, for example, guidelines for receptionists' telephone speaking behavior, instructions for how to screen job candidates over the telephone, motivational memos to the staff about increasing their clientele and the numbers of job candidates they interview per week, and sheets of paper with mottos about how to do good business, such as a "Whatever It Takes" packet, which contains "favorite insights" as reminders of FastEmp's "continued commitment to understanding and exceeding your expectations—whatever it takes."

Finally, I kept detailed field notes from observations of activities and interactions that occurred during the time that I was present at the site. Before focusing on the job interviews and events related specifically to them, my observations served the purpose of acquainting me with FastEmp's objectives and modes of operation. I observed the physical setting–the office layout, purpose of each space, ways the rooms were used and by whom. I also observed the everyday patterns and routines of the FastEmp staff. I sat in the back room— in which the copy machine, printer, job candidate files, and kitchen were located—and observed the comings and goings of the FastEmp staff. I observed the ways they related to each other, studied the FastEmp literature, and noticed hierarchical relationships.

By being present not only for the purpose of collecting data, but also as a temporary employee, volunteering to work as a receptionist at the front desk, I was exposed to interactions and events I would have missed, had I simply been there as a researcher. I noted significant events and interactions either immediately after they occurred or as soon as I left the site, and used them to contextualize and triangulate my research findings.

I approached the interviews between the participants and myself as a collaborative project in creating knowledge. It became necessary to recognize my own role in the creation of meaning during my interviews with both the job candidates and the staffing supervisors of FastEmp. That is, what they told me about their experiences in the job interview, as well as about their perspectives on other topics we covered, was directly influenced by my presence, and by the interaction that we coconstructed.[8]

A DAY IN THE LIFE OF FASTEMP

While the focal point for both the candidates and the staffing supervisors is the job interview, a number of other interrelated activities take place in the FastEmp office and influence the actions and interpretations of the participants in the job interview. The context for the job interviews is, therefore, better understood through a description of the general procedures of the job candidates and staffing supervisors on a typical day at FastEmp.

The Job Candidate's Procedure

A job candidate begins the job application process by calling the FastEmp receptionist on the telephone, faxing in a résumé, or walking in to make an appointment. Before scheduling an appointment, the receptionist screens the candidate's qualifications, inquiring about the caller's specific skills that might fulfill some of FastEmp's needs for current or potential position openings. She also obtains information about the caller's education, previous work experience, and, most importantly, "people skills"—those characteristics which indicate to the receptionist that this candidate is a potential "good representative" of FastEmp. If the candidate meets these preliminary qualifications, the receptionist schedules an appointment generally within the next 2 days. The job candidate is told to expect to spend 2 to 3 hours at FastEmp, filling out application forms, taking a battery of tests, and being interviewed by a staffing supervisor.

Approximately 50% of the job candidates who have appointments actually appear at FastEmp at the designated time for their interviews. Before the interview, they fill out a seven-page application form which includes biographical data, availability to work (time and location requirements or limitations), type of work sought (short term, permanent, professional, casual), information about education and work history, professional references, and a battery of tests. Light industrial job candidates are tested in proofreading, reading comprehension, arithmetic, filing, and on-the-job safety policies. Candidates for clerical positions take tests in proofreading, spelling, arithmetic, filing, and typing. Depending on their abilities and work interests, clerical applicants may also be assessed for data processing and word processing skills before or after their job interview.

---

[8] As stated by Holstein and Gubrium (1995), "interviewers are deeply and unavoidably implicated in creating meanings that ostensibly reside within respondents" (p. 3). This was as true of me, when I interviewed the participants, as it was of the staffing supervisors, when they interviewed the job candidates in the job interviews.

The job candidate spends anywhere from 20 to 90 minutes filling out the application forms and then waits to be called for an interview with a staffing supervisor. This wait can take from a few seconds to half an hour or more. When the staffing supervisor is ready, she leads the candidate to a conference room where the two seat themselves at one end of a large table. She then commences the job interview. They have relative privacy in the conference room, where the door is closed, but the walls are glass and there are occasional interruptions from the receptionist or other staffing supervisors who step inside to speak with the interviewer.

At the conclusion of the job interview, if the staffing supervisor does not require further tests of the candidate, the job candidate is free to go. Candidates are invited to make appointments to use software training programs available to them, should they wish to add skills to their repertoire in order to be eligible for more or better paying jobs.

The Staffing Supervisor's Procedure

Staffing supervisors' responsibilities include networking with clients (those companies that seek temporary or permanent employees through FastEmp), interviewing job candidates, and matching qualified candidates with appropriate jobs. They earn a base salary plus commission, which can be as much as 50% of their total income. They describe their positions as a stepping stone for young professionals planning to move up the corporate ladder. As Amy explains, "You can't do this job for a long time. . . . If you don't move up into management within a few years of doing this job, then you're really not gonna go anywhere in this industry. It's a burn-out industry."

While the staffing supervisors at South Bay FastEmp follow one interviewing protocol, each of them brings an individual gatekeeping style to the interviews, as well as to the follow-up with the job candidates. They differ, for example, in how they deal with documentation of the job interviews, in their attitudes about the importance of job candidates' references, and in average duration of their interviews. None of them is completely consistent in their treatment of the candidates. (Carol, for example, does not always check references before interviewing a job candidate, despite her claim that this is her regular practice). This is to be expected, given the variability of moods, candidates, schedules, and tasks to be carried out on any given day at FastEmp. We see in the following discussion that some candidates are given more leeway, or benefit of the doubt, than others who have similar weaknesses in their applications or interactions; this is relevant to the analysis of the distribution of successful and failed interviews. Findings regarding the staffing supervisors' differences, and how these differences affect the outcomes of their job interviews, are discussed later.

BEFORE THE EVENT

FastEmp staffing supervisors have expressed awareness of the linguistic diversity of their job candidates, and a concern that intercultural miscommunications during the job interviews with some of their NNS candidates have resulted in inappropriate job placements. They feel that the time is ripe for developing strategies for better assessing the skills of their candidates by understanding more about intercultural miscommunication, so as to find better matches for candidates and clients.

While, overtly, the verbal interactions are the focal point of the job interviews, they are affected by a myriad of nonverbal variables. Many of these are before-the-event factors, such as whether or not the candidate arrives to her or his interview punctually, what FastEmp's current needs are, and the preconceived notions of the interviewing staffing supervisor. Despite their awareness, in general, of issues of cross-cultural differences in the workplace, the staffing supervisors are not, for the most part, aware of how their own preconceived notions about L2 ability, ethnic/cultural background, social class, and type of work for which the candidates are applying influence their assessments of the candidates' applications and interviews. Their attitudes about different types of job candidates—light industrial versus clerical—result in their focusing on different questions with different candidates. The clerical candidates, in general, have more opportunities to demonstrate their areas of expertise through content of more open ended questions addressed in their interviews. In contrast, interview questions addressed to many of the light industrial candidates focus more on when and where they worked in the past, than on what they actually did in their previous positions. The following sections present examples of these different interview styles. The outcomes, also discussed below, illustrate an imbalance in success rates according to job types and, correspondingly, according to the racial distribution of the candidates.

DURING THE EVENT

Stylistic Differences

As mentioned earlier, each staffing supervisor takes an individual approach to the interviews. They differ in the overall amount of time they spend with each candidate, as well as in the areas they choose to emphasize.

Erin, whose light industrial interviews lasted 13 minutes and whose clerical interviews lasted 21.5 minutes on average, took the most time explaining to the candidates what the purpose of the interview was, giving them an overview of the job interview, and asking detailed questions about their work preferences and backgrounds. Amy, in contrast, had a more direct and expedient approach, which was manifested not only in the way she conducted the job interviews—which lasted on average 9.5 minutes for light industrial candidates and 12.5 minutes for clerical candidates—but also in the other tasks she carried out as part of her job. Sacrificing perfection for efficiency, Amy utilized the least amount of time for niceties, making less of an effort than her colleagues to build rapport with her interlocutors. Carol, like Erin, displayed more patience with her candidates, and a desire to help them feel comfortable in the interview. She often deferred to the expertise of Amy, however, because she was new to the job and felt the candidates sometimes asked questions she could not answer. Her job interviews were the shortest in length (both her clerical and light industrial interviews averaged 7.5 minutes), because, she explained, she was less knowledgeable than the other staff about FastEmp job opportunities. Renata took the approach of a teacher. In her interviews, after examining their résumés, Renata went over the candidates' strengths and weaknesses with them and made suggestions for improvements they could make in future versions of their résumés, in order to sell themselves as more attractive job candidates.

Verbal Evidence of Success or Failure

The verbal interactions of the job interview generally follow the sequence of components detailed earlier. Within these sections, a number of strategies and/or actions occur which can "make or break" the encounter. One of the critical verbal actions that can potentially lead to either a successful or failed job interview is the discussion of reasons for leaving previous places of employment. Depending on how the candidates choose to explain why they left their previous positions, they either arouse the suspicion of their interviewing staffing supervisor or assure the supervisor of their responsible conduct. In other words, beyond giving the staffing supervisor *truthful* answers to her questions, the job candidates are variably successful in offering *acceptable* reasons for their answers.

Mark.   In the case of Mark, a job candidate for light industrial work, distrust is established when he is asked by Amy (the staffing supervisor who interviewed him) to explain why and when he left a particular job listed on his application; consequently, Mark fails his interview. Mark is a fluent NNS, having completed his primary and secondary schooling in an English-speaking school in his home country, the Philippines.

(3)   Amy and Mark (L1 WHAT, light industrial candidate)

```
1    Amy      Okay. When you were um: (1.0) okay so you were at
2             Gromer and Zane, a cashier and customer service?
3    Mark     Yes::.
4    Amy      Okay, um: .. tell me a little bit about the duties
5             that you did there.
6    Mark     Uh: I was doing stocking, cashiering, .. uh::
7             helping: customers: direct them to what they nee/ded
8    Amy      Okay,
9    Mark     an:::d=
10   Amy      =Did you like /that job?
11   Mark     Yeah.
12   Amy      Why'd you lea:ve.
13   Mark     Uh: had I had a medical uh: I had a medical lea:ve
14            and  then I had personal problems plus I was looking
15            for advancement. An:d things were just weren't
```

```
16              working out right for I mean .. before .. it was::
17              y'know. /I need \some advancement and I'm just
18              barely surviving from there.
19    Amy       Okay, (·hhh) now- you said that your last day was in
20              May?
21    Mark      Yeah .. I jus:t yeah I jus:t I just got um I just
22              got done from that job over there.
23    Amy       When was your last /da:\y.
24    Mark      It wa::s two days ago.
25    Amy       Two days ago?=
26    Mark      =Yeah.=
27    Amy       =Okay. (3.0) And you said that you are on /me/di/cal
28              leave from there?
29    Mark      Well no I had um a: I had um: I had a medical
30              problem I had to go to the doctors. But then uh I
31              had um: a: I had a medicals leave from there but
32              then my excuse .. is .. is: is I d'know it's just my
33              my boss said it's like .. y'know they had to let me
34              go .. from that.
35    Amy       Okay so they let you go.
36    Mark      Yeah.
```

At first it appears in lines 1–5 that Amy is interested in knowing what skills Mark utilized in his job with Gromer and Zane. She does not want long, elaborate answers, however, and communicates this as follows. In response to Amy's request of Mark to tell her "a little bit about the duties that you did there" (lines 4–5), Mark begins to list some of the tasks he had, but when he slows down his pace with a long "an:::d," Amy takes the floor and asks a new question—whether he liked that job (line 10). Mark's monosyllabic answer, "yeah" (line 11), seems to suffice, as Amy again moves on to a new question, this time asking him why he left that job (line 12).

Now Mark takes a longer turn—without being interrupted—during which he offers four reasons for having left the job (lines 13–18). First, he states, he had a medical leave (line 13). Second, he had personal problems (line 14). Third, he was looking for advancement (lines 14–15); here, the implication is that he was not finding the advancement he was looking for at this particular job. Fourth, and as a way of summarizing his previously named three reasons, Mark states in more general terms that "things … just weren't working out right" at that job (lines 15–16). Mark then returns to his third reason, stressing the importance of advancement, and supports that statement with a further elaboration that he is "just *barely* surviving" at that job (lines 17–18). This set of reasons arouses Amy's suspicion enough that she then begins to verify his employment dates.

Amy verifies with Mark that his last day on the job was in May (lines 19–20)—the same month that this FastEmp job interview takes place. Mark confirms this, and also adds a slight amount of precision to that fact by stating that he "just got done from that job over there" (lines 21–22). Amy, seeking more precision, asks Mark when the last day was (line 23). Mark answers by telling her, "It wa::s *two* days ago." (line 24). Suspicious again, Amy repeats Mark's statement as a question (line 25), which Mark confirms again, allowing for no pause between their turns (line 26).

Amy's suspicion stems from the fact that, if Mark left his previous job for medical reasons only 2 days ago, chances are he should still be on medical leave; so why is he now looking for another job? After 3 seconds of silent pondering, Amy asks for clarification by restating as a question his claim that he is on medical leave from the job he left 2 days ago (lines 27–28). Mark hedges, answers in the negative to her yes/no question (line 29), and then fumbles to provide a better explanation for the evident incongruity. His fumbling is manifested through repetitions (line 29: "I had um a: I had um: I had a"); pauses and fillers (lines 32–33: "my excuse .. is .. is: is I d'know it's just my my boss said it's like .."); and a final new (i.e., fifth) reason for having left the job, that "they had to let me go" (lines 33–34).

As far as Amy is concerned, the fifth reason offered by Mark is the only reason that matters, and she sums up his somewhat confusing narrative with one sentence—"Okay so *they* let *you* go" (line 35), raising her volume on "they" and "you" to indicate she now understands that the employer is responsible for Mark's having left the job. Amy does not give him the benefit of the doubt by considering the possible legitimate reasons Mark may have been let go. Throughout the remainder of the interview, Amy focuses solely on dates and lengths of time Mark spent on various assignments, without showing any interest or giving Mark the opportunity to talk about what he actually did on those jobs, what skills he has, or what other characteristics and qualifications he has.

Predictably, Mark fails his job interview, for reasons which are identified by Amy in her assessment of him:

> I just didn't get a good feeling from him. . . . I think that he was trying to um, he was trying to cover up the fact that he had a lot of employment gaps until I delved in deeper. And so I didn't like that he was trying to be misleading.

LaQuita. In contrast to Mark's outcome, we see in the following excerpt from LaQuita's job interview that it is possible to provide an acceptable reason for having left a previous job, as well as to do so in such a way as to highlight some of the candidate's positive characteristics which might impress the staffing supervisor favorably. LaQuita is an African American NS in her mid-twenties, applying for a clerical position. In the following excerpt, Amy asks LaQuita about the size of the company for which she had previously worked, and then probes for the reason that she left this job.

(4) Amy and LaQuita (NS, clerical candidate)

```
1    Amy        Okay, okay \great /how big of \a /com\pany is it,
2    LaQuita    Oh gosh um .. ((laughs)) (·hhh) um I would say
3               immediately,.. yeah 's 'bout, /probly \like, probly
4               like three hundred or so=
5    Amy        =/Oh \okay so there's .. \hund/reds,=
6    LaQuita    =Yeah=
7    Amy        =Okay. Great. And- what was the reason that you
8               /left this position?
```

```
 9  LaQuita   Basically um I'm on an indefinite leave um I have
10            the um, I have the oppor/tunity to come \back which
11            is great had a big goin away party, /only /I'm I'm
12            think\ing I'm lookin' for somethin a little bit
13            mor:e stable as well as I'm goin' to school in the
14            evenings=
15  Amy       =mhmm=
16  LaQuita   =so I'm not really um, in terms of sure if I'm gonna
17            y'know go do that on a full time basis as of
18            yet,[that's]
19  Amy            [(·hhh)] What was instable about this job?
20  LaQuita   /Well, in terms of, \of the instability, I just
21            think we had a lot of .. comings and goings and when
22            you have a [manager]
23  Amy                  [lot of turnover?]
24  La Quita  /Yeah, \I think and just in terms of .. um .. the
25            peopl:e .. /I mean, \it's a good envir- I mean goo:d
26            company, oh in terms of the jo:b description that
27            I've gone on but /I think \in terms of stability,
28            y'know you kind of wànt a manager you kind of want
29            supervisors you kind of want a little more
30            structure=
31  Amy       =Mhmm=
32  LaQuita   =So I think um .. that that's definitely my reason
33            for taking a leave.
34  Amy       Okay.
```

In lines 1–6, Amy comes to understand that LaQuita worked for a relatively large company. Amy then asks her for the reason she left the position (lines 7–8). LaQuita's response to this query highlights four positive characteristics: First, the fact that she is on indefinite leave and can return to the job if/when she wants to indicates that the decision to leave the job was hers and not her employer's. Second, her colleagues like her so much that they gave her a going-away party, again implying that they would like to have her back, which in turn implies that she is a desirable employee. Third, the reason LaQuita offers for having left the job, and for applying for a different job, is that she seeks more stability than was offered at her previous job (lines 12–13). Stability, in general, is a frequently-occurring term in the language of staffing supervisors, who seek stable job candidates to hold stable positions. LaQuita's use of the word thus helps to establish co-membership with Amy, and connotes positive characteristics; she also subsequently explains, per Amy's request (line 19), that what she means by instable is a fast rate of turnover among her supervisors (lines 20–30). LaQuita's justification for needing a more stable work environment is that, in addition to wanting to work full time, she is going to school in the evenings (lines 13–14). The pursuit of further education in the culture of FastEmp implies ambition and a desire for self-improvement, also traits sought by the staffing supervisors in their potential employees. Thus we see that LaQuita has gone far beyond giving a literal answer to Amy's question about why she left her previous job: She demonstrates desirable traits such as being a "stable" employee, being well-liked by her colleagues, and being hardworking.

Amy's assessment of LaQuita provides further evidence of the success of her job interview. Amy identifies as of interest not only job skills LaQuita possesses, but also, in particular, her self-presentation and interactional style, which Amy sees as professional and appropriate for a job with FastEmp:

> She's good, I mean she, y'know obviously she has a good professional appearance. . . . She came off very well with her presentation. . . . She knows good things to say. She knows responses such as what are your strengths and she said immediately communication and flexibility. Y'know some people . . . kind of stop and pause and hem and haw and not know what to say but I mean she is poised and she is definitely sophisticated I think in her business sense so I think that is definitely a strength for her.

AFTER THE EVENT

Differential Treatment of Candidates

At the conclusion of each job interview, Erin and Carol generally have the candidates complete federal forms for tax and employability purposes, which qualify the job candidates for work assignments without having to return to FastEmp. Amy, on the other hand, is least concerned with accommodating the job candidates, and most concerned with efficiency. Reasoning that, if a candidate really wants the job, she or he would be willing to return to FastEmp to complete the paper work before starting the assignment, Amy generally does not deal with the legal documents, choosing instead to wait until the time that a candidate is assigned a job.

As with the paper work, the staffing supervisors also differ in their approaches to checking the job candidates' professional references. Carol is most rigid about checking candidates' references *before* their job interview, feeling that, especially in light of her lack of familiarity with her new position, she must rely on these references to help her assess the candidates during their interviews. She also acknowledges that other factors, such as the tests the candidates take, play into her final assessment of the candidates. Amy, on the other hand, feels comfortable making assessments of many of her candidates before checking their references. In fact, again in her effort to save time, she often postpones checking references until she has a concrete job possibility to offer the candidate.

Amy's standards for judging the reliability of the references vary considerably, depending on her overall impression of the candidate. The candidates are instructed on their application to provide names, titles, and phone numbers of three "professional/work" references—"references that are not related to you who have knowledge of your skill level." According to Amy, candidates are to list their prior supervisors here, despite the fact that, in the work history section of their applications, there is also a space where candidates are to list the names and phone numbers of their supervisors. The job candidates exhibit a range of interpretations of the written instructions, however. Some list their supervisors, coworkers, personal references (e.g., friends), or some combination of these. Amy's tolerance for candidates' interpretations which deviate from her expectations varies tremendously. Patty, for example—a white NS light industrial candidate—impresses Amy as nervous, not very believable, and a person who "didn't understand the things I was asking and was just giving me whatever answer came to her mind." Accordingly, Amy judges Patty's reference choices harshly. Patty provided the names of three coworkers, one of whom was a close friend as she revealed to Amy during the interview: "She w-worked with me at Alamo Rictor for a long time. She's like a retired woman and we're very close." Amy accused her, however, of providing only personal references, and explained to me in her debriefing interview that references must be supervisors and managers, as opposed to coworkers, "people that will be more objective than somebody that's her best friend."

In contrast, Amy responds more benevolently to Liz, a white NS clerical candidate who, similarly, does not provide the types of references Amy expects (see also Kerekes, 2003b). After Amy discovers that the first reference Liz has written down is a person Liz "never actually worked with," she simply asks Liz, "Okay, are any of these business references?" and then asks Liz's permission to contact some of the supervisors whose names Liz has not provided in the reference section of her application. Liz cannot provide the phone number for one of the references Amy proposed, stating, "You can call her if you can find her number. I have no idea where it is," to which Amy responds, "I'll just call the HR department." Amy overlooks Liz's failure to list supervisors as her references because Amy is impressed with her candidacy, and says of Liz, "I thought she was good. . . . I thought she was professional and serious about her job search." Amy is similarly unbothered by the fact that Linda, a white light industrial job candidate, does not list former employers as references. She simply looks at Linda's work history and asks for Linda's permission to call some of the supervisors she has listed in that section. In her interviews of four other high-level white candidates for clerical positions, Amy neglects to ask anything about their references during the interviews, and readily assesses them as highly employable in her debriefing interviews with me, despite the fact that she has not yet checked their references.

One area of agreement in the staffing supervisors' approaches to dealing with the job candidates is their style of rejection of job candidates; they unanimously choose to reject candidates indirectly. The staffing supervisors generally tell candidates whom they do not expect to place on an assignment that they are still checking the candidates' references. In the case of one candidate, Carol rationalizes this response with the following comment to me:

> What I told her was that we couldn't hire her at this time. We were awaiting still more references. And that is somewhat true. If I get another reference that comes back and it's good I may change my mind.

Carol does not actually check this candidate's other references, however.

The staffing supervisors never simply state to disqualified job candidates that the candidates will not be placed on an assignment through FastEmp. Even Nguyen, a candidate whose English ability Carol deemed so weak that he did not get to have a full job interview, was told that she would check his references and get back to him. In this case, Nguyen took Carol's message seriously, and he returned to FastEmp the next day to see if she had finished checking his references. Carol told him that she was still checking his references. Carol told me, meanwhile, that if Nguyen continued to come in or call FastEmp, she would have to "be more direct" with him to indicate he cannot be hired. Carol did not in fact intend to check his references, having classified him as not employable by FastEmp on the basis of his "poor command of English language." Nguyen came back later that week to check with Carol again.

In spite of Nguyen's apparent difficulty with English, his resume and test scores indicate competence in a variety of light industrial work settings. This raises the question of how important NNS candidates' L2 ability is as a qualification for some of the light industrial jobs. Here, again, the staffing supervisors differ in their perspectives on how to assess the candidates. On occasion, a job candidate arrives at the job interview with an interpreter (usually a family member or friend). Carol's perspective is that, since "applicants can't take their translators with them to the job," she cannot hire them if they need an interpreter for the interview. In the case of other NNSs, Carol uses the question, "What are your long-term goals?" to gauge their L2 ability. Carol's experience has led her to conclude that "if they don't have a good command of the English language, they don't understand that question." Amy, in contrast to Carol, takes the approach that NNSs with low English ability can be hired for jobs at which the supervisors can communicate with such candidates in their L1.

Successful, Failed, and Weak Job Interviews

On the basis of assessments offered in the debriefing interviews with the staffing supervisors, documentation of the job candidates' statuses, and transcripts of the job interviews, each of the job candidates in this study was categorized as having had a *successful*, *failed*, or *weak* job interview.[9] The success of a job candidate was revealed during debriefing, in the staffing supervisors' answer to the question, "Do you think you'll be able to place this person?" The staffing supervisor's answer to this question was an unequivocal "yes" for successful job candidates. The one exception to this rule was a candidate whom Carol (the staffing supervisor who interviewed her) wanted to place, but who became disqualified on the basis of a negative reference from her former employer. Job candidates who had failed interviews were those whom the staffing supervisor did not intend to place on an assignment. Several job candidates were categorized as weak because the staffing supervisor felt she could place them on assignments despite their interviews. That is, although they did not impress the staffing supervisor with their interviewing behavior, the skills they displayed

---

[9] 100% intercoder reliability was established for this categorization, using approximately 10% of the data (randomly chosen) and two coders.

and references they provided indicated to her that they could successfully carry out a FastEmp assignment.

The relative success of each candidate depended, however, on other factors as well, such as the current availability and/or need to fill particular work assignments, or projected needs in the near future. Some candidates who were seen as marginal at best (especially some of the light industrial candidates), were hired or given legal forms immediately after their interviews (thereby making them eligible to accept an assignment immediately, without having to return to FastEmp before starting a job), because they could be used to fill job orders that had already been placed by client companies of FastEmp.

Distribution of Outcomes

In their assessments of the job candidates, the staffing supervisors identified three salient areas in which the candidates are expected to be proficient: job skills, language use, and ability to conduct themselves skillfully in a job interview (interviewing competence). Many of the issues they discuss involve skills they feel can be specifically learned, practiced, and improved by job candidates in order to achieve better results in the future. These include the ability to predict questions that will be asked and to have prepared answers for these questions, specifically indicating character strengths such as enthusiasm, leadership or the ability to take initiative, flexibility, reliability, and trustworthiness. Now we shall see which of the candidates tended to have greater success and which had higher failure rates, on the basis of socioeconomic variables, including the types of jobs they seek, the candidates' genders, their race, and language backgrounds.

Distribution According to Job Type. Of the 24 job candidates who applied for clerical positions, 20 (83%) had successful interviews, one (4%) had a weak interview, and three (13%) had failed interviews. Of the 24 job candidates who applied for light industrial positions, in contrast, only 11 (46%) had successful interviews. In other words, nearly twice as many clerical candidates as light industrial candidates had successful job interviews. Eight (33%) of the 24 light industrial candidates were not hired (i.e., they had failed interviews; these numbers include Nguyen, the candidate who was disqualified because of his L2 ability before he could have a job interview). The remaining five (21%) were

Table 4.2. Job Interview Success Rate, by Job Type

Job type	Success rate		
	Successful	Weak	Failed
Light industrial	11	5	8
Clerical	20	1	3
Total	*31*	*6*	*11*

categorized as weak because, even though they qualified for work, their interviewing skills were deemed inadequate by the staffing supervisors who assessed them. Table 4.2 illustrates the distribution of successful, weak, and failed job interviews across light industrial and clerical job candidates.

   Distribution According to Language Background and Job Type. Overall, the success rates according to language background did not differ notably, nor was there much difference in the success rate by job type. Within each of the categories described earlier, we can see the distribution according to language status and race in Table 4.3. Of the successful light industrial workers, 7 (63%) are NNSs (all people of color, since, in this study, all of the NNSs are people of color), and 4 (36%) are NSs, including two African Americans and two whites. Of the light industrials who had weak or failed interviews, 7 (54%)are NNSs (again, all people of color) and 6 (45%) are NSs (three African American and one White).

   Of the five NNSs who failed their interviews, two were disqualified on account of their inadequate L2 ability, according to the staffing supervisors' assessments (one of these was Nguyen, who did not have a complete job inter-

Table 4.3. Job Interview Success Rate, by L1 and Job Type

Job type	Language status	Success rate (by background)		
		Successful	Weak	Failed
Light industrial	NNS	7 (4A, 2L, 1P)	3 (3L)	4 (2A, 2L)
	NS	4 (2B, 2W)	2 (1B, 1L)	4 (3B, 1W)
Clerical	NNS	8 (6A, 2L)	1 (1P)	1 (1A)
	NS	12 (3B,1L,8W)	0	2 (2W)
Total		*31*	*6*	*11*

Note. A = Asian; B = Black/African American; L = Latino; P = Pacific Islander; W = White/European American. (Indicates background information)

view). In addition, staffing supervisors mentioned minor concerns about the L2 ability of five of the NNSs who, nevertheless, had successful job interviews.

They were also concerned about the L2 ability of one job candidate who had a weak interview, but who was subsequently placed successfully on an assignment.

Distribution According to Gender and Job Type.   For both the clerical and light industrial job types, more of the female candidates were successful than the male candidates. Of the 24 female job candidates, 20 (83%) had successful interviews, whereas only 11 (46%) of the 24 male candidates had successful interviews (Table 4.4); nearly twice as many women as men had successful interviews.

In terms of gender and job type, the least successful group of candidates in this study were the male light industrial candidates. Of the 14 male light industrial candidates, only four had successful interviews. Ten of the 14 male light industrial candidates, or 71%, had weak or failed interviews. Not only did these candidates (the male light industrials) differ from the staffing supervisors in gender, but also in educational and socioeconomic backgrounds; the staffing supervisors, unlike the male light industrial job candidates they interviewed, had all received at least 2 years of higher education and came from middle-class backgrounds. Many of the light industrial candidates came from self-described working-class backgrounds. In other words, the candidates who had the least in common with their interviewers had the highest failure rate. In terms of race, we see that, of the 10 who failed or had weak interviews, all of them (100%) were men of color (two Asians, three African Americans, and five Latinos).

Distribution According to Interviewer.   Finally, there were also differences in success rates of job interviews depending on which staffing

Table 4.4. Job Interview Success Rate, by Gender, Job Type, and Ethnic Background

Job type	Gender	Success rate (by background)		
		Successful	Weak	Failed
Light industrial	Male	7 (2A, 2B, 1L, 1P, 1W)	0	3 (1B, 1L, 1W)
	Female	4 (2A, 1L, 1W)	5 (1B, 4L)	5 (2A, 2B, 1L)
Clerical	Male	13 (3A, 3B, 3L, 4W)	0	1 (1W)
	Female	7 (2A, 1L, 4W)	1 (1P)	2 (1A, 1W)
Total	*Male*	*20 (5A, 5B, 4L, 1P, 5W)*	*0*	*4 (1B, 1L, 2W)*
	Female	*11 (4A, 2L, 5W)*	*6 (1B, 4L, 1P)*	*7 (3A, 2B, 1L, 1W)*

Note. A = Asian; B = Black/African American; L = Latino; P = Pacific Islander; W = White/European American. (Indicates background information)

Table 4.5. Job Interview Success Rate, by Staffing Supervisor, and Job Type

Job type	Success rate in number of interviews					
	Successful		Weak		Failed	
Light industrial	Amy	2	Amy	0	Amy	6
	Carol	7	Carol	3	Carol	2
	Erin	1	Erin	2	Erin	0
	Renata	1	Renata	0	Renata	0
Clerical	Amy	9	Amy	0	Amy	1
	Carol	4	Carol	0	Carol	0
	Erin	7	Erin	1	Erin	2
	Renata	0	Renata	0	Renata	0
Total	*Amy*	*11*	*Amy*	*0*	*Amy*	*7*
	Carol	*11*	*Carol*	*3*	*Carol*	*2*
	Erin	*8*	*Erin*	*3*	*Erin*	*2*
	Renata	*1*	*Renata*	*0*	*Renata*	*0*

supervisor conducted the interview (Table 4.5). Amy, who conducted the highest number of job interviews in this study (totaling 18) had the highest total number of failed interviews (7, or 39% of her interviews) and no weak interviews. Although Erin and Carol each had fewer total interviews, each having three weak and two failed interviews, the ratio of success to failure was similar across all three interviewers. (Erin's weak and failed interviews amounted to 38% of her inter-views, and Carol's weak and failed interviews amounted to 31% of her interviews.) The rate of successful interviews was 61% for Amy, 62% for Erin, and 69% for Carol.

Amy's interviewing style reflects her relative lack of tolerance, in comparison to Erin and Carol, for inconsistencies in the job candidates' self-presentation and answers to her questions. This may explain why she failed more of the candidates and made a clearer distinction between successful and failed candidates (with no marginal, weak candidates) than the other staffing supervisors.

DISCUSSION

The findings from this study show a connection between the job candidates' race, gender, and the success of the job interview. The fact that the three main staffing supervisors in this study are European American middle-class women is not coincidental (most staffing supervisors in this industry are). Beyond these biographical similarities, they also share goals and values: All of them are between the ages of 25 and 30; they have similar ambitions; their positions as staffing supervisors are stepping stones to attaining other career goals; they are part of corporate America; they value higher education, and plan to continue their own educations in the near future.

The group of job candidates whose failure rate is highest consists of male applicants for light industrial positions, and they are all minority races (two

Asians, two African Americans, and one Latino; see Table 4.4). They have less education and fewer plans to continue their education than the staffing supervisors have; the type of work in which they are interested is vastly different from the world of work with which the staffing supervisors are familiar; they are of the opposite gender from the staffing supervisors; and, in general, there is little overlap between their world and that of the staffing supervisors.

The female job candidates in this study had greater success than the male candidates, either because they were better able to figure out how to act in an acceptable manner, or because doing so came more naturally to them. Following the argument that similar backgrounds breed similar Discourses (Gee, 1996),[10] immediately in favor of the female job candidates is the fact that they are of the same gender as the staffing supervisors. One of the characteristics of about one third of the successful job interviews was the existence of rapport-building chit-chat during the interviews. Incidental topics which were discussed included common acquaintances, raising children, and getting married. Involvement of this nature has been associated by some scholars with a female conversational style (Tannen, 1990). While, in this study, four of the nine candidates who employed chit-chat (demonstrating comembership) with the staffing supervisor during the job interview were men, all nine who did so had successful interviews. One could argue that, whether or not characteristic of female speakers, chit-chat is certainly one of the characteristics of the interactional styles of the female staffing supervisors in this study. By engaging in informal chit-chat during the interview, the job candidates find common ground with the staffing supervisors' discourse styles, and vice versa. Because of lack of data from male staffing supervisors (of whom there are none at FastEmp), we cannot say that the chit-chat phenomenon is gender-specific, but we can say that it characterizes some successful gatekeeping encounters.

In the case of FastEmp, a common discourse style shared by the interlocutors more likely results in a positive interaction than when the interlocutors' discourse styles are vastly different from one another; the staffing supervisors represent a higher prestige discourse style than their light industrial job candidate. The negatively evaluated differences between their discourse style and that of the light industrial candidates result in less favorable interactions, because the staffing supervisors react more positively to discourse styles similar to their own. One's discourse style reflects one's family background, educational background, and class. In this study, the staffing supervisors reacted more favorably to those candidates whose backgrounds more closely resembled their own.

---

[10] Discourses (spelled with a capital "D"), as defined by Gee (1996), are ways of displaying membership in particular groups, through a display of values and beliefs related to one's social identity. These are expressed through a speaker's ways of acting, talking, writing, and interacting with others, and can involve not only the language itself, but also gestures, physical appearance, and even other props which communicate one's identity (e.g., a symphony musician who carries her instrument with her, or a job applicant's briefcase).

Before, During, or After?

We have seen a number of influences on the staffing supervisor's evaluation of a job candidate, some of which operate before the staffing supervisor meets the candidate face-to-face, others which operate immediately upon their first meeting in person, and yet others which come into play during the actual job interview. Beyond these, however, still another source influences the staffing supervisors' assessments of the candidates: the greater context of the interaction, or the "pretext" (Hinnenkamp, 1992, cited in Meeuwis, 1994). The staffing supervisors' preconceived notions of job candidate types, based on gender, race, education, and the type of job for which they are applying, prompt those supervisors to have certain expectations of the individual job candidates and to interact with them accordingly. Similarly, the job candidates' predetermined ideas of FastEmp itself, and of the employment agency job interview setting in general, influence those candidates' behavior and reactions during the gatekeeping encounters.

Among the staffing supervisors, the label "light industrial" conjures up images of candidates who are "casual," "lax," "not professional," and who have "weak" speaking skills (e.g., "poor grammar").[11] Light industrial candidates are, therefore, at a disadvantage in comparison to their clerical counterparts, whom the staffing supervisors do not automatically expect to be below par regarding professionalism. Demographic trends at FastEmp are such that, if a candidate is both male and a racial minority, he is more likely to be applying for light industrial work than for clerical work. As a light industrial candidate, he already has points against him before he commences his job interview. Negative expectations of light industrial candidates get transferred to more general, negative expectations of African American, Latino, and Asian male candidates. These negative expectations cause staffing supervisors to be intolerant of candidates' deviations from ideal job interviewing conduct. While these candidates may be able to compensate for the initial negative judgments they face, they must work hard to do so. Clerical candidates and those candidates whom the staffing supervisors generally label as professional, on the other hand, are more likely to be given the benefit of the doubt if and when they deviate from expected job interviewing conduct.

The interviewer constrains the possible discourse types that are used—those of the dominant cultural group (Fairclough, 1989). Participants' preconceived ideas about their interlocutors, or about the culture/people they believe their interlocutors represent, are influenced by their ideological presuppositions (Foucault, 1972; Shea, 1994) and related discourses (Gee, 1996). Interlocutors' power differences on the basis of skin color, gender, and lifestyle can serve to legitimize and reproduce boundaries between members of different groups;

---

[11] These descriptors are in quotes because the words are taken from the staffing supervisors' assessments of various light industrial job candidates.

these are manifested in their verbal interactions (Bernstein, 1996; Fairclough, 1989). Therefore, even when saying essentially the same thing, if speakers look different (e.g., different races or different genders) or speak differently (e.g., a British accent versus an Indian accent)—that is, if different expectations are held of the speakers (Tannen, 1993a, 1993b)—they are likely to be interpreted differently as well (Gumperz, 1982b) This is often to the detriment of speakers of low-prestige varieties of English (including nonnative and nonstandard varieties). Different interpretations can lead to misunderstandings which are not necessarily recognized or acknowledged: "The absence of superficial problems of meaning exchange is no indication of the absence of miscommunication at deeper levels" (Coupland, Wiemann, & Giles, 1991, pp. 6-7).

In addition to preconceived biases or stereotypes the staffing supervisors may have of the job candidates, the amount of data from which the staffing supervisor forms her impression of the candidate before commencing the job interview varies tremendously, and is often determined by chance occurrences and/or chance timing of the occurrences. Depending on the current demand from clients for temporary employees, how many staffing supervisors are in the office, the time of day, and numerous other factors, the staffing supervisors will be more or less familiar with a candidate's résumé, application, test scores, and references before the interview commences. However accidental the set of factors is which contributes to the preinterview impression, it clearly affects the interactions that subsequently occur during the interview. Add to these impressions the staffing supervisor's immediate impression upon seeing the job candidate—Is the job candidate on time? What is she or he wearing? How professional does this candidate look?—and the staffing supervisor likely has quite a distinct idea about this candidate's eligibility for work before the job interview has even begun.

Can a Judgment Be Reversed?

Job candidates who are received by the staffing supervisors with negative expectations are not automatically doomed to fail their interviews, but they must be able to implement compensatory strategies in order to (re)gain their interlocutors' trust, against the odds. One light industrial candidate—a Mexican male in his 20s—impressed the staffing supervisors when he arrived at his interview dressed in slacks and a white dress shirt. Mild-mannered and clean-cut, he impressed them with his "professionalism." Stated another way, although he was applying for light industrial work, he looked and acted like their prototypical, successful, clerical candidate; his appearance thus worked in his favor.

In the case of a job candidate who is distrusted by a staffing supervisor because of gaps in her or his work history, the staffing supervisor is likely to focus her questions on the precise dates and locations of the candidate's previous assignments, rather than asking the candidate about her or his strengths and experiences in former positions. The way the candidate chooses to answer her questions can serve to establish either legitimacy or illegitimacy. For example, in the case of Martin, an African-American NS light industrial candidate, spending 4 months looking for work was not viewed as a legitimate reason for gaps in his work history; in contrast, taking time off to rest and relax at Lake Tahoe was considered legitimate, as in the case of Peter, a White NS clerical candidate (Kerekes, 2003a, 2003b). Initially, Peter aroused Amy's suspicion on account of his written application, which indicated gaps in his work history; he was able to compensate for the flaw in his application by giving Amy an acceptable reason for the gap, however.

Another way the candidates establish legitimacy is by knowing when to elaborate on their answers. The successful—and trusted—job candidates volunteered more information about themselves and their circumstances than the distrusted candidates, who often answered the staffing supervisors' questions literally, without adding any information other than that which was specifically solicited. Similar results were found in studies of Oral Proficiency Interviews of NNSs, in which candidates who provided minimal instead of elaborated answers risked underrepresenting their L2 ability and thus receiving lower proficiency ratings (Ross, 1998; Young & Halleck, 1998). Even within the realm of elaboration, however, the candidates must know what sort of elaboration is legitimate in the gatekeeping encounter.

Going into great details about one's technical expertise in an area with which the staffing supervisor is not very familiar, for example, is not an appropriate kind of elaboration. Because, especially in the case of light industrial positions, the staffing supervisors do not possess the expertise to be able to assess the candidates' field-specific job qualifications, they emphasize the skills they are more able to evaluate: interpersonal skills, general professionalism, and trustworthiness. These criteria have been chosen as the focal areas for consideration in this mediated interviewing situation not necessarily because they are the most crucial, but because they are most compatible with the staffing supervisors' areas of expertise. The avoidance of qualities the staffing supervi-sors cannot judge well (e.g., a light industrial candidate's familiarity with various tools and pieces of equipment) and attention to those a staffing supervisor feels competent to judge involves a shift from professional qualifications to personal qualities.

Are Successful Interviews Successful?

In this chapter, we have seen that, while clerical candidates had a higher success rate than their light industrial candidates, and female candidates were more successful than their male counterparts, there was no obvious advantage to being either a NS or NNS of English; neither was there an advantage to having a particularly high level of L2 ability, for the NNSs. Successful encounters were related to the ability to demonstrate desirable employee characteristics, which proved equally possible for job candidates with a variety of language backgrounds.

What we have not seen is how accurate, or inaccurate, the staffing supervisors' judgments of the job candidates proved to be. What must still be questioned is just how effective the interviewing process is for determining who will succeed and who will not, on the job. Since data collection took place over several months, it was not possible to follow up equally on the progress of all of the candidates. What I did find, however, was that, at the time of my departure, of the 37 job candidates who had originally been assessed by the staffing supervisors as employable, eight had since been fired from FastEmp (for poor job performance or for not showing up for a job assignment), and another six had never been offered any work opportunities through FastEmp, despite their eligibility. Of the remaining 23 candidates eligible for employment through FastEmp, 11 were currently on assignments; 4 were not working but were available to be placed on assignments; and 8 had become inactive in the database, meaning that they were no longer being considered for assignments (this may have been because they had found full-time employment, were no longer interested in working for FastEmp, or were not any longer seen as suitable for FastEmp assignments). A high number of job candidates who had successful job interviews did not end up being successful on their assignments; we can only wonder how many of the candidates who had failed interviews may have ended up working out well on the job, had they been given the chance. Although it is in the interest of job candidates to learn how best to impress the staffing supervisors with their interviewing competence, it is in the interest of FastEmp staff to consider how to raise the success rate of their interviewing process— taking success to mean an accurate evaluation and resulting placement (or nonplacement) of the job candidates.

REFERENCES

Akinnaso, F. N., & Ajirotutu, C. S. (1982). Performance and ethnic style in job interviews. In J. J.Gumperz (Ed.), *Language and social identity* (pp. 119-144). New York: Cambridge University Press.

Bernstein, B. (1996). *Pedagogy, symbolic control, and identity*. London: Taylor & Francis.

Coupland, N., Wiemann, J. M., & Giles, H. (1991). Talk as "problem" and communication as "miscommunication": An integrative analysis. In J. Wiemann (Ed.), *Miscommunication" and problematic talk* (pp. 1-17). Newbury Park, CA: Sage.

Denzin, N. K., & Lincoln, Y. S. (1994). Introduction: Entering the field of qualitative research. In Y. S. Lincoln (Ed.), *Handbook of qualitative research* (pp. 1-17). Thousand Oaks, CA: Sage.

Erickson, F., & Shultz, J. (1982). *The counselor as gatekeeper: Social interaction in interviews*. New York: Academic Press.

Fairclough, N. (1989). *Language and power*. London: Longman.

Foucault, M. (1970). *The order of things: An archaeology of the human sciences*. New York: Random House.

Gee, J. P. (1996). *Social linguistics and literacies: Ideology in discourses* (2nd ed.). London: The Falmer Press.

Gumperz, J. J. (Ed.). (1982). *Language and social identity*. Cambridge, England: Cambridge University Press.

Gumperz, J. J. (1992). Interviewing in intercultural situations. In J. Heritage (Ed.), *Talk at work: Interaction in institutional settings* (Vol. 8, pp. 302-327). Cambridge, England: Cambridge University Press.

Holstein, J. A., & Gubrium, J. F. (1995). *The active interview* (Vol. 37). Thousand Oaks, CA: Sage.

Kerekes, J. (2001). *The co-construction of a successful gatekeeping encounter: Strategies of linguistically diverse speakers.* Unpublished doctoral dissertation., Stanford University, Stanford.

Kerekes, J. (2003a). Distrust: A determining factor in the outcomes of gatekeeping encounters. In S. Ross (Ed.), *Misunderstanding in social life.* London: Longman/Pearson.

Kerekes, J. (2003b). *Winning an interviewer's trust in a gatekeeping encounter.* Manuscript submitted for publication.

Meeuwis, M., & Sarangi, S. (1994). Perspectives on intercultural communication: A critical reading. *Pragmatics, 4*(3), 309-313.

Ross, S. (1998). Divergent frame interpretations in language proficiency interview interaction. In A. W. He (Ed.), *Talking and testing: Discourse approaches to the assessment of oral proficiency* (Vol. 14, pp. 333-353). Amsterdam: John Benjamins.

Schiffrin, D. (1994). *Approaches to discourse.* Cambridge, MA: Blackwell.

Shea, D. P. (1994). Perspective and production: Structuring conversational participation across cultural borders. *Pragmatics, 4*(3), 357-389.

Tannen, D. (1990). Gender differences in topical coherence: Creating involvement in best friends' talk. *Discourse processes: A multidisciplinary journal, 13*(1), 73-90.

Tannen, D. (1993a). The relativity of linguistic strategies: Rethinking power and solidarity in gender and dominance. In D. Tannen (Ed.), *Gender and conversational interaction* (pp. 165-188). Oxford, England: Oxford University Press.

Tannen, D. (1993b). What's in a frame? Surface evidence for underlying expectations. In D. Tannen (Ed.), *Framing in discourse* (pp. 14-56). New York: Oxford University Press.

Young, R., & Halleck, G. B. (1998). "Let them eat cake!" or how to avoid losing your head in cross-cultural conversations. In A. W. He (Ed.), *Talking and testing: Discourse approaches to the assessment of oral proficiency* (pp.355-382). Amsterdam: Benjamins.

Young, R. F., & He, A. W. (1998). Language Proficiency Interviews: A Discourse Approach. In A. W. He (Ed.), *Talking and testing: Discourse approaches to the assessment of oral proficiency* (pp. 1-24). Amsterdam: John Benjamins.

APPENDIX

Transcription Conventions and Illustrations

[ ]	overlap
=	latching
..	pause less than 0.5 second
...	pause greater than 0.5 second and less than 1 second
(1)	timed pause (in seconds)
:	elongation
—	cut-off
.	final falling tone
,	slight rise
?	final rising tone
?,	weaker rising tone
/	higher pitch in following syllable(s)
\	lower pitch in following syllable(s)
!	animated tone
italics	slightly louder volume
CAPITALS	much louder volume
° °	softer volume
(hhh)	audible aspiration (out-breath)
(·hhh)	audible inhalation (in-breath)
(text)	transcriptionist doubt; a good guess at an unclear segment
((phenomenon))	vocal or nonvocal, nonlexical phenomenon which interrupts lexical stretch
( )	unintelligible speech
(ʌ ʌ)	unintelligible speech with a good guess at the number of syllables indicated by number of x's
{((phenomenon)) text}	vocal or nonvocal, nonlexical phenomenon that co-occurs with lexical segment indicated between curly brackets.

5

Discourse Strategies in the Context of Crosscultural Institutional Talk: Uncovering Interlanguage Pragmatics in the University Classroom

Catherine Evans Davies
The University of Alabama
Andrea E. Tyler
Georgetown University

A number of researchers have noted that the field of interlanguage pragmatics (ILP) has focused primarily on comparisons of the L2 learners' production of speech acts to those of native speakers (e.g., Bardovi-Harlig, 1999; Kasper, 1992; Kasper & Schmidt, 1996). Kasper and Schmidt (1996) suggested that ILP studies have remained comparative in nature, at least in part, because they have primarily been modeled on crosscultural pragmatic analyses in which the purpose is to examine the similarities and differences between two distinct speech communities, rather than to understand the L2 learner's development of target-like pragmatic competence. Moreover, the majority of these studies have relied on data elicited from various forms of discourse completion tasks (DCT). The weaknesses and limitations of this method of data collection are well known (See Introduction, this volume). Thus, the foci of interlanguage pragmatics have been highly limited in methodology of analysis (comparative), data (elicited responses to DCTs), and theoretical framework (speech act theory). The purpose of the present chapter is to begin to address all three of these limitations. The primary goal is to demonstrate that naturally occurring institutional talk is a rich source of data that, when analyzed from a triangulated, interactional sociolinguistic perspective, can yield significant insights into the various discourse dimensions which contribute to interlanguage pragmatics.

We present an example of naturally occurring institutional talk that illustrates interlanguage pragmatics in the discourse of an advanced L2 learner. Rather than simply comparing the L2 learner's production to that of native speakers, the analysis considers the norms of both the speaker's L1/C1 (first language/first culture) and the target language/culture. The analysis reveals that the L2 learner uses a number of discourse strategies that appear not to be representative of the norms of either his native language, Korean, or the target language, U.S. English. Interfaces between two cultural systems are what Kramsch (1993) calls "third places." Like instances of interlanguage in the areas of syntax or phonology, this finding constitutes evidence of a stage in the development of the L2 learner's interlanguage pragmatics that cannot be straightforwardly explained as simple interference from the L1 or negative language transfer. Additionally, we present an analytical framework for uncovering such instances of interlanguage pragmatics that is grounded in interactional sociolinguistics (Gumperz, 1982, 1992) and relies on triangulation of the data through video playback with the participants and ethnographic interviews with members of the participants' speech communities, as well as the analysts' detailed examination of the discourse.

Previous Research on Which This Chapter Builds

The present analysis builds on Tyler and Davies (1990) which examined a portion of this same extended interaction. That analysis focused on a discussion of grades and found mismatches in discourse management strategies, schemas, interpretive frame, interpretation of participant roles, and discourse structuring cues in the linguistic code. In that paper, we offered a working hypothesis concerning a crosscultural difference in expectations for discourse-level organization patterns and discourse management styles in discussions of grades between teachers and students. We hypothesized that American teachers would tend to adopt a "deductive/assertive" strategy when asked to explain why a student received a low grade, probably starting with an overall summary of the student's execution of the assignment or with the point the instructor considered most important. In contrast, Korean teachers would tend to use an "inductive/ collaborative" strategy by which they introduced a number of small problems with which the student would be expected to agree and gradually move to articulation of the major problem. By analogy with written genres, the American would be more likely to begin with a thematic statement or topic sentence and then back it up; the Korean would be more likely to save the topic sentence for the end and rely on the listener to make the connections along the way.

We also noticed, but did not pursue in the earlier analysis, an embedded discussion concerning possible cheating on the part of the student. We were particularly struck by the apparent shift in discourse strategy to a "deductive/assertive" style by the Korean teacher in this section of the interaction. As native speakers of English, we were frankly surprised by the directness and deductive rhetorical organization the ITA used in this section of the interaction and felt strongly that it violated norms of the U.S. classroom. In Tyler and Davies (1990) we suggested that the topic under discussion might be a significant variable affecting discourse management strategy. In particular, we hypothesized that in a discussion of cheating, the norm for an American teacher would be the "inductive/ collaborative" style while the norm for a Korean teacher might be the "deductive/assertive" style. Thus, our initial hypothesis was that this apparently problematic discourse management strategy was the result of negative transfer from the L1/C1. The present analysis, which includes additional data from in-depth interviews with representative members of the relevant speech communities, reveals that the issue is not so simple.

An Interactional Sociolinguistic Approach

In contrast to Conversation Analysis (Markee, 2000), the framework we adopt rejects the notion that a full understanding of a crosscultural interaction can be established solely from the text. This is because an interactional sociolinguistic perspective accepts as fundamental the postulate that the lexical items and the syntax in which they occur always underdetermine the rich interpretation assigned to any interaction (Green, 1989; Grice, 1975; Gumperz, 1982). Analysis of the text alone is insufficient for uncovering participants' inferences (which are by definition implicit) that are crucial elements of the interpretation and the emergent context. Gumperz points out that every language/culture develops a set of implicit implicatures which are associated with constellations of features at different levels of linguistic organization (prosodic, phonetic, lexical, grammatical, pragmatic, etc.) that constitute what he calls contextualization cues. These cues channel interpretive processes.

Because much of the interpretation by an interlocutor stems from implicit, speech-community-specific, contextualization cues, the analyst cannot reliably establish the interlocutors' interpretation of the ongoing crosslinguistic/ crosscultural interaction nor the motivation for an interlocutor's contribution by examining only the text. Triangulation involving participants' commentary and the commentary of representative members of the relevant speech communities is also essential. The triangulated analysis evolves out of an interweaving of careful attention to the discourse (including paralinguistic elements), commentary by the participants, which is elicited through video play back, and commentary from representative members of the relevant speech communities. The analyst can independently identify specific aspects of the discourse which reveal tensions or difficulties through careful attention to rhythm, pausing, stress, interlocutor's utterances, discourse management strategies, body language, etc. (Erickson & Shultz, 1982). These can form the basis for guided video playback, but the analysis does not fully emerge until all three sources of data have been integrated.

Our approach relates to at least two established traditions within SLA in the study of classroom discourse (Ellis, 1994). One is the tradition of the ethnography of speaking and communication (Hymes, 1974; Saville-Troike, 1989). Ethnographic dimensions of our approach are the focus on context, the use of video- and audiotaping, participant observation, the elicitation of interpretations by members of the appropriate speech community, and triangulation of methods. The other related approach is ethnographically oriented discourse analysis that seeks to understand necessary sociocultural background knowledge on which interpretations are based. We also seek evidence from within the discourse itself of how interlocutors are reacting to each other, positioning themselves, and interpreting the ongoing interaction.

Discourse analysis from an interactional sociolinguistic perspective considers simultaneously occurring, multiple layers of the discourse as it occurs within a situated context (Duranti & Goodwin, 1992; Gumperz, 1982, 1992).

Contextualization cues can arise from any of these facets of the interaction. The situated context provides important norms of expectation for multiple aspects of the interaction. For instance, the situated context of the U.S. university classroom provides norms for the participant roles of instructor and student. For space reasons, we will limit the present analysis by placing primary focus on discourse management strategies. We will argue that the discourse produced by the L2 learner in this exchange represents an amalgam of the learner's L1 pragmatics, a partial understanding of the target language pragmatics, and the particular restrictions and resources of the institutional setting in which the interaction occurred.

Discourse management strategies are purposeful linguistic maneuvers that provide both an overall ordering to the shape of an extended stretch of discourse, as well as more local stratagems for accomplishing a particular communicative goal in spoken interaction. Specific speech communities appear to privilege particular discourse management strategies such that they often achieve the status of cultural schemas that have an ideological component. They are also shaped by more specific institutional cultures and local dynamics of the emergent context.   Within SLA and applied linguistics, perhaps the closest affinity would be with work in "contrastive rhetoric" (e.g., Connor, 1996; Hinds, 1987; Kaplan, 1966), which attempts to find prototypical patterns of exposition, persuasion, or argumentation associated with different cultural traditions. Work in contrastive rhetoric, however, primarily deals with written language. Discourse management strategies[1] are part of ordinary everyday interaction, thus they occupy another realm in which the prototypical schemas learned as part of the socialization process are typically not available to consciousness of the speaker.[2]

Bardovi-Harlig (1999) has also pointed out that interlanguage pragmatics has tended to try to artificially separate grammatical from pragmatic competence. The interactional sociolinguistic approach to discourse adopted

---

[1] Our use of the word "strategy" differs from those found in the mainstream SLA literature (cf. Ellis, 1994; Faerch & Kasper, 1983). There is one tradition of the "learning strategy," with relation to speakers' development of interlanguage (Dulay & Burt, 1975), which has received comprehensive treatment by Oxford (1990). The other tradition is that of the "communication strategy," traced by S. Pit Corder (1983) to Selinker's (1972) "strategies of communication" to account for learner errors in spontaneous speech. Canale and Swain (1980) accordingly defined "strategic competence" as the ability to cope with problems in communication, and thus this use of "strategy," arising out of error analysis, has been defined specifically as a response to a breakdown in communication. The instantiation of this use of "strategy" is found in taxonomies such as Haastrup and Phillipson (1983), and Bialystok (1983): e.g., generalization, word coinage, restructuring, paraphrase, language switch, foreignizing native language terms, transliteration, semantic contiguity, description. All of these "strategies" appear to be local and specific from a discourse perspective, oriented to a problem in a particular part of an utterance. Perhaps Ellis's (1999, p. 251) expression of "doubts regarding the centrality afforded to discourse repair in mainstream SLA, suggesting that its importance for L2 acquisition may have been overestimated," may liberate the word "strategy" for new uses.
[2] Some work on speech acts within interlanguage pragmatics (e.g., Trosborg, 1987), to the extent that the analysis talks in terms of "strategies" for achieving, for example, an apology, is shifting more toward the use that we are adopting.

here is more holistic. All levels of linguistic organization are potentially significant in signaling communicative intent through contextualization cues. Within this framework, pragmatic competence cannot effectively be analyzed separately from grammatical competence; in fact, it may be the case that "pragmatics provides the most general support system for mastery of the formal aspects of language" (Bruner, 1981, p. 32). Taking an even broader perspective, the notion of "discourse strategy" allows us to move in the direction of the concept of "interactional competence" (Hall, 1995; Kramsch, 1986) at the discourse level.

THE DATA

The primary data under consideration is the video recording of a naturally occurring interaction from a routine observation in an American university classroom between an International Teaching Assistant (ITA) from Korea and an American undergraduate. At the time of the original data collection both authors were faculty within the institution, and Tyler directed a program for improving the oral communication skills of International Teaching Assistants. For discussion of routine observations and video playback sessions, see Tyler and Davies (1990), Davies et al. (1989), Davies and Tyler (1994), Tyler (1994). We consider the ITA an advanced English learner based on his TOEFL score of 620 and his SPEAK score of 240. The SPEAK test is the institutionally-administered version of the Test of Spoken English produced by the Educational Testing Service. Two additional sources of data are verbal reports by the ITA during several video play back sessions and interviews with representative members of the relevant speech communities. (See more discussion of "representative members of the relevant speech communities" below when we talk about American and Korean interviewees.)

The physical setting of the interaction is a physics lab. Students sit in assigned pairs at lab tables. There is an instructor's desk at the front of the room. At the beginning of the lab session, while the students were taking a quiz, the ITA had handed back the graded homework and a quiz from the previous week. At the top of one of the quizzes the ITA had written: "Please do not cheat." That student's lab partner was absent and so did not receive her quiz, which had the same warning at the top. As the other students started their experiments, the student in question came to the front of the classroom to ask about the grades he received. The discussion began with the points received on the homework; in this stretch of the interaction the ITA used an inductive/collaborative discourse management strategy. In the 1990 paper, we argued that this strategy was unexpected for the American undergraduate and contributed to the escalating miscommunication in which the student repeatedly challenged the ITA's explanations. After a lengthy and rather testy exchange about the homework which ended in the student acquiescing to the ITA's explanation, the student pulled out his quiz and asked why the ITA had written "Please do not cheat" at the top.

To provide the conversational context of the discussion of cheating which we investigate here, we provide a traditionally formatted transcript of the extended interaction between the ITA and his student. The "grade" and "cheating" portions are labeled. This is an impoverished representation of the spoken language data because intonation contours and non-verbal information are missing. Our purpose here is to provide the reader with the conversation leading up to the "cheating" episode, and also to present our data for the first time in a format that the reader may already be familiar with. (For the fully elaborated transcript of the "discussion of grade" section, along with the analysis of the "inductive/collaborative" strategy, please see Tyler and Davies [1990].) In the version of the transcript presented here we have accommodated spoken language to written language conventions, and we have underlined words that receive strong stress so that the reader can have a better idea of how the interaction sounds. A backslash indicates overlapping speech (as in the T's second turn with "And"), and unclear segments are indicated with square brackets (as in the T's second turn after "should").

Discussion of Grade

The student has just asked why he received such a low grade on the homework:

T: Let me see your paper. Well, you've written all these numbers all over your graph.
S: It says to. It says to. In the other paper it says plot your...it says write the numbers of your points. That's why I did it.
T: \And............let's see...you have no enclosures. You should [ ]...ah..if you have point here,
S: ah huh
T: then you should ...ah...because of this..this..because this is graph...this [you will] need...connected. And if...with connection.. (may, make) .the point may not be seen. You should enclose this point with some shape.
S: [Well, I] ....if you can't see the points there...
T: I know, but it is mandatory...for your [graph, factor] analysis. See...see this one.   And........graph B...maybe this ah.... We have four graphs, so each graph will be four points [ ]
S: \Wai-wai-wait. What about the calculations?
T: Oh.   In this case I didn't take off any number....any scores...for calculations, because
S: \Wai-ai-ai-ai. I wrote three pages of calculations and I'm not going to get any credit for it?
T: No. I mean, I didn't take off.
S: You mean you didn't give credit.
T: Maybe...maybe.these calculations   is demonstrated on your graph B. Sorry, you almost missed the important, difficult point of this lab assignment. Sorry, but graph B is on log-log paper.
S: It is.
T: But you [you didn't] draw this graph on this paper.
S: This is log-log paper, isn't it?

T: Is this log-log <u>paper</u>?
S: I thought it <u>was</u>.
T: Oh, sorry. Hi, hi, Dave, would you please show me the log-log <u>paper</u>? So there's no point here.
(Dave brings paper.)
T: Thank you. This one. This and <u>this.</u>
S: I thought that was lo<u>g-log</u> paper.
T: Log-log <u>paper</u> means….you know what the log-log paper
S: \ I know exactly what it <u>means</u>. I thought that was log-log <u>paper</u>.
T: But I can't give you any…any <u>numbers</u>…any <u>points</u>..for this <u>graph</u>. And if you want to find <u>slopes</u>, or if you want to ah ana- <u>analyze</u> this graph, you should i<u>gnore</u> this [point].
S: I <u>should</u>. Yeah. I just wrote it in there to show you that I came <u>up</u> with it.
T: \And…….but find the slope of this…<u>graph</u>…you should ah…you should ah..you should have some <u>straight</u> lines. That's the sense of <u>line</u> fitting. Your data points should not be…will not lie on the exact…straight <u>line</u>. They should be scattered [ ] [ ]. But you should…you should make…a best <u>guess</u>. Make straight line <u>here</u>. This…<u>look</u>. <u>No</u> sense. It has <u>no</u> sense. To find some [ ] [ ] [ ] [ ] [ ]. The same for <u>this</u> one.

Discussion of Cheating

The student takes out his quiz and asks why the ITA had written "Please do not cheat" at the top. The ITA also has the quiz of the other student who is suspected of cheating. The ITA lays the two quizzes down side by side on the desk and says something like "Let's look at these quizzes. Let's see what's written here."

T: The figures are exactly the <u>same</u>. The symbols you use   is exactly the <u>same</u>.
S: Well you <u>have</u> to use the law of co-sines to get the answer
T: \<u>I</u> know <u>I</u> know   I know you <u>should</u> but
S: \Look at her answers <u>here</u>. They're just like <u>mine</u>. She didn't even <u>have</u> anything there. I had most of <u>that.</u>
T: \But But I was <u>confident</u> that <u>she</u> or <u>you</u> have cheated.
S: haaaah
T: Maybe you <u>didn't</u> cheat but ah you are supposed to <u>protect</u> your <u>answers</u>. Am I <u>right</u>? Know what I <u>mean</u>? You understand? Is there any proper <u>reason</u> to this special coincidence?
S: Well, you have to work--- everyone worked them out the <u>same</u>, I bet.
T: <u>I</u> know but because of their personalities and their information and knowledge [ ], there… these two answers should <u>not</u> be (the)same. But this is from my experience.
S: So I don't get any <u>credit</u> for the quiz.
T: Maybe ah if you just apply for this… if you just apply the <u>quiz</u>, there you have <u>C</u>. Then you have <u>C</u>. Is equivalent to <u>one</u> point. It's <u>fair</u>.
S: I've been <u>reamed</u>.
T: Sorry.

TRANSCRIPTION AND ANALYSIS

This section first presents the elaborated transcription of the "cheating" interaction, followed by an analysis that considers several dimensions of the discourse (nonverbal, prosodic, lexical, syntactic, pragmatic). The discourse analysis leads to key questions for which a structured process of video playback and interviews with representative members of the relevant speech communities yields crosscultural data concerning norms, schemas, and interpretations of the situated interaction. This data in turn allows both a fuller understanding of the interaction and some theoretical conclusions concerning discourse strategies and interlanguage pragmatics in crosscultural institutional context.

In the following transcription we have tried to represent the speakers' utterances and their nonverbal behavior in an approximation to real time. Each numbered horizontal space (containing in reality three lines) represents a stretch of time within which the speakers are interacting. The nonverbal behavior is described on the uppermost line, the ITA's utterances are on the second line, and the student's utterances are on the third line. We have used standard punctuation to indicate prosody. A falling intonation is signaled by the use of a period (.) and a rising intonation is signaled by the use of a question mark (?). Words or syllables that receive noticeable stress have been underlined.

There is a short gap in the tape here. Our observational notes and notes from interviews with the ITA indicate that the ITA responded with something like, "Let's look at these quizzes." The ITA has the quiz of the other student who is suspected of cheating (the missing lab partner), finds it and lays the two quizzes down side by side on the desk and says something like, "Let's see what's written here." After a few remarks concerning an erroneous written comment made by the ITA, the discussion of cheating begins:

```
1. ============================================================
ITA points to two test papers lying side by side on the desk
T: The figures are exactly the same.   The symbols you use is
S:
2. ============================================================
                        whiny, challenging student has leaned into lower
                        position than ITA
T: exactly the same
S:                      well you have to use the law of co-sines to get the answer
3 .============================================================
            ITA oriented to student
T: I know I know     I know you should but but
S:                                   Look at her answers here.
They're just like mine.  She didn't even have anything there I had most of that
4. ============================================================
                    drop in volume on "cheated"
T:  but I was confident that she or you have cheated.
S:                                         haaaah
                                           Looks away
```

5. ==
T: Maybe you <u>did</u>n't cheat but ah you are supposed to pro<u>tect</u> your <u>ans</u>wers.
S:
6. ==
lower volume—student does not meet his gaze   return to typical volume
T: Am I <u>right</u>? Know what I <u>mean</u>? You under<u>stand</u>? Is there any proper
S:
7. ==
                              long pause---student does not meet gaze
T: <u>rea</u>son to this special co<u>inc</u>idence?
S: Well
8. ==

T: <u>I</u> know but
S: you have to work…everyone worked them out the <u>same</u> I bet.
9. ==

T: because of their perso<u>nal</u>ities and their infor<u>ma</u>tion and <u>know</u>ledge[ ]
S:
10. ==
                                                  gestures toward
                                                  own chest
                                                  student avoids gaze
T: There...these two answers should <u>not</u> be (the) same.   But this is from my
S:
11. ==
                          ITA orients away from student to grade book
T: exp<u>er</u>ience.   Maybe ah if you just
S: So I don't get any <u>cred</u>it for the quiz.
12. ==
                  student stands up so that he is taller than ITA, looks at him
T: app<u>ly</u> for this. If you just apply this <u>quiz</u>, there you have <u>C</u>. Then you
S:
13. ==
                                    not addressing ITA
T: have <u>C</u>. Is equivalent to <u>one</u> point. It's <u>fair</u>.   Sorry.
S: I've been <u>reamed</u>.

Initial Discourse Analysis

In an initial discourse analysis the analyst looks at the video carefully, and pinpoints trouble spots and key questions to be pursued with the participants and other consultants. The primary perspective represented in the discourse analysis at this point is inevitably that of the analysts, in this case Americans with university teaching experience. For the American analysts, there is a striking difference between this interaction and the discussion of grades as analyzed in Tyler and Davies (1990). Cheating is bad behavior, and American universities are concerned about its apparent increase among students. The suspicion of cheating charges the atmosphere of the entire conversation with a moral/ethical weight. The Korean ITA's treatment of the suspicion/accusation of cheating, in contrast to his inductive/collaborative discourse strategy in the discussion of grading, is very direct and even confrontational. In dealing with this topic, the ITA appears to act in a very authoritarian way, explicitly asserting his conclusions without allowing the student much opportunity to respond to the accusation, thus using a very face-threatening version of a deductive/assertive strategy. Even though the American analysts respond, as does the student, with extreme discomfort to this authoritarian approach, they are also aware that such responses to moral/ethical transgressions are in fact part of the repertoire within American society, and might assume that such responses are more typical in other societies. Such assumptions might lead the analysts to prematurely conclude that what is happening here is a transfer of discourse strategy from a Korean context to an American one.

It may be useful to have an overview of what we are calling the ITA's assertive/deductive strategy before we offer the more detailed discourse analysis

- A framing of the interaction by writing the message "Please do not cheat" at the top of the page on the quiz. It presupposes the fact of cheating on the quiz as well as exhorting appropriate behavior on future quizzes. (There is a strange mismatch of the use of "please" with the imperative concerning cheating. And, in fact, the use of "please" seems incongruous with the ITA's treatment of the cheating situation in his face-to-face interaction with the student.)
- A strong statement of the facts that demonstrate cheating (while pointing to quizzes).
- An immediate statement of conviction that one or the other student has cheated.
- A statement that even if this student hasn't cheated, he is still guilty of not shielding his answers.
- Three questions in a row demanding/attempting to solicit agreement concerning behavior norms in a testing-taking situation.
- One (potentially sarcastic) question demanding(?) an explanation.
- A statement of his experience as a teacher to back up his conclusion that cheating has occurred.
- An explicit judgment that his treatment of the situation is "fair."

We suggest that you now follow the transcript closely as you read the discourse analysis. In lines 1–2 the ITA begins with an observation about the two quizzes that constitutes the evidence for his conclusion that the students have cheated, and then follows it up immediately with his judgment in line 4. In his first two statements concerning the quiz, the ITA uses syntactic parallelism which repeats the heavily stressed phrase "exactly the same." There is no equivocation here. When the student responds in line 2 that everyone would have had to use the same "law" to work the problem, the ITA responds in line 2 with repetitions of "I know" that sound dismissive to the American ear because the stress is on "I" rather than "know." The ITA then asserts in line 4 that "I am confident that you or she have cheated." The ITA does lower his volume on the final word, *cheated*, in line 4. This might be a move to mitigate the face threat to the student by de-emphasizing the words that explicitly carry the accusation and also to potentially provide a bit of privacy for the student since the interaction is taking place in front of the other students. Even though the statement might be considered to be mitigated in some sense because the possibility is presented that the student is not the cheater (but rather that it is the absent female student), the use of the predicate adjective "confident" in line 4 to describe his level of sureness is quite strong for the ITA.

The unexpected directness of the accusation is registered through the student's uptake at that point: He looks away while expelling breath with the sound "haah" at line 5, indicating "seriousness" and strong emotion. It should be noted that even though the ITA states that he is "confident" that one of the students has cheated, this utterance is not a direct speech act of "accusation" of the student standing in front of him. Neither is there a direct response from the student. During this interaction the ITA is physically oriented to the student, who seems to be expressing his ambivalence physically toward the ITA. On the one hand he is expressing deference by leaning over so that his body is literally at a lower level than the ITA. On the other hand he is expressing disrespect (in American terms) by avoiding eye contact.

The ITA's next utterance in line 5 at first appears to be mitigating ("Maybe you didn't cheat"), but it is followed immediately by a clause that appears to blame the student for his behavior ("but ah you are supposed to protect your answers."). The way the ITA frames the situation makes the student guilty in any case (even if he didn't cheat, he didn't shield his answers and thereby allowed the other student to cheat).

Following this utterance, the ITA produces a series of questions in lines 6 and 7 ("Am I right? Know what I mean? You understand? Is there any proper reason to this special coincidence?") which seem to shift gradually from rhetorical to authentic questions. The first three questions appear to be rhetorically asserting and then seeking confirmation for the claim concerning normative behavior for test-taking. These three questions are produced at lower volume with orientation to the student. The final question appears to be demanding an explanation from the student for the similarity of the answers on the two quiz papers. Following on the blaming statement about protecting answers, such a series of questions is highly face-threatening. The lack of interactional space granted by the ITA for a response after each of the first three questions contributes to the intimidating effect. Even though the ITA's final question might appear to presuppose (through the use of the words "special coincidence") the student's innocence here, given the previous interaction and stance that the ITA has taken, the final question could sound almost sarcastic to an American ear. The use of the adjective "proper" to modify "reason" is also potentially interpretable as sarcastic; it suggests that the student may have "reasons" but not ones judged by the ITA to be proper or satisfactory. Whereas the utterances appear to challenge the student, there is some ambiguity in the ITA's lower volume and physical orientation to the student. It may be the ITA's lack of lexical and grammatical competence that contributes to the challenging quality of the last question.

Discourse-data-internal evidence of the significant impact of this series of questions is the length of the pause before the student responds. When he finally does respond, it is lamely to assert in lines 7 and 8 that "Well you have to work. . .everyone worked them out the same I bet." The use of the opener "well" suggests a weak disagreement, but the student's shift of subject in mid-clause in line 8 suggests a retreat in response to the strong face-threat presented by the ITA. He begins with generic "you," claiming knowledge of how such problems must be worked out. He then apparently realizes that he is, in fact, speaking inappropriately to the teacher and backs down from such a claim to authority, shifting to a statement about the students in the class (represented by "everyone" in subject position), which is then further hedged by a final "I bet."

The student avoids responding directly to the four questions the ITA has just posed—neither does he respond to the accusation of cheating. The ITA responds with another "I know" that again sounds dismissive—because of stress on "I" rather than "know"—and then concludes with a final assertion of his authority in lines 8–10. He states that "but because of their personalities and experience and knowledge, there. . .these two answers should not be the same." Even though the initial subordinate clause is unclear (although he appears to be getting at individual differences among students), the final clause is very strong, with the use of the modal "should." This response by the ITA then culminates in a powerful statement at line 10 of his authority as the teacher, even though it is prefaced with "but:" "But this is from my experience." The "but" here sounds like a conventional nod in the direction of self-effacement that is not to be taken seriously.

The ITA asserts his authority through the implication that he has had extensive experience with students in this sort of situation. This stands in contrast to the way he handles the situation about log–log paper in the discussion of grades in the previous study (Tyler & Davies, 1990). In the log–log paper situation, when the student challenges his statement that the student hasn't used log–log paper, he doesn't assert his authority verbally, but rather asks another student for a sample of log–log paper and then shows the student the difference, which the student accepts. A statement, "But this is from my experience," is unanswerable by the student who clearly cannot claim such experience for himself. When the student does respond, he begins his utterance with "so," linking his statement to the previous discourse by casting the discussion of the quiz as the premise from which he now draws his conclusion, at lines 10–11, that "I don't get any credit for the quiz." At this point the ITA seems to have put the student in a position of drawing a conclusion and accepting it. Notice, however, that the conclusion is not "yes, I cheated" or "I didn't cheat but I clearly failed to shield my answers"—but rather appears to be something like an implicit acknowledgment of cheating or of failing to shield, together with an acceptance of the ITA's power in the situation. It is a "conclusion" that acknowledges his defeat in the attempt to get more points on the quiz. The student initiates a shift here away from the moral to the logistical.

The ITA's next series of utterances are logistical, in terms of points and course grade, etc., along with an explicit moral judgment at line 12 concerning his handling of the situation: "It's fair." The ITA orients away from the student as he consults the grade book. It is noteworthy that even though the student doesn't admit to cheating, the ITA is penalizing the student with points as if he had cheated. This may be because the ITA has framed it that whether the student actually cheated or not, he is still guilty of not having shielded his answers. Moving out of his position of physical deference, the student stands up to his full height and looks down at the ITA as he hears the grades that he will get. The student's defeat is registered by his loser's comment, not uttered in the direction of the ITA, "I've been reamed," at line 13. This is quite rude, with sexual connotation, although the student may not be consciously aware of that dimension of the expression. The passive construction suggests a lack of blame on the part of the student. The student is ultimately penalized in terms of points for the quiz.

Key Questions

At this point we have established from the discourse analysis that the Korean ITA apparently switched his discourse strategy from an inductive/collaborative one in the discussion of grades to a deductive/assertive strategy in handling the suspected cheating. He also assumes a much more assertive role which emphasizes his experience and authority. The next step is to try to discover both Korean and American norms concerning cheating in order to shed light on the interlanguage pragmatics dimension of the situation. In the stress of the situation is the Korean transferring a version of a Korean discourse strategy for this particular topic and situation? What can American TAs tell us about their schemas for this situation and what the American undergraduate was probably expecting?

Creating Structured Techniques for Answering the Questions. After we had obtained IRB approval for the project involving human subjects, we sought appropriate Koreans and Americans to be interviewed. Potential interviewees were told they would be asked about issues of importance to teachers cross-culturally. We used interviews from six Koreans who had some experience of teaching in university contexts in Korea and who hadn't been too Americanized by their experience at American universities. We had release forms ready and obtained permission to taperecord the interviews if it seemed appropriate. Otherwise, we took notes on the interviews. Individual interviews were conducted in university offices, and tape recording was done using a Radio Shack tietack microphone positioned between the interlocutors. For the American TA interviews we selected one university English teacher with 20 years of experience, one with about 5 years of experience, and one who had just begun as TA the previous semester and thus had just recently received orientation as an American university teacher. The interview protocols are included in the appendix. We created questions that moved from abstract (in order to get at norms) to very specific and situated when we asked the interviewees to look at the videotape and comment on the Korean ITA's handling of the suspected cheating. The questions were intended as general guides and prompts to initiate open-ended responses. Challenges were to provide appropriate contextualization for the transcript and videotape, and to prepare the interviewee for viewing the tape. We read descriptions of the context and immediately preceding situation to the interviewees, in order to create consistency across interviews. Anticipating that the transcript as given above might be confusing in the interview situation, we created a less detailed version of the transcript, treating it as a screenplay. While the interviewees followed along with the transcript, we read it aloud to them, maintaining stress patterns as marked with underlining and generally imitating the ITA and student. We asked for any questions on points needing clarification, and then we played the videotape. Interviewees were asked to comment on anything that struck them. Comments were followed up in relation to specific moments in the interaction; for example, a comment that "the ITA doesn't give the student a chance to talk" would be referred immediately to the transcript to find what was happening in the discourse from the interviewee's point of view and what aspects of the discourse were being used as contextualization cues. For example, the Americans confirmed our analysis that the stress on "I" rather than "know," together with the lexical choice of "know" rather than "understand" on the part of the ITA were significant in creating the impression that he was dismissing the student's response rather than expressing sympathy at line 2.

Findings From the Representatives of the Speech Communities

The interviews served both to validate and further inform our initial discourse analysis and also to provide rich data on the relation between discourse strategy and topic in the institutional context of the university. Interestingly, both the Korean and the American teachers commented that a more skillful teacher would have prevented this situation from ever arising, and discussed appropriate classroom management techniques.

Americans. For the Americans, the data represent a situation fraught with moral and ethical issues; "cheating" is considered to be morally wrong. There is concern that university students are engaging in more and more of this behavior, and American universities are taking up "academic misconduct" as an important issue. The Americans expressed shock at the "confrontational" way that the Korean ITA handled the discussion of potential cheating. All of them said that they would handle a comparable situation in a very indirect way, with some version of what we have called an "inductive/collaborative" discourse strategy.

It was clear from their responses that the Americans were affected by ideological, cultural, and institutional constraints. The ideological dimension (in terms of the basic principle of "innocent until proven guilty") was least overt but appeared to motivate a reluctance to make a direct accusation in the circumstances. The Americans also expressed a sense of the student's privacy being violated and noted that such a discussion would never happen in front of the entire class. A related issue was the cultural fact of the current litigiousness of American society; teachers are now worried about being sued over statements that they make to students. The institutional constraints are most obvious in the current trend (in place at both of the researchers' universities) to remove the teacher from any confrontation with the student in cases of suspected academic misconduct. The least-experienced teacher, who had just gone through TA orientation, seemed most aware of current policies concerning how she should handle cases of suspected academic misconduct. A teacher is explicitly directed to avoid any situation like the one in the data, submitting evidence of cheating to a departmental or college committee. Policies governing the handling of academic misconduct through departmental and university review boards can be located on American university websites.

Thus we see that the constraints imposed within the culture of an institution (here as part of a national trend) can affect discourse strategy in a profound way in relation to a particular topic. Whereas we might assume a cultural preference for the "deductive/assertive" style in many situations, given overt American norms for speeches and expository essays, we need to be careful about inappropriate generalization. When the topic is cheating, Americans appear to opt for an "inductive/collaborative" style. Even when one of the Americans responded initially that she would "confront" the student privately with the evidence of cheating, probing revealed that what she really meant was that she would simply show the evidence to the students and ask them to explain, but would offer no verbal conclusions (i.e., she would opt for an extremely indirect form of the inductive/collaborative strategy).

Koreans. The Koreans consistently emphasized that cheating is treated very seriously, especially in secondary school because the competition to get into good universities is stiff. They also noted that, unless the student uses high tech, cheating is difficult. High school teachers go to elaborate lengths to prevent the possibility of cheating. Students are often physically positioned so that they are sitting at a maximal distance from one another. Two of our interviewees related experiences in which teachers had students stack backpacks on chairs situated between students in order to create physical barriers between students as a way of curtailing the possibility of students looking at each other's papers. In addition, they reported there were often additional proctors roaming the classroom, looking for any signs of cheating. Three of the informants said that teachers also give specific instructions on how individual students should guard their work so that other students cannot see their answers. Two noted they had seen teachers take away test papers if students were sitting in such a way that it appeared they were allowing other students to see their answers.

In response to the question of what Korean teachers do when they have evidence of cheating but have not actually seen the students engaged in cheating, the Korean participants unanimously said the teacher would most likely treat the situation cautiously. One informant said he felt that the strength of the teacher's reaction would be in proportion to the importance of the test or assignment. He noted that small quizzes are unusual in Korea, but if the assignment were not worth much, the teacher might not react strongly to suspected cheating. The Koreans reported a range of responses they had heard of or observed. The teacher might caution the entire class about cheating and then increase the vigilance in looking for cheating by bringing in extra proctors or dividing the class into smaller groups and testing each group in different classrooms, but not specifically accuse the suspected parties. As a way to create a group reaction against cheating, the next quiz would often be much more difficult than the previous one. They uniformly reported that they had never heard of a Korean teacher writing a message like "Do not cheat" at the top of a test. Neither had they ever heard of a teacher publicly accusing a student of cheating if the teacher had not actually observed the student in the act of cheating.

The Korean interviewees also stressed that a Korean teacher had much more authority than an American instructor and if a teacher determined that students had cheated, he or she might simply give the student an F or a lowered grade with no discussion. In many instances quizzes and tests are not returned, so the students are not always sure as to why they receive a particular grade. The presumption is that if the students had cheated, they would accept the lower grade without question. If a student thought he or she had done well and received a lower grade than expected, an option might be to privately and humbly ask the instructor about the grade. But in this situation, the student would not challenge the teacher's assessment, so the question of cheating might never arise.

Another practice is that the teacher might tell the suspected students to "follow him to his office." The interviewees noted that this command in itself is often considered a serious reprimand. Once in the office, the teacher would likely show the students the written material that made the teacher suspect cheating. In this case, the strong expectation would be that the student(s) would immediately confess without the teacher having to explicitly accuse the student. In other words, if the instructor chose to discuss cheating, the preferred discourse management strategy would be an inductive, nonconfrontational one. In some ways the strategy is not significantly different from the typical discourse strategy employed by American instructors. There are some important differences, however, primarily having to do with the authority of the teacher to make a determination of cheating and act on it without informing the student.

As we reported in Tyler and Davies (1990), the ITA felt confused about how to handle the entire interaction. His initial instinct was to postpone the discussion of grades until after the class. However, he had also been warned by other Koreans that American students ask many questions in the classroom (something that is unusual in Korea) and that the teacher is expected to answer the questions. He was unsure if it would be considered appropriate to postpone the discussion until after class and so determined that he should answer the student's questions during the lab, when the other students were present.

Although the ITA had attempted to make adjustments to the informality of the U.S. classroom (he dressed in shorts and a tee shirt and joked with the students) and to the greater consideration/authority given American students (he addresses students by their first names and elicits their questions), in the video playback sessions he stated that he was taken by surprise at the student's repeated rejections of his explanations for the student's poor grade on the homework assignment. He was not prepared for the student to so boldly question the instructor's judgment and authority. He clearly articulated a sense of growing tension during the interaction, pointing out places on the video where he held his back more and more stiffly as the exchange continued. Although he attempted to pursue the goal of calmly explaining in detail the problems with the student's homework, after 10 minutes he felt that the student was being unduly quarrelsome.

It was at this point that the issue of cheating arose. Based on his experience in Korea, he never thought a student would question a teacher's judgment about cheating. Thus, he found himself in a situation he would never encounter in Korea.

In our initial interviews, we asked the ITA why he had written "Please do not cheat" on the quizzes. He stated that the quiz was a small part of the overall grade and while he wanted to discourage further cheating, he did not feel that cheating on the quiz warranted a discussion in his office. This squares with our other informants' remarks about the seriousness associated with being told to go to the teacher's office. This ITA wanted to warn the students not to cheat without penalizing them too severely. He pointed out that, rather than giving the students zeros, he gave some credit for the quiz. He was hesitant to alert the entire class to the fact that he suspected some of the students of cheating, as he was aware that American teachers were expected to build friendly relations with students and such a general warning might impair that rapport. His sense was that a written warning given individually would be a face saving move that would avoid involving the entire class.

DISCUSSION

Our triangulated data suggests that the discourse management strategies used by the ITA in this interaction cannot be explained simply as a matter of negative transfer from the L1/C1. In fact, we haven't found evidence that a Korean teacher, even with greater authority than an American teacher, would use this overall assertive/deductive strategy in a comparable situation. We hypothesize that the ITA found himself in both a physical and cultural setting that was substantially different from what he had encountered in Korea. Moreover, the student–teacher interaction in which he found himself was quite different from those he had encountered in his native culture. There is evidence of attempts on his part to adjust his discourse management strategies and his enactment of his participant role as teacher to the norms of the U.S. classroom, but it is also clear that his understanding of those norms was incomplete. Although he drew on certain aspects of his L1/C1 schemas, it seems that many aspects of his discourse management strategies are outside the norms of either his L1/C1 or the target U.S. language/culture. Thus, we see several instances of true interlanguage pragmatics.

One of the clearest instances and arguably the most important in terms of the failure of the interaction, is his decision to respond to the indirect, written evidence of cheating by writing "Please do not cheat" at the top of the students' papers, issue partial credit for the quiz, and return the papers without planning to discuss the issue with the accused students. The message presupposes the fact of cheating on the quiz as well as exhorting appropriate behavior on future quizzes. The enactment of this strategy serves as a framing for the ensuing interaction with accused student.

The circumstances that led the ITA to use this strategy are complex. In grading the quizzes, the ITA found himself in a situation that would rarely occur in Korean classrooms because of the difference in physical arrangements when quizzes and tests are administered. Our Korean informants uniformly told us that various physical precautions would be taken to lessen the possibility of a student copying from another. The strategy of physically separating the students is not available to the ITA in the U.S. physics lab. Moreover, in the Korean context, if students are suspected of cheating, the teacher is likely to bring in additional proctors to carefully monitor the students and keep further cheating from occurring. Again, this is not a possibility in the U.S. situation.

The Korean informants also told us that the teacher might issue a warning to the entire class if the cheating were considered serious. After such a warning the next quizzes would be more difficult. However, the ITA was reluctant to issue such a warning because of the potential negative effect on his rapport with the entire class, especially since only two students out of the entire class were involved. Moreover, small, regular quizzes seem not to be typical in Korean classes, while they are an institutional requirement in the course the ITA is teaching. In the Korean situation, tests that carry more weight seem to be the norm. Thus, the ITA is again in a situation in which there is no analog in his native culture. One of our informants suggested that how strongly the teacher reacts to an instance of cheating is somewhat dependent on the importance of the test itself. Thus, another factor in the decision not to talk to the students about the cheating seems to be that the weight of the quiz was so small in the overall grade. Nevertheless, the ITA does not want the cheating to continue. The ITA seems to have made the decision that the quiz grade was not significant enough to warrant a public warning to the entire class and opts for the private written warning. All the Korean informants indicated that this was a strategy that was outside the norms of the Korean classroom. Thus, we see a strategy emerging which is influenced by certain aspects of Korean academic culture but which plays out in a discourse strategy that would not typically be found in the Korean classroom.

The norms for the participant roles of teacher and student in the Korean context are much different from those of the U.S. context. In this area, the ITA seems to have relied on his understanding of the teacher having absolute authority in deciding the students' grades and in making the determination that cheating has taken place. Recall that our informants told us that a Korean teacher might give a student a low grade because the teacher had determined cheating had taken place. In such cases, many Korean teachers might opt not to discuss the issue with the suspected student. If the test were not returned, which is apparently often the case, the student might not ever be aware that the teacher had made that determination. The ultimate strategy followed by the ITA in this interaction was to make the determination that cheating had occurred (which he felt was unquestionably supported by the written evidence) and act on his authority by issuing a lower grade to both students. In making this determination, he did not feel compelled to find out which student had actually done the copying. Here his thinking seems to be largely determined by the strong Korean ethic that each student is responsible for shielding his or her answers and that students who do not do so are judged as complicitious. These elements of the strategy seem to involve transfer from the norms of the Korean classroom. By giving a written warning, he is indicating to the students that he is aware that some cheating has occurred and that he wants it to stop. However, in contrast to the Korean situation, the quiz had to be returned to the students. In returning the quizzes with the written warning, the students are made aware of the teacher's assessment. This creates a situation different from either the typical Korean or U.S. norm.

For the U.S. student, any allegation of cheating constitutes a serious threat to the individual's personal integrity. In this situation, even a guilty student may feel the need to defend his or her honor. The Korean informants suggested that if the student were innocent, he or she might privately discuss the matter with the teacher, but if the teacher were firm in his or her decision, the student would acquiesce. The guilty student would likely stay quiet and accept the lower grade. Thus, the ITA is taken by surprise when the student publicly asks for an explanation. (In truth, we find the student's behavior to be outside the typical norms of the U.S. classroom. Our sense, which was confirmed by interviews with the U.S. informants, is that this type of conversation is most likely to take place in private, at least in part because the student wants to avoid being embarrassed in front of the other students.) In the Korean context, the student would never ask the question, especially after having a testy discussion of a homework assignment. Once again, the ITA is in unknown waters. Still following his filtered understanding that in the U.S. classroom the teacher has to answer the student's question, he forges ahead with a strong statement of the facts that demonstrate cheating (while pointing to quizzes), "The figures are exactly the <u>same</u>. The symbols you use is exactly the <u>same</u>." The accusation of cheating followed by explicit presentation of the evidence on the part of the teacher represents a deductive discourse management strategy which strikes the U.S. listener as confrontational. It also struck the Koreans as unusual. They suggested that the teacher would show the two quizzes to the two students and wait for one or both to confess.

At this point, the student challenges the teacher's evidence, "well, you <u>have</u> to use the law of cosines to get the answer." The Korean informants indicated that students in Korea would never offer such a challenge. Even in the face of such a confrontation, the ITA still attempts to be responsive by indicating that he understands the student's point of view. His lexical choice, however, of "know" rather than "understand," and a stress on "I" rather than on the verb, creates an impression that he is being dismissive rather than sympathetic. Being in the unexpected position of having his judgment and authority directly challenged, the ITA, becomes even more direct, "But I was <u>con</u>fident that <u>she</u> or <u>you</u> have cheated." This statement is followed by a rapid fire series of questions that have the effect of aggressively challenging the student to offer an explanation. Our Korean informants were very uncomfortable with this exchange. They saw the ITA as aggressive, but they also saw the student as disrespectful. The ITA himself revealed that he was surprised and somewhat insulted by the student's challenge and felt the need to defend himself. Again, it seems that the ITA is implementing discourse strategies that only partially reflect his L1 pragmatics. The strategy of aggressively pointing out the evidence of cheating and demanding that the student offer an explanation is outside the norms of Korean teacher behavior largely because the dynamics of the Korean classroom are such that the student would never offer such a challenge. Simultaneously, the ITA is influenced by his sense that the teacher should not be challenged and that as the teacher he had the right to make the assessment that cheating had occurred. One of our Korean informants explained that some "scary male teachers" in high school are very aggressive and even use corporal punishment if they feel students are disrespectful. Thus, the discourse management strategies that emerge, while reflecting aspects of the Korean schema of participant roles, also differ from typical Korean classroom behavior.

An irony of the situation is that "positive transfer" of a collaborative/inductive discourse strategy by the Korean ITA might have provided a better match with typical American behavior in this context.

Existing Institutional Processes as a Source of Data

The Use of Videotaping in the Preparation of Teachers.   With the prevalent use of videotaping as a tool in the preparation and supervision of teachers, such tapes can be an important source of institutional talk as data for research on interlanguage pragmatics. Bardovi-Harlig and Hartford (chapter 1, this volume) provide information on the logistics of this important tool. Perhaps the most complex use of videotaping in teacher preparation and supervision is the kind of process out of which this particular data emerged. In this model, routine taping and playback methodology (cf. Davies & Tyler, 1994; Davies et al., 1989; Tyler & Davies, 1990) are an integral part of the process.

The Kinds of Data Created. Videotaping and analysis of the sort described would provide data for at least three sorts of studies within the framework of interlanguage pragmatics (cf. Bardovi-Harlig, 1999): (1) longitudinal data with individual ITAs; (2) data to track the effects of specific instruction; (3) an opportunity to match taped data of actual teaching performance with other sorts of evaluative data, in particular with student evaluations of teaching. The examination of actual teaching performance in such cases might yield some interesting findings concerning the relative importance of pragmatic competence in relation to other sorts of competence (i.e. that an ITA with well-developed pragmatic competence might be able to compensate very effectively for a lack of competence in other areas of language—pronunciation, grammar, lexicon, etc., as we saw in the case of Wes [Schmidt, 1983]). And that an ITA with excellent pronunciation, for example, but lack of pragmatic competence might get very poor teaching evaluations from students. This would challenge "commonsense" notions about language proficiency and interactional competence.

Existing Institutional Processes as Part of a Methodology

Triangulation of Multiple Perspectives. Institutional arrangements for teacher supervision that involve discussion of the videotapes also provide an important source of data for methodologies that require triangulation from the perspectives of the participants in addition to the perspective of the analyst. Playback methodology with the videotapes also allows the elicitation of inter pretations from other members of the interpretative communities represented by the participants. This is key to providing crucial insights that the analyst, limited by his or her own cultural assumptions, does not have access to from the transcript alone. Such a methodological procedure also helps to tease out the cultural from the individual.

The Identification of Key Problematic Situations. Routine collection of institutional talk (i.e. systematic gathering of natural data in a range of institutional contexts) allows the researcher to identify key problematic situations where communication breaks down. The value of such data from this theoretical perspective is that it allows the analyst to use miscommunication for insight into the taken-for-granted schemas underlying successful communication (Erickson & Shultz, 1982; Gumperz & Tannen, 1979). This orientation to the data contrasts with a "strategic" approach (Canale & Swain, 1980) in which the focus is on discovering what learners do to compensate for miscommunication with the assumption that their linguistic behavior in these contexts is important to the process of language acquisition. Our assumption, in contrast, is that the learner is unlikely to "acquire" more targetlike pragmatic competence or gain insight into the state of his or her interlanguage pragmatic competence without instruction of a sort that is much more like a process of explicit socialization (cf. Bardovi-Harlig et al., 1991; Davies, in press; Davies & Tyler, 1994; Gumperz & Roberts, 1980; Tyler, 1994). Analysis of data of miscommunication in key problematic situations allows insight into both crosscultural and interlanguage pragmatics, and such insights can be used in preparing curriculum for instruction of the sort just described (cf. Tyler, 1994). In this sort of instruction the videotapes are a central element, subject to joint analysis by the supervisor and teacher/learner.

CONCLUSION

In analyzing this example of interlanguage pragmatics and explicating our methodology, we hope to have addressed limitations of current research in interlanguage pragmatics in terms of methodology, data, and theoretical framework. Through our interactional sociolinguistic analysis of this discourse data we have shown that simple notions of "transfer" are not adequate to understanding interlanguage pragmatics. Rather, each crosscultural situation is potentially a new context, a "third place" (Kramsch, 1993) in the interface between cultural and linguistic systems. We have seen that the L2 learner in our data produced discourse that was a complex construction built of L1 pragmatics and of a partial understanding of the target language pragmatics filtered through his perception of the target culture. The discourse was further shaped by resources and constraints of particular institutional contexts.

We also hope to have established the notion of "discourse strategy" as a dimension of interlanguage pragmatics and as an interesting area for research. We take "strategy" to mean a purposeful linguistic maneuver that provides both an overall ordering to the shape of an extended stretch of discourse, as well as more local stratagems for accomplishing a particular communicative goal in spoken interaction. Each language/culture privileges particular discourse strategies in particular situations. Like other aspects of language, L1 discourse strategies can potentially be transferred in L2 production (as demonstrated in Tyler & Davies, 1990). Understanding the circumstances under which such transfer takes place, with either felicitous or infelicitous results, is an important component of bettering our understanding of the development of pragmatic competence. Conversely, understanding the circumstances under which an L2 learner uses discourse strategies which match neither the L1 nor the L2 adds importantly to our understanding of ILP.

Within an analytical approach to interlanguage pragmatics/discourse analysis it might seem "logical" to separate out different levels of language or dimensions of competence and then try to study them separately. Such an analytical approach is presumably based on the assumption that, for example, the learner builds up from grammatical to pragmatic competence, or that there are certain a priori elements that can be isolated and studied (e.g., speech acts), which are then strung together to create a "discourse strategy." In contrast, we hope to have demonstrated that a holistic approach to the data is essential, one that makes clear the potential role of all levels of linguistic organization in "interlanguage pragmatics" and the importance of context at the cultural and institutional level as part of the interpretive process.

Finally, we also hope to have demonstrated that naturally occurring institutional talk can be a valuable and accessible resource for researchers.

References

Bardovi-Harlig, K. (1999). Exploring the interlanguage of interlanguage pragmatics: A research agenda for acquisitional pragmatics. *Language Learning, 49* (4), 677-713.

Bardovi-Harlig, K., Hartford, B. A., Mahan-Taylor, R., Morgan, M. J., & Reynolds, D. W. (1991). Developing pragmatic awareness: Closing the conversation. *ELT Journal, 45,* 4-15.

Bialystock, E. (1983). Some factors in the selection and implementation of communication strategies. In C. Faerch & G. Kasper (Eds.), *Strategies in interlanguage communication* (pp. 100-118). New York: Longman.

Bruner, J. S. (1981). The social context of language acquisition. *Language and Communication, 1,* 155-178.

Canale, M., & Swain, M. (1980). Theoretical bases for communicative approaches to second language teaching and testing. *Applied Linguistics, 1,* 1-47.

Connor, U. (1996). *Contrastive rhetoric: Cross-cultural aspects of second-language writing.* New York: Cambridge University Press.

Corder, S. P. (1983). Strategies of communication. In C. Faerch & G. Kasper (Eds.), *Strategies in interlanguage communication,* 15-19, New York: Longman.

Davies, C. E. (in press). Developing awareness of crosscultural pragmatics: The case of American/ German sociable interaction. *Multilingua: Journal of Cross-Cultural and Interlanguage Communication.*

Davies, C. E., & Tyler, A. (1994). Demystifying cross-cultural (mis)communication: Improving performance through balanced feedback in a situated context. In C. G. Madden & L. M. Cynthia (Eds.), *Discourse and performance of international teaching assistants* (pp. 201-220). Alexandria, VA: TESOL Publications.

Davies, C. E., Tyler, A., & Koran, J. J. (1989). Face-to-face with English speakers: An advanced training class for international teaching assistants. *English for Specific Purposes, 8,* 139-153.

Dulay, H. C., & Burt, M. K. (1975). A new approach to discovering universal strategies of child second language acquisition. In D. P. Dato (Ed.), *Developmental psycholinguistics: Theory and applications* (pp. 209-233). Washington, D.C.: Georgetown University Press.

Duranti, A., & Goodwin, C. (Eds.). (1992). *Rethinking context: Language as an interactive phenomenon.* New York: Cambridge University Press.

Ellis, R. (1994). *The study of second language acquisition.* New York: Oxford University Press.

Ellis, R. (1999). *Learning a second language through interaction: Studies in bilingualism, Vol 17.* Philadelphia: Benjamins.

Erickson, F., & Shultz, J. (1982). *Counselor as gatekeeper: Social interactions in interviews.* New York: Academic Press.

Faerch, C., & Kasper, G. (Eds.). (1983). *Strategies in interlanguage communication.* New York: Longman.

Green, G. M. (1996). *Pragmatics and natural language understanding* (2nd ed.). Mahwah, NJ: Lawrence Erlbaum Associates.

Grice, H., P. (1975). Logic and conversation. In P. Cole & J. L. Morgan (Eds.), *Syntax and semantics: Speech acts, Vol. 3* (pp. 41-58). New York: Academic Press.

Gumperz, J. J. (1982). *Discourse strategies.* New York: Cambridge University Press.

Gumperz, J. J. (1992). Contextualization cues and understanding. In A. Duranti & C. Goodwin (Eds.), *Rethinking context* (pp. 229-252). New York: Cambridge University Press.

Gumperz, J. J., & Tannen, D. (1979). Individual and social differences in language use. In W. Wang & C. Fillmore (Eds.), *Individual differences in language ability and language behavior* (pp. 305-325). New York: Academic Press.

Gumperz, J. J., & Roberts, C. (1980). *Developing awareness skills for inter-ethnic communication.* (Occasional Paper No. 12). Singapore: SEAMEO Regional Language Centre.

Hall, J. K. (1995). 'Aw, man, where you goin'?': Classroom interaction and the development of L2 interactional competence. *Issues in Applied Linguistics, 6*(2), 37-62. .

Haastrup, K., & Phillipson, R. (1983). Achievement strategies in learner/native speaker interaction. In C. Faerch & G. Kasper (Eds.), *Strategies in interlanguage communication* (pp. 140-158). New York: Longman.

Hinds, J. (1987). Reader versus writer responsibility: A new typology. In U. Connor & R. Kaplan (Eds.), *Writing across languages* (pp. 141-152). Reading, MA: Addison-Wesley.

Hymes, D. (1974). *Foundations in sociolinguistics: An ethnographic approach.* Philadelphia: The University of Pennsylvania Press.

Kaplan, R. (1966). Cultural thought patterns in intercultural education. *Language Learning, 16*, 1-20.

Kasper, G. (1992). Pragmatic transfer. *Second Language Research, 8*, 203-231.

Kasper, G., & Schmidt, R. (1996). Developmental issues in interlanguage pragmatics. *Studies in Second Language Acquisition, 18*, 149-169.

Kramsch, C. J. (1993). *Context and culture in language teaching.* Oxford, England: Oxford University Press.

Kramsch, C. J. (1986). From language proficiency to interactional competence. *The Modern Language Journal, 70*(4), 366-372.

Markee, N. (2000). *Conversation analysis.* Mahwah, NJ: Lawrence Erlbaum Associates.

Oxford, R. (1990). *Language learning strategies: What every teacher should know.* Rowley, MA: Newbury House.

Saville-Troike, M. (1989). *The ethnography of communication: An introduction* (2nd ed.). Malden, MA: Blackwell.

Selinker, L. (1972). Interlanguage. *IRAL, 10*, 209-231.

Schmidt, R. (1983). Interaction, acculturation and the acquisition of communication competence. In N. Wolfson & E. Judd (Eds.), *Sociolinguistics and second language acquisition.* Rowley, MA: Newbury House.

Trosberg, A. (1987). Apology strategies in natives/non-natives. *Journal of Pragmatics, 11*, 147-167.

Tyler, A. E. (1994). Effective role-play situations and focused feedback: A case for pragmatic analysis in the classroom. In C. G. Madden & C. L. Myers (Eds.), *Discourse and performance of international teaching assistants* (pp. 116-133). Arlington, VA: TESOL Publications.

Tyler, A. E., & Davies, C. E. (1990). Cross-linguistic communication missteps. *Text, 10*, 385-411.

6

English for Specific Purposes and Interlanguage Pragmatics

Elaine Tarone
University of Minnesota

Although research on interlanguage pragmatics (ILP) has made substantial strides over the last decades, it is my thesis in this chapter that ILP research can benefit by incorporating central constructs of English for Specific Purposes (ESP), specifically *discourse community* and *genre*, and by awareness of research findings in ESP.

SIMILARITIES BETWEEN ILP AND ESP RESEARCH APPROACHES

Pragmatics examines the way in which speakers and hearers communicate more than is explicitly said. This ability to infer meaning is particularly strong when speaker and hearer share experience as members of the same *social group* or *speech community* (Yule, 1996). Research on interlanguage pragmatics examines the way in which members of a native language speech community acquire the pragmatic speaking norms of a target language speech community.

Research on English for specific purposes examines ways in which members of particular discourse communities use language varieties (genres) to communicate with one another in their pursuit of common professional or work-related goals. Pragmatic effects are often at the center of ESP research, which stresses the way discourse communities agree to use language for work-related purposes. As Widdowson (1998) pointed out, the study of English for specific purposes is inherently a study in pragmatics. The reason why insiders can understand "special purpose genres" not intelligible to outsiders is that they are "able to infer the relevant discourse because of their professional competence as members of this discourse community." The discourse is shaped the way it is because members of the discourse community, like all speakers, "design utterances to key into the context of recipient knowledge in the most economical way" (p. 4). Thus, special purpose genres have their origins in pragmatic principles of communication, and it is because of pragmatic principles that they are processible on an ongoing basis by members of the discourse community.

DIFFERENCES BETWEEN RESEARCH APPROACHES
IN ILP AND ESP

Interlanguage Pragmatics Research

In research on interlanguage pragmatics, the subjects are nonnative speakers (NNS) of the target language, and are usually compared with native speakers (NS) of the target language with regard to their pragmatic knowledge and performance. Learners are viewed as moving from one speech community with native language norms to a new speech community with target language norms.

An idealized construct of "speech community" has been central in the study of ILP. Although definitions of the construct "speech community" vary slightly, here we can follow Hymes (1972): A speech community is a group of people who share conventions of speaking and interpretation of speech performance. Within the English-speaking world, there are of course many speech communities. Preston (1989) argued, for instance, that second-language classrooms can be viewed as speech communities, with internally agreed-upon formal and informal speech styles appropriate for use with teachers vs. students. However, in the interest of efficiency, in ILP research it seems to have been generally agreed to treat as a single speech community, with a single set of pragmatic norms, all speakers of one of the standard varieties of English (e.g., American English). Although Beebe and colleagues (e.g., Beebe & Takahashi, 1989) have sometimes dealt with speech acts like rudeness in the context of a smaller speech community such as New York, participants' membership in discourse communities or more specialized speech communities within the idealized target language speech community has not generally been a factor in ILP research. We can exemplify this stance with the following statement: *A request is a request, across all social contexts; NNSs must master the general norms of NSs of the idealized speech community.*

A perennial issue for discussion by researchers in interlanguage pragmatics has to do with the sort of data one should use in this sort of study. If one is studying a particular speech act, should they limit their data collection to the taping of natural oral interaction? Such data collection methods, used for example by Bardovi-Harlig and Hartford (1996) in examining the pragmatic features of academic advising sessions, have the virtue of face validity: They show how learners actually behave in the real world. In addition, they allow researchers to go beyond documentation of general group patterns, as they permit the researcher to analyze deliberate individual choices to flout pragmatic norms (e.g., Broner & Tarone, 2001; Nelms, 2002; Rundquist, 1990; Tarone, 2000). However, such studies may also have certain disadvantages:

- they may be extremely time-consuming and inefficient, since the target speech act or pragmatic behavior may not occur very frequently in general social interaction;

- there is a problem of comparability, of the learners with each other and of the learners with speakers of the target language variety;
- there is a problem of generalizability, since only a few learners can be observed at a time and it is unclear whether these are representative; and
- there is a competence/performance problem, since observations alone record behavior, but not the learner's or the fluent speaker's perspective on behavior.

As a result, some researchers have relied on the use of tools such as discourse completion tasks (DCTs) to access a larger number of learners' and native speakers' introspections about the speech acts which ought to be performed in a range of hypothetical speaking situations. Such techniques obviously have their own opposite shortcomings:

- They use taxonomies and frameworks structured by the researcher that may bias the results in unforeseen ways;
- they may permit subjects too much time for reflection and for self-flattery, and thus not predict actual behavior;
- they provide insufficient contextualization so that study participants are asked to respond with idealized responses to idealized situations;
- they emphasize group norms, with no ability to analyze individual choices, such as sarcasm (e.g., Nelms, 2002) and other forms of language play (e.g., Broner & Tarone, 2001; Tarone, 2000).

In the study of pragmatics, social context is critical, and it is imperative to find ways to study pragmatics in natural interactions, using techniques that minimize the shortcomings outlined above.

In sum, work in ILP focuses on participants' status as native speakers or nonnative speakers, on "general pragmatic norms" of an idealized TL speech community (as discussed on p. 157 of this chapter), and on the degree to which individual second language learners conform to those general pragmatic norms. ILP research has tended to rely on data elicitation devices and not observation of natural interaction in social contexts.

English for Specific Purposes Research

Research on English for Specific Purposes, in contrast to what has been described earlier, focuses on the norms of strictly delimited discourse communities, the grammar and pragmatic characteristics of genres used within those communities, and on the distinction between expert and novice performance.

Research on ESP is quite diverse, and includes both corpus linguistics and genre analysis. In this chapter, I focus on genre analysis as this approach has evolved in the field of English for Specific Purposes, particularly following the model of John Swales. LSP (Languages for Specific Purposes) and ESP (English for Specific Purposes) are fields of study focusing on the description of the language production and judgments, not of second language learners, but of expert speakers of some language variety or genre used by members of a specific discourse community. The term discourse community is used in different ways in different fields of study. In this chapter, discourse community is defined, following Swales, as a specialized type of speech community defined solely by shared common public goals—often professional or vocational goals. Importantly, the discourse community is defined, not as a group of people whose shared linguistic conventions derive from shared ethnic background, or geographical space, or social class. The discourse community is defined more narrowly by the common goals the members of the community share. Typical examples of discourse communities are professional groups, academic departments, and hobbyists. Swales (1990) gives the example of his stamp-collecting club, which consists of people who are brought together by their common goal of collecting stamps. In pursuing that common goal, members of a discourse community use genres to communicate with one another in furthering their common purpose; in Swales' example, there is a club newsletter genre in which discourse community members advertise various stamps they wish to sell or buy, using technical terms and phrases whose meaning is opaque to outsiders but crystal clear to them.

The essential linguistic assumption underlying the notion of genre is that when a discourse community uses language for a specific purpose such as writing a research paper in microbiology, a technical manual for a computer, nursing notes, or a stamp-collectors' newsletter—or for oral activities such as a history lecture—that language becomes specialized in both information structure and linguistic form. The discourse community agrees that information should be organized in a particular way in that genre, and that linguistic forms should be used in mutually agreed-upon ways to signal that organization. As Hymes would say, members of the same discourse community share the same conventions for writing or speaking the genres that are used by that community in pursuit of its common public goal.

The focus of research on LSP or ESP is empirical and practical: It describes the characteristics of these different genres, or language varieties, so as to establish what it is that novices to the discourse community need to learn. Louis Trimble often pointed out that no one is a native speaker of any variety of English for specific purposes; everyone has to learn new norms when joining a new discourse community as an adult (personal communication, 1971). And, increasingly, expert members of an English-speaking discourse community may or may not be native speakers of English. The important distinction for ESP is on the expert–novice distinction, not the NS–NNS distinction, and on what it is that novices need to learn about the forms used in target genres to perform pragmatic functions. We can exemplify the general stance in ESP research with the following statement: *A request may fail or succeed in a discourse community depending on whether its realization fits genre norms. All novices (native speakers or not) must master genre norms.*

Let us now turn to an exploration of the twin constructs of discourse community and genre and their relevance for research in interlanguage pragmatics.

THE CONSTRUCTS *GENRE* AND *DISCOURSE COMMUNITY*

The construct of genre was memorably defined by John Swales (1990, p. 58) as a class of communicative events used by a discourse community to serve some agreed-upon set of communicative purposes. Those purposes have an impact on the information structure and the linguistic characteristics of the genre.

The discourse community itself is a group of people with shared common public goals. The discourse community has expert members who know the community norms and can transmit them to novices. Expert members of the discourse community share common assumptions about the purposes and structure of genres used by that community. Members of the discourse community use genres as a means of communication to pursue their common goals.

Use of these twin constructs, discourse community and genre, can enhance ILP research in several ways. First, they can make it possible for researchers on interlanguage pragmatics to gather natural data in highly comparable social circumstances, and thus to compare the performance and perception of experts and novices, native speakers and nonnative speakers. The structure of the genre is highly stylized and mutually agreed upon within the discourse community. Because the speaker or writer's general goal is clear when producing a genre, the problem of inability to identify speaker intention that has bedeviled ILP researchers focusing only on free conversation can be greatly ameliorated.

A second advantage conveyed by use of the construct of discourse community is the notion that such communities contain *expert members*: members who know the content of the field and the conventions of the discourse better than others. Such experts are usually easily identified by other members of the community. The primary focus of genre analysis researchers in ESP has been upon description of genres as used by expert members of the discourse community. As outsiders to the discourse community, researchers themselves do not have the professional competence to understand the discourse; they need to consult with expert members, just as any anthropologist or ethnographer must find a way to consult with, and describe the perspective of, members of the community being studied. Selinker (1979) laid out the reasons why ESP researchers need the input of such "subject specialist informants," and set out guidelines for working with them as informants. Researchers, he suggested, need to have informants because they themselves, as outsiders to the discourse community, do not have good intuitions about the genre. Researchers should seek informants who are known by other discourse community members to be good at producing the genre and who in addition have the ability to reflect consciously and analytically about the language they use in producing the genre. Recall that there are no native speakers of ESP genres: Because expert specialist informants have themselves learned the rules of their genres relatively late in life, their knowledge of these rules seems to be more accessible to analysis and reflection than is the case with earlier-acquired native languages (see Preston, 2000, for a discussion of the relative automaticity of early and late acquired language varieties). Even so, some informants are better able than others to talk with the researcher about exemplars of the genre, providing reasons why the language in the genre is organized and structured the way it is.

Genre analyses such as those described in Gibbs (2002; chapter 7, this volume) and Kuehn and Tarone (2000) would have been impossible without the input of expert members of the discourse community. Basically, what expert members of the discourse community can do is to lay out the prototypical structure of given genres that are used by the discourse community. They can act as informants, showing the researcher prototypical choices made in exemplars of the genre. For example, when we were trying to describe the grammatical/rhetorical structure of journal articles in astrophysics, a subject specialist informant told us that research paper writers in this field choose the passive rather than the active voice in a systematic and principled way, using the passive for verbs referencing standard procedures and the active for verbs referencing unique choices made by the researcher (cf. Tarone, Gillette, Dwyer, & Icke, 1998). Our informant glossed every verb phrase in two astrophysics journal articles, showing us how every choice of active or passive followed this pattern in the information structure of those articles.

But expert members of the discourse community can do more than just indicate what is prototypical about a genre; they can also tell us when individual speakers or writers make idiosyncratic choices, deliberately violating the prototypical structure of a genre for some individual purpose such as language play (cf. Myers, 1989). An expert member can also indicate when the norms of the genre themselves appear to be changing. For example, Fernando's (2001) informant in plant genetics could point to cases where a younger colleague writing a journal article chose to use language that was more directly critical of others' work than the expert member himself would have chosen. He commented that this was an example of a growing trend among some members of his discourse community, not one he himself participated in, but one which he recognized as part of a change in the genre.

The construct of discourse community in research on interlanguage pragmatics can also be helpful in that it naturally shifts the focus of analysis away from the "idealized native speaker" of an idealized target language, and allows us to analyze instead the actual performance and interpretation of expert members of real discourse communities. Such experts may as easily be nonnative speakers of English as native speakers. The focus is on expertise within the discourse community and not on native speaker background. This is important because in today's world, given the increase in World Englishes, and the use of English among nonnative speakers of English worldwide, it seems less and less relevant to focus solely on the native speaker variety as the goal of learning.

A final factor favoring a focus on language use inside discourse communities has to do with the goal of English language learners worldwide. More and more, learners are not motivated so much to learn English to become members of U.S. or British society (a traditional view of *integrative motivation*) as to join professional discourse communities in which English is the language of choice. If integrative motivation exists, it is increasingly focused on the desire to join discourse communities, rather than the desire to change citizenship; English language learners want to be accepted into the professional discourse community of doctors, or lawyers or engineers. If this is the case, then their interactions within these discourse communities are the logical locus of research on interlanguage pragmatics, because these are the settings in which they will naturally be most focused on using and learning their new second language.

Let us now turn to some examples of studies in English for Specific Purposes that use the constructs of discourse community and genre to analyze interlanguage pragmatics in natural settings.

EXAMPLES OF STUDIES IN INTERLANGUAGE PRAGMATICS USING ESP CONSTRUCTS

Social Services Intake Interviews

The social services oral intake interview was identified by Kuehn and Tarone (2000) as a genre that is used by social service workers to screen applicants for social services. In this setting, the discourse community consists primarily of social services financial workers, who have the common goal of identifying individuals entitled to social services benefits, and distributing those benefits to entitled applicants. The community may also include the applicants themselves, who may begin as novices but become expert over time, but who have a very constrained role in the community. The purpose of the oral intake interview as a genre is to enable a financial worker (who is the interviewer) to review information given by the applicant on a written application form in order to determine whether and how much financial assistance should be given to the applicant. The script for this genre is agreed upon by the community as the most effective communicative means to that goal, and involves the performance, by the interviewer and the applicant, of a script: a predictable sequence of speech acts. The language used by the participants—the lexis and the structure of the script itself—is not easily understood by outsiders or novices, yet within the discourse community these are assumed to be common knowledge.

In Kuehn and Tarone (2000), the first author had been a social worker in the office studied, and provided her own script (expected sequences of speech acts and typical problems) for the intake interview. In addition, two native speaker intake interviewers were asked to provide their scripts for what typically happens during the intake interview. The scripts provided by the two interviewers and the first author were the same, as one would expect, given the theoretical framework of genre analysis which posits a discourse community with substantial agreement among its expert members on the purpose and structure of its genres. The information structure of the written application form was analyzed. Then, three oral interviews were audio taped, two of them with native speaker applicants, and one with a Hispanic applicant and her daughter, who acted as an interpreter. The interviews were transcribed and analyzed. Tapes of the three interviews were played to the two intake interviewers for comment.

The paper draws several conclusions. First, the second language learners' script includes a section that is missing in the interviewers' scripts, namely, giving reasons why she was applying for assistance. The financial aid workers said in the later interviews that this was a common occurrence with novice applicants, whether native speakers or nonnative speakers of English. Novices commonly wanted to provide this information, but the financial workers did not want or need it. Second, a common cycle in the script involves the financial workers' paraphrase of information on the application form, with the expectation that the applicants will explicitly confirm their paraphrase. The nonnative speaker of English does not explicitly confirm this to the extent the native speaker applicants did. Third, there is evidence, in the conversation in Spanish between the applicant and her daughter, that the nonnative applicant often misunderstands the financial worker's requests for confirmation. Possibly they do not understand the paraphrases provided by the financial workers. The applicant and her daughter clearly also misunderstand some directives; they do not respond to them, discuss them in Spanish, or obey them later. The form of the directive "I need you to. . . ." seems particularly hard for the NNSs to understand. Finally, the financial workers are observed to use a large number of technical words and phrases (e.g., "proofs," "go retroactive," "retromedical coverage," "SSI," "RSDI") without explaining them and also to use slang ("hunky-dory") which nonnative speakers of English (or even young native speakers) are unlikely to understand.

The authors point out the parallels between the interactional context of the welfare office and that of the university office advising session (Bardovi-Harlig & Hartford, 1996). Both the office advising session and the oral intake interview are genres performed in private within the discourse community, and can be thought of as private encounters of individuals of unequal status in institutional settings (cf. Bardovi-Harlig & Hartford, 1996). It is virtually impossible under such circumstances for novices to access good input ahead of time as to the appropriate L2 performance in such settings. Thus, they must learn the genre as they take part in it, responding in interaction with a more powerful, high-status interlocutor. A similar context may be the doctor's office.

Doctor-Patient Interviews

Ranney (1992) examines the cross-cultural pragmatics of the doctor–patient office interview using the construct of "script" to analyze the genre. In this study, the genre is the doctor–patient interview, an oral interaction whose purpose is to enable the doctor to obtain enough information from the patient to assist him or her to reach a diagnosis of the problem which brought the patient to the office, and possibly to prescribe treatment or medication. The discourse community has members that include doctors, nurse practitioners, nurses and other medical workers who assist the doctor in orienting to the problem that brings the patient to the office. Doctors are the expert members of this community. Patients are typically novice members of the discourse community, but if they participate frequently in the doctor–patient interview they may achieve increasingly expert status, just as the welfare office applicants did.

Ranney's study uses the construct of script to collect data and analyze the pragmatic structure of the genre. Her data collection methodology involves the elicitation of learner and expert scripts. She proposes that Schank and Abelson's (1977) notion of *script* be extended beyond an expected sequence of actions to include an individual's expectation of a sequence of speech acts that typically occur in a particular cultural event or speech event. So, for example, we all have a script, or set of expectations, based on our previous experience, about what typically happens and is said when one enters a restaurant and orders a meal, when one buys stamps at the post office, or when one meets with one's academic advisor to seek approval for a proposed class schedule. Because these scripts are based on previous experience, they are culture-bound. And because they are basically a set of expectations about what is likely to happen, and what speech acts are likely to occur in what order, scripts can be elicited in much the same way speech acts can be elicited by Discourse Completion Tasks (DCTs). The advantage of script elicitation is that it enables the researcher to discover the learners' expectations of discourse patterns: their ideas as to which speech acts are going to be appropriate for particular settings and roles and their under-standing of the order speech acts generally follow in a given speech event.

Using a script framework, Ranney compares college students' scripts for the genre of the doctor–patient interview. Nine were native speakers (NSs) of English and nine were NSs of Hmong and learners of English L2. She found that the NNS scripts were less well developed than the NS scripts. In addition, there were cultural differences between the scripts the two groups had for the medical consultation. For example, the American patients were more likely to expect to be given a diagnosis at the end of the interview, while the Hmong patients did not expect this. On the other hand, the Hmong patients were more likely to expect to be given medication at the end of the consultation. Although they considered it important to use respectful verbal and nonverbal behavior in the presence of a doctor, they were also much more likely to use on-record strategies for requesting medication or refusing surgery than the American patients were. It is unclear whether this Hmong preference for on-record strategies was because of their presupposition that medication was to be expected, or because they lacked linguistic competence to use more indirect strategies such as questions, modals such as *would*, or complex sentence embeddings in making possibly face-threatening requests.

Nursing Notes

The discourse community in this study consists of nurses working in an English-medium hospital in Montreal, Canada. The genre of interest is "nursing notes": documents for the patient's file that record essential information on the patient's condition and actions taken by nursing staff. The francophone nursing students in the Parks and Maguire (1999) study were fortunate to have an ample supply of mentors and coworkers in the discourse community who worked with the students collaboratively over time in a variety of ways to help them learn how to produce nursing notes in English.

Parks and Maguire point out that genre analysis has traditionally focused on the product, or the nature of the genre, but can also focus on the process of learning how to use a new genre. They offer a longitudinal case study of a francophone nursing student learning to produce nursing notes in English in a Canadian hospital. The study focuses on how this novice acquires the new genre on the job through the supportive mentoring of experts in the discourse community. An interesting feature of this study is the inclusion in the published paper of one francophone learner's hand-written first, second, and third drafts of nursing notes, progressively incorporating more and more pieces of input obtained from these mentors and coworkers, who told him what he had to include, in what order, and how it should be phrased.

Hotel Housekeeper Call-Ins

In chapter 7 of this volume, Gibbs (see also Gibbs, 2002) examines the difficulty that hotel workers have in making a particular kind of telephone call on the job. In her study, the discourse community consists of hotel workers in two departments: Housekeeping, and Room Service/Convention Services. This discourse community had expert members, who trained novice members on a regular basis. The genre under study is referred to in the discourse community as a "call-in." As Gibbs explains, a call-in is a phone call made by a housekeeper to a worker in Room Service/Convention Services to perform a request for removal of refrigerators, trays, roll-away beds and other items. The prototypical purpose of the call-in is thus to perform a Request speech act.

Gibbs taped call-ins made by a novice nonnative speaker of English and by an expert housekeeper. The fact that the call-in is a genre with a clearly identified goal and a prototypical structure allows us to compare the naturally-occurring pragmatic performance of the expert and novice housekeepers. In (1) below, we see an example of the expert housekeeper's call-in:

(1)   "Call-in" performed by expert housekeeper:

    T-O Ring.
    T-1 R: Hello.
    T-2 H: Pick up in room 936, refrigerator.

T-3 R: 936.
T-4 H: Yep. (Hangs up)

In (2) below we see an example of a call-in made by the non-native speaking novice housekeeper, a call-in that results in pragmatic failure:

(2) Failed "call-in" performed by novice NNS housekeeper:

T-O Ring.
T-1 R: Hello. Convention Services.
T-2 H: This is J. I'm- (.8) [housekeeping]
T-3 R: [how can]
            How can I help you?
T-4 H: I am housekeeping.
T-5 R: To call housekeeping you need to dial 52.
T-6 H: Housekeeping. Pick up.
T-7 R: Please dial 52.
T-8 H: Pick up. Room 1717.
T-9 R: I will call housekeeping to come help you. Good bye. (hangs up)

Gibbs contacted the Convention Services worker immediately after the call-in transcribed in (2) to ask why he had treated a housekeeper so poorly. He responded that he hadn't had any phone calls from any housekeeper all morning.

So let us compare the structure of the two call-ins. In the successful call-in in (1), the topic is introduced without any personal identification of caller or receiver, and there is no greeting sequence, as is normally the case in social phone calls (cf. Schegloff, 1986). In successful call-ins, housekeepers do not identify themselves. The request is performed bald on record with no mitigation. Gibbs shows that the novice hotel worker's failure with call-ins is a result of erroneously using the structure of the social phone call, trying to provide personal identification in Turn 2. When he does this, he is identified in as a guest by the worker in Convention Services, who responds to him as a guest in Turn 3. In spite of numerous attempts to self-identify as a housekeeper in subsequent turns, the novice housekeeper is unable to do so. For this reason, he is unsuccessful in achieving his work-related goal of Requesting. (It is interesting that the learners' difficulty was compounded by a hotel training tape [described in Gibbs, 2002] that actually trained them to make call-ins the wrong way—that is, it modeled call-ins that included personal identifications and greetings.) Gibbs concludes by showing that when the novice nonnative speaker hotel housekeepers were taught the correct structure of the call-in, they achieved success in being correctly identified in call-ins and in achieving their work-related goals.

CONCLUSION

Research in ESP can enrich work in interlanguage pragmatics in a number of ways. First, in our search for research methodologies for future studies of interlanguage pragmatics, ESP research can provide theoretical constructs, and methodological ideas. For example, the theoretical framework undergirding genre analysis, which posits the existence of discourse communities with common goals, shared communicative genres, and expert members who all share knowledge about the community's discourse conventions, is very useful. Operating within the assumptions of genre analysis, the researcher can elicit and describe the discourse knowledge of one or two expert members of a given community with some confidence that their knowledge is truly representative of the knowledge base of the whole discourse community. We have seen that techniques such as script elicitation and genre analysis can be useful research tools in describing the pragmatic competence of such informants. Such expert members can tell us not only what the prototypical structure of a genre in that community is, but also tell us when individual writers or speakers depart from that prototypical structure, and what such departures communicate.

Because ESP as a subfield generates descriptions of the way language is actually used in specified discourse communities, it can provide researchers on IL pragmatics with research methodologies and with data on the way in which second language learners actually perform pragmatic functions in the real world, using the language for real purposes. In this sense, we have seen how ESP studies have documented the way learners acquire L2 scripts and speech acts on the job or in institutional settings. ESP studies provide data on learner performance in relatively high-stakes social contexts, such as academic advising sessions, applications to college, and applications for social services.

Another trait of ESP as a subfield is its strong emphasis on establishing the goal of learning empirically, with baseline information on the performance and judgment of expert users of the genre in the target discourse community. Thus, ESP as a subfield can bring to the discussion on IL pragmatics information both on prototypical and idiosyncratic expert language use, and on novice language use in the same genres, either to support existing theories of interlanguage pragmatics or to challenge them.

A final advantage of cultivating a connection between ILP and ESP research is the fact that the ESP framework provides a view of learners as participants in the social/institutional event/practice rather than as merely nonnative speakers. What matters in this framework is not the native vs. non-native distinction, but rather the expert vs. novice distinction. Avoidance of an overemphasis on the native/nonnative distinction is also a very powerful result of adopting the ESP-genre analysis framework.

The studies in the Appendix are selected to provide a representative cross-sampling of genre analyses that include both oral and written data produced by both expert and second-language learning novice members of a range of discourse communities. The subfield of applied linguistics that is called English for Specific Purposes is extremely varied and rich; however, other studies of interest to ILP researchers undoubtedly exist. I hope to have provided such researchers with a useful starting place in searching for studies of interest to them. Further, I hope to have provided a good case for the argument that the theoretical frameworks and research methodologies being used in ESP are both useful and interesting to ILP researchers, and can help to extend the range, usefulness, and sophistication of research on interlanguage pragmatics.

ACKNOWLEDGMENT: Paper presented at AAAL '02, Salt Lake City Colloquium on Revisioning Interlanguage Pragmatics Research (A. D. Cohen, Organizer), and at the University of Illinois, Champaign-Urbana, Nov. 14, 2002.

REFERENCES

Bardovi-Harlig, K., & Hartford, B. (1996). Input in an institutional setting. *Studies in Second Language Acquisition, 18*, 171-188.

Beebe, L., & Takahashi, T. (1989). Sociolinguistic variation in face-threatening speech acts: Chastisement and disagreement. In M. Eisenstein (Ed.), *The dynamic interlanguage: Empirical studies in second language variation* (pp. 199-218). New York: Plenum.

Broner, M., & Tarone, E. (2001). Is it fun? Language play in a fifth grade Spanish immersion classroom. *Modern Language Journal, 85*, 363-379.

Brown, P., & Levinson, S. (1978). *Politeness: Some universals in language usage.* London: Cambridge University Press.

Eades, D. (1994). A case of communicative clash: Aboriginal English and the legal system. In J. Gibbons (Ed.), *Language and the law* (pp. 234-264). London: Longman.

Flowerdew, J., & Miller, L. (1996). Lectures in a second language: Notes towards a cultural grammar. *English for Specific Purposes, 15*, 121-140.

Fernando, M. M. (2001). *Use of passive, stative and active verb forms in two plant genetics research publications.* Unpublished masters qualifying paper, University of Minnesota, Minneapolis.

Gibbs, T. (2002). *Misidentification of limited proficiency English speaking employees in hotel call-ins.* Unpublished masters qualifying Paper, University of Minnesota.

Gimenez, J. C. (2001). Ethnographic observations in cross-cultural business negotiations between non-native speakers of English: An exploratory study. *English for Specific Purposes, 20*, 169-193.

Hymes, D. (1972). On communicative competence. In J. Pride & J. Holmes (Eds.), *Sociolinguistics.* Harmondsworth, England: Penguin.

Jacobson, Wayne. (1986). An assessment of the communication needs of non-native speakers of English in an undergraduate physics lab. *English for Specific Purposes, 5,* 173-188.

Kuehn, K., & Tarone, E. (2000). Negotiating the social services oral intake interview, *TESOL Quarterly, 34*, 99-126.

Maier, P. (1992). Politeness strategies in business letters by native and non-native English speakers. *English for Specific Purposes, 11*, 189-206.

Maley, Y. (1994). The language of the law. In J. Gibbons (Ed.), *Language and the law* (pp. 11-50). London: Longman.

Myers, G. (1989) The pragmatics of politeness in scientific articles. *Applied Linguistics, 10*, 1-35.

Nelms, J. (2002, April). The role of sarcasm in NS-NNS (mis)-communication. Paper presented at the annual convention of the American Association for Applied Linguistics, Salt Lake City, UT.

Nishiyama, T. (1990). *A study of class discussion and participation skills.* Unpublished masters Plan B Paper, University of Minnesota.

Parks, S., & Maguire, M. (1999). Coping with on-the-job writing in ESL: A constructivist-semiotic perspective. *Language Learning, 49*, 143-175.

Preston, D. (1989). *Sociolinguistics and second language acquisition.* Oxford, England: Basil Blackwell.

Preston, D. (2000). Three kinds of sociolinguistics and SLA: A psycholinguistic perspective. In B. Swierzbin, M. Anderson, C. Klee, & E. Tarone (Eds.), *Social and cognitive factors in second language acquisition: Selected proceedings of the 1999 Second Language Research Forum* (pp. 3-30). Somerville, MA: Cascadilla Press.

Ranney, S. (1992). Learning a new script: An exploration of sociolinguistic competence. *Applied Linguistics, 13*, 25-50.

Rundquist, S. (1990). *Flouting Grice's maxims.* Unpublished doctoral dissertation, University of Minnesota.

Schank, R., & Abelson, R. (1977). *Scripts, plans, goals, and understanding: An inquiry into human knowledge structures.* Hillsdale, NJ: Lawrence Erlbaum Associates.

Schmidt, M. (1981) Needs assessment in English for specific purposes: The case study. In L. Selinker, E. Tarone, & V. Hanzeli (Eds.), *English for academic and technical purposes: Studies in honor of Louis Trimble* (pp. 199-210). Rowley, MA: Newbury House Publishers.

Selinker, L. (1979). On the use of informants in discourse analysis and "language for specific purposes". *International Review of Applied Linguistics, 17*, 189-215.

Selinker, L., & Douglas, D. (1985). Wrestling with 'context' in interlanguage theory. *Applied Linguistics, 6*, 190-204.

Swales, J. M. (1990). *Genre analysis: English in academic and research settings.* Cambridge, England: Cambridge University Press.

Tarone, E. (2000). Getting serious about language play: Language play, interlanguage variation and second language acquisition. In B. Swierzbin, F. Morris, M. Anderson, C. Klee, & E. Tarone (Eds.), *Social and cognitive factors in SLA: Proceedings of the 1999 Second Language Research Forum* (pp. 31-54). Somerville, MA: Cascadilla Press.

Tarone, E., Gillette, S., Dwyer, S., & Icke, V. (1998). On the use of the passive and active voice in astrophysics journal papers: With extensions to other languages and other fields. *English for Specific Purposes, 17*, 113-132.

Widdowson, H. G. (1998). Communication and community: The pragmatics of ESP. *English for Specific Purposes, 17*, 3-14.

Willing, K. (1992). *Talking it through: Clarification and problem-solving in professional work.* Sydney, Australia: National Centre for English Language Teaching and Research, Macquarie University.

Yule, G. (1996). *Pragmatics.* Oxford, England: Oxford University Press.

APPENDIX

Selected Annotated Bibliography of ESP Studies in Interlanguage Pragmatics

Eades, D. (1994). A case of communicative clash: Aboriginal English and the legal system. In J. Gibbons (Ed.), *Language and the law* (pp. 234-264). London: Longman.

Analyzes Australian Aborigines' use of a range of speech acts in English, and the ways in which their pragmatic practices disadvantage them in Australian courtrooms. In Aboriginal conversations, for example, rather than ask directly for information, the questioner presents a proposition for confirmation or correction. When Aboriginals seek substantial information, such as important personal details or reasons, they do not use questions; rather, the information-seeking process must be indirect and requires that the information-seeker contribute some of their own knowledge on the topic, followed by silence. Other characteristics of Aboriginal pragmatics that affect interaction in the courtroom include use of silence in conversation, preferred ways of responding to either–or questions, and difference in eye-contact patterning.

Flowerdew, J., & Miller, L. (1996). Lectures in a second language: Notes towards a cultural grammar. *English for Specific Purposes, 15*, 121-140.

An ethnographic research study of lectures produced by ten native speakers of English at a university in Hong Kong, and the way in which L1 Cantonese speakers understood those lectures. Data were collected over a period of 3 years, via questionnaires, in-depth interviews with the lecturers and students, participant observation of 11 lectures, reflective diaries kept by lecturers and students, field notes, recordings and transcriptions of three lectures. The study showed that lecturers and students had very different assumptions as to the purpose of lectures: to deliver facts vs. to develop students' judgment and thinking skills. Their views also differed as to the role of lecturers, acceptable lecture style, permissible listener behavior during lectures, and the role of humor in the lecture. Most of the lecturers' attempts to simplify their language were generally viewed by their students as ineffective.

Gibbs, T. (2002). *Misidentification of limited proficiency English speaking employees in hotel call-ins.* Unpublished masters qualifying paper in Linguistics, University of Minnesota.

The researcher describes the conversational structure of the "call-in", a type of phone call made by hotel employees to other hotel staff. The function of the call-in is to perform a Request speech act. Call-ins made by native speaker and non-native speaker hotel staff are taped and described. Native speaker call-ins are shown to have a quite different structure from that of a social phone call: call-ins lack a greeting sequence and a personal identification sequence. This difference is problematic for nonnative speakers, whose training materials compound the problem. Communication breakdown occurs when NNS hotel staff try to make call-ins using the conversational structure of social phone calls and are misidentified as hotel guests. Training in the actual structure of the call-in results in successful performance of the Request speech act by LEP hotel employees.

Gimenez, J. C. (2001). Ethnographic observations in cross-cultural business negotiations between non-native speakers of English: An exploratory study. *English for Specific Purposes, 20*, 169-193.

The researcher analyzes NNS–NNS negotiations in business interactions and finds that sellers make more Commitments and Promises, using high self-disclosure, while Buyers perform more Warning speech acts (e.g., warning that they may go to competitors). Bargaining style can be either monochronic (a linear temporal orientation, with a rational decision criterion) or polychronic (an indirect, circular approach, with an intuitive decision criterion). The researcher analyzes the performance of "Reject" and "Suggest" speech acts; other important moves are "Establishing credentials", "Negotiating prices". Cross-cultural differences in strategy use are analyzed.

Jacobson, W. (1986) An assessment of the communication needs of non-native speakers of English in an undergraduate physics lab. *English for Specific Purposes, 5,* 173-188.

The researcher audiotaped students engaged in pair work in an undergraduate physics lab at the University of Minnesota. The oral interactions of native-speaker pairs are compared to the interactions of nonnative speaker pairs. Much more information was exchanged orally when the partners were both NSs than when one or both were NNSs. The communicative failure of a NNS student attempting to perform a Request for assistance from a TA is analyzed. In comparison to NS Requests, this student's Request was not sufficiently specific. It did not include enough background information about attempts to solve the problem that had already been tried. The NNS responded to TA inquiries with only affirmative or negative signals. As a result, the TA was unable to assist him in a timely fashion, spending more than 20 minutes with him during the lab period.

Kuehn, K. and Tarone, E. (2000). Negotiating the social services oral intake interview, *TESOL Quarterly, 34*, 99-126.

The study describes the script followed in the oral intake interview of a social services office, showing how it is related to the printed application form the applicant had filled out. A NNS applicant is shown to have a different script from the interviewers, to provide minimal back channel cues, and to misunderstand such speech acts as Confirmation Requests and Directives made by the interviewers.

Maier, P. (1992). Politeness strategies in business letters by native and non-native English speakers. *English for Specific Purposes, 11,* 189-206.

The researcher asked native and nonnative English speakers to write business letters in response to a role-play situation. In this situation, the writers have missed a job interview due to transportation problems, and have to write a letter requesting a new appointment for an interview. Native and non-native writers are shown to use quite different politeness strategies: the NNSs tended to use more positive politeness strategies, stressing their strong desire to secure the position and their optimism that they would be able to obtain a second interview, while the NSs tended to use negative politeness strategies, apologizing profusely for the imposition of having missed the first appointment, and stressing the interviewer's freedom to deny them a second interview.

Myers, G. (1989). The pragmatics of politeness in scientific articles. *Applied Linguistics, 10*, 1-35.

Myers shows how the Brown and Levinson (1978) model of politeness (previously applied only to oral discourse) can elegantly account for a wide range of seemingly unrelated phenomena in the written genre of research articles—phenomena such as hedging in making claims, affectation of modesty in referring to one's contributions, patterns of citation (or not) of others' work, and the use of humor in naming phenomena. Myers suggests that we view the research article as a delicate balancing act between the opposing pragmatic forces of performing the face-threatening act of making a claim, while mitigating that act. To mitigate, the writer uses positive and negative politeness strategies to preserve the faces of colleagues in the discourse community who may be threatened by that claim. Negative strategies include use of hedging devices such as modals in making claims. Positive strategies include expressions of dismay at the limitations of positions threatened by the claim, and the use of language play in the form of humor and puns.

Nishiyama, T. (1990). *A Study of class discussion and participation skills.* Unpublished masters. plan B paper, University of Minnesota.

The researcher audiotaped one hour of a class session of a graduate course, MBA 8045 (Marketing Management) that used the case study approach. This technique is based on class discussion and group decision-making. The researcher also analyzed questionnaires returned by 21 of the 42 students in the class, of whom 5 were nonnative speakers of English. Unlike the NSs, the NNSs indicated class discussions were the most problematic aspect of the course. The researcher identifies 3 types of interaction in the class, and analyzes the differing roles of the teacher in those interactions. She concludes that NNSs need to understand the way the teacher uses a range of conversational moves to signal to the students what is and is not relevant to the discussion.

Parks, S., & Maguire, M. (1999). Coping with on-the-job writing in ESL: A constructivist-semiotic perspective. *Language Learning, 49*, 143-175.

This longitudinal case study of a francophone nursing student learning to produce nursing notes in English focuses on how a novice acquires a new genre on the job through supportive mentoring of experts in the discourse community. Three consecutive drafts of the student's notes on a case are shown, together with the revisions that were suggested at each stage by more experienced nurses. The study shows how experts' suggestions are incorporated in each subsequent learner draft.

Ranney, S. (1992). Learning a new script: An exploration of sociolinguistic competence. *Applied Linguistics, 13*, 25-50.

This study compares scripts for the medical interview of 9 NSs of English and 9 NSs of Hmong and learners of English L2 (all college level). Nonnative speakers had systematically different scripts for what they expected to take place and what they expected to be said in a doctor-patient office interview. For example, Americans expected to be given a diagnosis at the end of the interview, while the Hmong expected to be given medication at the conclusion. NSs were more indirect than the NNSs in making requests.

Schmidt, M. (1981) Needs assessment in English for specific purposes: The case study. In L. Selinker, E. Tarone, & V. Hanzeli (Eds.), *English for academic and technical purposes: Studies in honor of Louis Trimble* (pp. 199-210). Rowley, MA: Newbury House Publishers.

The lecture comprehension and note-taking strategies of an Asian business student are analyzed in a college-level business class. The student's strategy of taking notes in Chinese is shown to backfire when she has to take an essay exam in English, because she doesn't have a record of the English language discourse needed to display what she knows on the exam in English. Though she accurately copies down a table written on the board, she is unable to explain the relationships it represents in English (a problem of information transfer, translating information from a visual form to words, or vice versa).

Willing, K. (1992). *Talking it through: Clarification and problem-solving in professional work.* Sydney, Australia: National Centre for English Language Teaching and Research, Macquarie University.

The researcher integrates frameworks of speech act analysis, conversation analysis, script analysis to analyze the interactive signaling used by native and nonnative speakers of English as they work together on problems and tasks onsite in white collar professional, multicultural workplaces. Participants are equipped with pocket tape recorders, which they switch on when engaged in conversational problem solving with their coworkers in dyads and small groups. The researcher describes clarification strategies deployed in dealing with cross-cultural and pragmatic communication difficulties.

7

Using Moves in the Opening Sequence to Identify Callers in Institutional Settings

Tara Leigh Gibbs
University of Minnesota

Students often come to teachers with questions about what to say in a particular situation. It is tempting to answer these questions with a spontaneously created dialogue and some appropriate vocabulary or syntax. Rarely, however, does the answer describe the various pragmatic moves the addressee is expecting or how the addressee will interpret deviations in the moves. Yet research suggests that the greatest source of difficulty in communication may not come from syntax and phonology, but rather from a failure to meet the pragmatic expectations of the discourse community.

This chapter examines the pragmatic structure of a particular type of institutional phone call, known as a *call-in*, performed daily by staff at a large conference hotel. After describing the setting for this research, this chapter reviews the structure of the opening of social telephone conversations identified by Schegloff (1986). Then, it describes differences between social and institutional phone conversations discovered by Hopper, Doany, Johnson, and Drummond (1990) and Wakin and Zimmerman (1999). Next, it describes the methodology employed in this study and analyzes the structure of a call-in by an expert member of the hotel's discourse community and the structure of call-ins by unsuccessful novice speakers. Finally, it compares these with the previous research described at the beginning of the chapter.

The Research Setting

Call-ins are phone calls in which employees, especially housekeepers, request services from another department, services such as the pick-up from a guest room of a tray, roll-away bed, or refrigerator, or the repair of something by maintenance. At least three largely unsuccessful attempts were made by the hotel to train its Limited Proficiency English Speaking (LPES) employees to perform call-ins prior to the ESL course from which this research material derives. The three attempts included two ESL programs prior to 1999 and a video created by the hotel and shown during new employee orientations.

In 1998, an ESL program which included a job shadowing component was initiated. In *job shadowing* the ESL teacher follows workplace ESL students one-on-one while they are working in order to encourage the students to use the English they are practicing in the classroom and to learn what types of language they are struggling with on the job. Job shadowing often included videotaping, audiotaping, or photographing in order to produce authentic material for the students to practice with in the classroom. The telephone conversations analyzed in this chapter were collected by me, the ESL teacher, during job shadowing and were used by the students in their class in order to become more aware of errors which led to unsuccessful call-ins and the nuances of the task they were trying to perform.

The results, presented below, were bewildering at first, especially when viewed in light of the familiar social phone call, and suggested a great deal of insensitivity on the part of the Convention Services employees with whom they interacted; however, this did not jive with what I knew of the Convention Services employees. The root of the problem became more apparent when a Convention Services employee was interviewed immediately after an unsuccessful call-in was recorded and said, "But, no one from Housekeeping has called all morning." He had misidentified the caller as a guest rather than as an employee.

Various learning challenges, such as, "Why aren't LPES employees successful when making call-ins?" and "How can we help the LPES employees to make call-ins?" did not seem answerable simply by watching what the workplace ESL students did while working. As a result, the concept of job shadowing came to be expanded in this program to also include shadowing expert speakers (native or nonnative speaking supervisors and coworkers who were successful in their communicative tasks) to find out how they performed their jobs.

Shadowing expert speakers at their jobs, in addition to shadowing the novice speakers, allowed differences in the pragmatic expectations of the expert speakers and the novice speakers to become apparent. This in turn allowed the 1998 ESL program to educate workplace students on the correct call-in structure, rather than on creative, but incorrect, structures which resulted in unsuccessful call-ins.

BACKGROUND AND LITERATURE REVIEW

Social Telephone Calls

Schegloff (1968, 1979) studied 450 telephone calls in a variety of settings, including personal phone calls and phone calls to businesses. Excluding all phone calls that did not begin with a "hello–hello" sequence (e.g., "American Airlines, how can I help you?"), Schegloff (1986) identified a series of *adjacency pairs* (p. 117) that almost invariably occur at the beginning of social telephone calls and that always impute a special meaning, for example, irritation, when they do not occur.[1] This sequence, known as the *opening*

---

[1] Adjacency pairs are sequences in which the first part obliges the second part, for example, a question and an answer, a greeting and a response, a display for identification and a display that

sequence, is composed of a summons–answer sequence followed by an identification sequence followed by a greeting–return greeting sequence, followed by a how-are-you sequence. Only after this opening sequence does the caller typically introduce the topic. Example (1) illustrates a minimal opening without a how-are-you sequence (Levinson, 1983, p. 312).[2]

(1)   Canonical opening sequence

```
        C: ((rings))    ((SUMMONS))
   T1   R: Hello.       ((ANSWER))
                        ((DISPLAY FOR RECOGNITION))
   T2   C: Hi.          ((GREETINGS 1ST PART))
                        ((CLAIM THAT C HAS RECOGNIZED R))
                        ((CLAIM THAT R CAN RECOGNIZE C))
   T3   R: Oh, hi::     ((GREETINGS 2ND PART))
                        ((CLAIM THAT R HAS RECOGNIZED C))
```

Schegloff (1968), Sacks, Schegloff, and Jefferson (1974), Levinson (1983), Psathas (1995), Markee (2000) and others state that all conversation is governed locally via two-part action sequences called adjacency pairs. The first utterance in the pair is called a *first,* and the second utterance in the pair is called a *second.* In the foregoing example, turn zero, the summons, is considered a first. The responsive action, the answer, in T1, is considered the second.[3] Most actions, such as the introduction of topic, have preferred seconds (acceptance of the topic) and dispreferred seconds (rejection of the topic). A *preferred second* is the most common or expected utterance in the given situation. A *dispreferred second* is an uncommon or undesired utterance in the given situation. According to Sacks et al. (1974), a first always demands a second. Failure to provide one carries special meaning and implications, while providing a dispreferred second may require additional rhetorical support.

Seconds often double as firsts for the next adjacency pair. In Example (2) I indicate the adjacency pairs for T1 of Example (1). T1, in bold, shows this doubling of duties, known as *interlocking organization* (Schegloff, 1986).

(2)   Interlocking organization

```
        C: ((rings))    1st        ((SUMMONS))
                        |
   T1   R: Hello.       2nd        ((ANSWER))
```

---

identification has or has not occurred, an introduction of topic and an uptake/acceptance/rejection of that topic, or a move to close a conversation and an agreement/rejection of that move. They are canonically adjacent, hence the name, *adjacency pair.*

[2] Later descriptions of the Opening Sequence tend to omit the "How are you" sequence. It may be that the "How are you" sequence is actually a presequence opening up the topic. As a result, this portion of the canonical sequence is abridged in its description here, inasmuch as the relevant point of the analysis is that the topic opens AFTER the identification and greeting sequences are completed and that this is true regardless of the interpretation of the "How are you" sequence.

[3] See Schegloff (1986) for an explanation of why this is an answer, not a greeting.

```
                     1st              ((DISPLAY FOR RECOGNITION))
                      |
T2   C:  Hi.         2nd              ((CLAIM THAT C HAS RECOGNIZED R))
```

Sometimes, a single utterance can initiate two firsts. In Example (3) I again indicate the adjacency pairs found in Example (1) and highlight T2 which, in addition to illustrating interlocking organization, also initiates two firsts. In response, T3 replies with two seconds.

```
(3)   Packing two firsts into a single utterance
            C: ((rings))   1st              ((SUMMONS))
                            |
      T1   R:  Hello.       2nd              ((ANSWER))


                            1st              ((DISPLAY FOR RECOGNITION))
                            |
      T2   C:  Hi.          2nd              ((CLAIM THAT C HAS RECOGNIZED R))


                            1st (a)          ((CLAIM THAT R CAN RECOGNIZE C))
                            |   1st (b)       ((GREETINGS 1ST PART))
                            |   |
      T3   R:  Oh, hi::     |   2nd (b)       ((GREETINGS 2ND PART))
                            2nd (a)           ((CLAIM THAT R HAS RECOGNIZED C))
```

The compression of two firsts into a single utterance or two seconds into a single utterance, rather than taking two turns or using two sentences to get the ideas across, will be referred to as *packing* since I am unaware of a common term to describe this phenomena. A more precise definition of *packing* would be: the occurrence of two firsts or of two seconds in one turn constructional unit. According to Levinson (1983), turn constructional units are blocks of speech that are used to build turns in speech. The end of a turn constructional unit constitutes a transition relevance place because the next turn can transition to another speaker just at this point in time. A turn constructional unit may be composed of sentences, clauses, noun phrases, or even single words. A turn may actually be composed of several turn constructional units if the speaker refuses to yield the floor at a transition relevance place, or if the current speaker is also allocated the next turn constructional unit.

Packing the greeting and claim for recognition together seems fairly common in the telephone calls Schegloff studied. Schegloff (1968) explained this by noting that callers know whom they hope to reach, though not necessarily who is answering the phone, and the receiver does not have knowledge, initially, as to who the caller is (remembering that Schegloff's work was done prior to caller I.D., of course). Thus, there is and must always be an identification sequence at the beginning of a phone call, even if it is not overtly realized. An example of an overt realization would be someone saying, "Hi, this is Mary. Is this Bert?" whereby the turn has three turn constructional units and three actions—greeting, claim the caller can be recognized, and claim the caller has recognized the receiver—as compared to T2 of Example (3) which has one turn constructional unit and all three of these same actions.

Institutional Telephone Calls

There is evidence that the canonical opening sequence identified by Schegloff may be altered in institutional settings. This section describes research by Hopper et al. (1990) which examines a phone call to a doctor's office by a patient, and research done by Wakin and Zimmerman (1999), Whalen and Zimmerman (1987, 1990), and Zimmerman (1992), which investigates phone calls from citizens to emergency dispatchers and to telephone directory information operators (henceforth referred to by their respective 3-digit phone numbers in the United States—*911 calls* and *411 calls*). In each of these phone calls the interactions are between outsiders to a particular discourse community (patient or citizen) and members of the particular discourse community (receptionist or dispatcher/operator).

Hopper et al. (1990) observed that data on telephone openings in doctors' offices include more examples that deviate from the canonical opening sequence than examples that conform to it. In light of openings such as that in Example (4), Hopper et al. (1990, p. 372) suggest that "strangers or previously unacquainted parties often display *reduced* formats compared to openings between acquaintances."[4] In Example (4), I have added the turn information and action sequences and changed the names to simply C for caller and R for receiver. The opening sequence in Example (4) displays a summons–answer sequence, part of an identification sequence, and an introduction of topic. It does not display a greeting sequence, nor does it display a how-are-you sequence. However, T2 does show an overt answer ("yes") to the move in T1, which I interpret as a claim that the caller has identified the receiver, or at least the fact that she is a receptionist at the clinic he is trying to reach. This is followed by an overt identification of self by the caller, and, after a pause, an introduction of topic. The sequence includes a number of pauses and disfluencies, which might be indications of attempts to allocate turns or to give dispreferred seconds, such as "I don't recognize you." Hopper and colleagues do not analyze this in detail, and so my suggestions regarding these disfluencies are followed by question marks.

---

[4] Hopper et al. state that in conversations between strangers there are fewer presequences, sequences that set up a move such as the introduction of topic or the closing of a conversation. (For more information on closing sequences see Schegloff et al. (1973). However, in Example 4 it appears to me that the "U::m" in T2 might be interpreted as a presequence setting up the introduction of topic, albeit with substantially reduced overt content. Likewise, the pause of four-tenths of a second could be a failure by the receiver to reject the move to introduce a topic and thus allocation of the next turn constructional unit to the caller, who then proceeds to introduce the topic.

(4)   Opening sequence of a call to a doctor's office

T0:	C:	((Ringing))	((SUMMONS))
T1:	R:	Central Allergy Associates	((ANSWER))
		this is Bonnie?	((DISPLAY FOR RECOGNITION))
		(0.9)	((Turn allocation? Claim by C not to recognize the name Bonnie?))
T2:	C:	Ye:s	((CLAIM OF RECOGNITION OF R))
		This is Rick Harrell	((DISPLAY FOR RECOGNITION))
		(0.4)	((Turn allocation? Claim by R not to recognize C?))
		U::m	((Request to initiate topic?))
		(0.4)	((Permission to initiate topic?))
		couple a days ago I saw	((INTRODUCTION OF TOPIC))
		Doctor: uh (0.4) Hart on a	
		uh (1.0) I was having coughing	

Similar findings for institutional phone calls to 411 (directory assistance) and 911 (emergency dispatchers) are reported by Whalen and Zimmerman (1987). Whalen and Zimmerman attribute such altered opening sequences to the idea that relational constraints are often not separable from the communicators' goals. Wakin and Zimmerman (1999), Whalen and Zimmerman (1990), and Zimmerman (1992), document monofocal phone calls to 411 and 911 in which citizens are calling professionals at these phone numbers. They report the omission of three sequences from the opening sequence: the identification sequence, the greeting sequence, and the how-are-you sequence.[5] They find that the goals of these calls override the need for these sequences, and that the preemption of these sequences demonstrates the orientation of the parties to the common goal: getting a phone number and reporting an emergency.

In Example (5), Wakin and Zimmerman (1999, p. 416) have used D for Dispatcher instead of R for receiver and they have numbered the dialogue by turn constructional unit rather than by turn. I have added the actions in italics for which they did not offer an analysis.

(5)   Opening Sequence of a 911 Call

00		((Ring))	((SUMMONS))
01	D:	Mid-City emergency::,	((ANSWER))
			((IDENTIFICATION))
02		(0.1)	*((??))*
03	C:	U::m yeah.	*((CLAIM OF RECOGNITION?))*
04		Somebody just vandalized my car.	((INITIATION OF BUSINESS))

---

[5]   In the 911 calls identification does occur as part of the subsequent talk, albeit not usually during the opening. Additionally, when callers do identify themselves during the opening sequence, the dispatcher doesn't seem to orient towards this at all at this point in time and later re-requests identification.

Zimmerman and Wakin express concern that the monofocal nature of these phone calls may make the structures ungeneralizable to other institutional phone calls. When comparing the phone call to the doctor's office with the phone call to 911, we can observe differences in the identification sequence and in the moves to introduce the topic of discussion. However, there are also similarities. Both phone calls omit the greeting sequence and the how-are-you sequence, and in both cases, mutual, personal identification has not occurred by the time the topic is introduced. A fourth, potential commonality is the disfluency preceding the introduction of topic. Thus, there may be some characteristics that can be generalizable to other institutional phone calls.

The calls to the doctor's office, to 411, and to 911 are all calls made by people who are not members of the institution's discourse community to people who are members of the institution's discourse community. The data in this chapter, however, are from members of an institutional discourse community calling other members of the same discourse community. Fairchild (1995), who studied politeness in institutional phone calls, suggested that it may be possible to identify callers as clients or employees even without their identifying themselves overtly as such. Thus, in addition to asking whether institutional calls are different from social calls, we should also ask if members of the institutional discourse communities talk with each other the same way they talk with outsiders to the discourse community.

Genre and Discourse Communities in Institutions

Swales (1990) defined genre as a property of a discourse community. A discourse community is a group of individuals who share a set of common public goals, use mechanisms of intercommunication to provide information, use one or more genres to pursue their goals, use some special lexis, and include members with content and discourse expertise (pp. 24-27). Swales offers the following five criteria for a genre:

1. A genre comprises a class of communicative events used by a discourse community to further its common goals.
2. The class of events share a single communicative purpose
3. The events vary in their prototypicality, but their structure is highly predictable
4. The speech event occurs frequently within the discourse community.
5. The speech event is clearly recognized by experts in the discourse community.

The goal of genre analysis seems to be the explication of the forms used in a particular situation with a particular meaning.

The call-in appears to meet Swales' (1990) criteria for a genre. Specifically, there is a discourse community with expert members who recognize the call-in as a speech event that occurs frequently and who have sought to train others to conduct this speech event. The call-in is part of a class of communicative events with a single goal: requesting another department to do something. Finally, the call-in varies in its prototypicality—not every call will be word-for-word the same, and some calls will flout the rules to various ends—but its structure is highly predictable as this chapter will show, and expert members of the discourse community expect and utilize this structure as members of the discourse community in order to display themselves as employees and recognize each other as employees.

The genre analysis framework assumes the existence of expert members of the discourse community who know, understand, and use the discourse rules of the community, and novice members of the discourse community who may not yet know, understand, or use the discourse rules of the community (Swales, 1990; Tarone, chapter 6, this volume). Examples of novices are university students learning how to write academic research papers (Swales, 1990), and, as this chapter shows, housekeepers learning to make call-ins.

RESEARCH QUESTIONS

Given our goal of understanding why the novice speakers are unsuccessful in making call-ins, we would like to see if there are any differences between the structures of successful and unsuccessful call-ins which might account for this and if, provided an accurate model, novice speakers are able to perform a successful call-in.

METHOD

As the ESL teacher for the course which was training students to perform call-ins, I quickly became aware that the students avoided call-ins because they were "difficult," despite their success in calling each other room-to-room during classroom role plays of call-ins. Since one of the principles of the curriculum development was to bring as much of the job into the classroom as possible and as much of the classroom into the job as possible, permission to record the students making call-ins was quickly received during informal meetings with the hotel administration. Arrangements were made during a weekly chat with the head of housekeeping and during a daily exchange of greetings with the head of human resources by the photocopier. I had hoped that listening to their own calls would help novice housekeepers build confidence, identify problem areas, and bridge the gap between role play and reality. An expert speaker was also recorded to provide an instructional model for the students.

Data Collection

The data analyzed in this chapter were gathered as part of the needs analysis and curriculum development materials for an ESL class. Three types of data were utilized in this study: transcripts of call-ins, interviews with employees, and an informal listening survey of expert English-speaking employees.

Both expert English-speaking and limited-proficiency English-speaking housekeepers were recorded during job shadowing. Job shadowing was scheduled after every class for approximately 1 hour. Call-ins were recorded with a Marantz PMD222 tape recorder that was plugged into the telephone in the rooms being cleaned or with a Radio Shack suction-cup Telephone Pick-up plugged into a Sony TCM-353V cassette-recorder. The expert English-speaking supervisor was recorded when I followed her on her rounds. She received no specific instructions regarding the call.

The limited-proficiency English-speaking housekeepers were recorded twice. A year prior to the first recording, a handful of the students had been in a different ESL classes and had practiced making call-ins. In addition, most of the students had seen a video of a call-in during the new employee orientation. In my class, prior to the first recording, the students had role-played making a call-in with each other. The role plays were spontaneous and unscripted. At the time of the first recording, learners had not been given an authentic call-in dialogue to use while making call-ins, and thus, they were spontaneous and unrehearsed.

Approximately 2 weeks later the novices were recorded a second time. Before the second recording, they received instruction on making a call-in. The instruction consisted of providing the learners with a transcript of the expert supervisor's call-in with blanks for the room number and item to be picked up. The students practiced calling a supervisor in another guest room using this new dialogue worksheet. During job shadowing students were encouraged to attempt making a real call-in to Convention Services and these calls were again recorded just as the first calls had been recorded.

On some occasions, expert English-speaking employees who were involved in the recorded conversations were also interviewed in order to determine whom they believed they had been talking to. In particular, this happened in person after the primary subject's first recording, and it happened several other times over the phone when I called Convention Services after a student had hung up and asked them if they thought they had been talking to an employee or a guest. However, after a few calls they began to realize why I was calling, which made their responses less spontaneous.

In the last stage of data collection, the recording of the supervisor was played for 16 expert English-speaking employees. The employees were approached individually and in small groups during lunchtime and asked informally to listen to a conversation on tape and to identify the participants in the conversation as employees of the hotel or guests of the hotel. Recordings of the limited-proficiency English-speaking novices were not played for expert English-speaking employees in order to avoid embarrassment, since the employees may have recognized each other's voices.

Participants

The primary novice participant is a 50+ year-old male Vietnamese Limited Proficiency English Speaking (LPES) housekeeper who had worked at the hotel for more than 1 year and who attended a mandatory worksite ESL course 1.5 hours a day, 2 days a week. He also participated in job shadowing with the ESL instructor after each class. He was chosen as the primary subject for the analysis because his data was the most complete data in the curriculum archive (see the following section on data collection), including a worksheet with his conversation and a worksheet recording his pause lengths for an exercise on holding the floor in a conversation. Finally, it was after taping his call-in that I talked with the employee in Convention Services who claimed not to have spoken with any housekeepers "all morning." Thus, there was additional triangulation of the data regarding this conversation.

As the course progressed, I began following one of the supervisors around during job shadowing in order to observe her interactions with the students. Her calls were extremely striking in their speed, abruptness, and consistency, so I asked her if I could record one of her calls to use as a dialogue model. The primary expert subject is a 50+ year-old female expert English-speaking housekeeping supervisor who had worked at the hotel for over 20 years and who was training a new native English-speaking housekeeper at the time of the recording. Each time she came to a Limited English Proficiency Employee and they reported call-ins which needed to be made, she performed a call-in.

The secondary subjects were 16 expert English-speaking supervisors and expert English-speaking employees in Housekeeping, Human Resources, Room Service and Convention Services, and 18 LPES housekeepers participating in the ESL course and job shadowing. The LPES housekeepers had various language backgrounds, including Spanish, Amharic, Oromo, Somali, and Vietnamese. Their ages ranged from 19 to 62.

RESULTS AND DISCUSSION

This section presents six transcripts of call-ins to Convention Services. The first transcript is of a successful call-in by the expert speaker. This is followed by three transcripts of unsuccessful call-ins by novice speakers, and two successful call-ins by novice speakers. The section ends with two successful call-ins by the first and third unsuccessful novice speakers after they have been trained on the dialogue of the expert speaker.

Expert Speaker Call-in

Example (6) shows an expert speaker's call-in.

(6) Expert Speaker: Successful call-in

T0:	C:	Rings	((Summons))
T1:	R:	Hello,	((Answer))
			((Display for recognition))
T2:	C:	Pick up in room	((Claim C has recognized R))
		936, refrigerator.	((Claim R can recognize C))
			((Intro. of topic—Request))

T3:	R:	936.	((Granting of Request—Uptake of Topic))
			((Claim R has recognized C))
			((Question))
T4:	C:	Yep. (Hangs up)	((Answer))
			((Closure))
T5:	((presumably R hangs up, too))		((Closure))

(Transcript of Z., recorded in May, 1998)

In T0 and T1 (Turn 1) of the expert speaker's transcript, we see a first, the summons in T0, with an answer as its second in T1. T1 also serves as a first, a display for recognition. T2 provides a second, a claim the caller has recognized the receiver, and it provides a first, an introduction of topic as a request. Based on Schegloff's argument that there must be identification occurring for both the receiver and the caller, and his action-sequencing for telephone calls, an identification sequence must have occurred prior to the introduction of topic. Because T2 is the first time that the caller speaks, the claim the receiver can recognize the caller cannot occur earlier than T2. As the topic is clearly introduced in T2, this leaves only one conclusion—that T2 provides two firsts. Thus, in addition to introducing the topic—a request—T2 also makes a claim that the receiver can identify the caller.

T3 offers a second to both of these firsts. By confirming the room number, the receiver is taking up the topic and granting the request. Additionally, based on our acceptance of the theory that a first requires a second, we must assume that the receiver is implicitly confirming his identification of the caller as a housekeeper. Notice that this analysis has the introduction of topic occurring before the identification sequence is completed. In a subsequent interview, the man who answered the phone in Convention Services after the phone call indicated that "a housekeeper had called." An interview with the housekeeper after the conversation indicated that one of the "young guys" had answered the phone in Convention Services. Thus, the call had successfully enabled mutual identification, in terms of the institutional role of the caller and receiver, to take place.

The identification process was also verified when this phone call and three other models were played for 16 native English speaking employees in the lunch room from various departments, including Convention Services, Housekeeping, Maintenance, and Security. They were asked to determine whether the caller was a guest or an employee. All identified the caller as a hotel employee. Several added that the caller was probably a housekeeper. Note that identification occurs, not in terms of individual identity, but in terms of the role of the caller and receiver.

Structure of a Call-in by a Novice Speaker

Analyzing the novice speaker's transcript in terms of Schegloff's categories yields the sequences seen in Example (7). Note that in the sections in which repairs occur, the caller's interpretations of the actions are indicated in bold, while the receiver's interpretations of the actions are indicated in italics.

(7) First novice speaker: Unsuccessful call-in

T0:	C:	*Rings*	1st ((Summons))
T1:	R:	Hello.	2nd ((Answer))
		Convention Services.	1st ((Claim that C can recognize R))
T2:	C:	This is J. I'm-	2nd ((Claim that C has recognized R))
		(.8)	
		[housekeeping.]	1st ((Claim that R can recognize C))
T3:	R:	[How can-]	2nd ((Claim that R has recognized C))
		How can I help you?	1st ((Offer/Request for intro. of topic))
T4:	C:	I am housekeeping.	**1st ((Repair of T3: Claim that R has recognized C: assertion: Claim that R can recognize C))**
			2nd ((Introduction of topic: Answer))
			1st ((Request for housekeeping))
T5:	R:	To call housekeeping you need to dial 52.	*2nd ((Uptake of request: Answer))*
			1st ((Directive))
			2nd ((Rejection of repair: directive to call himself))
T6:	C:	Housekeeping. Pick up.	**1st ((Repair of T3: Claim that R has recognized C: assertion: Claim that R can recognize C))**
			1st ((Introduction of topic: request for pick-up))
			2nd ((Rejection of directive to call housekeeping))
			1st ((Request for housekeeping))
			2nd ((Uptake of request: Answer))
T7:	R:	Please dial 52.	*1st ((Directive))*
			2nd ((Rejection of repair))
			2nd ((Rejection of topic))
T8:	C:	Pick up. Room 1717.	**1st ((Repair of introduction of topic: request for pick-up))**
			2nd ((Rejection of directive))
			1st ((Request for housekeeping))
T9:	R:	I will call housekeeping to come help you.	*2nd ((Answer))*
			1st ((Decision to circumvent pre-closure))
		Good-bye.	*1st ((Closure))*

T10: C: Pickup. Is- (.8)   1ˢᵗ ((Repair))

           I-(.8)   ((??))

           There-(1 sec)?   ((??))

(Transcript of J. recorded in April, 1998)

In Example (7), T0 is a first, a summons to the phone. T1 is a second, an answer to the summons. It is also a first, a claim that the receiver can recognize the caller, also called a display for recognition. T2 is a second, a claim the caller has recognized the receiver. T2 is also a first, a claim the receiver can identify the caller, also called a display for recognition. This display is overt. The caller also begins a second sentence, apparently an attempt at further clarification of his display for recognition, however, he is unable to come up with the term *housekeeper* and after a long hesitation offers the word "housekeeping" instead.

In T3 we see that since the caller has displayed himself for recognition in T2, the expectation is that the receiver will either make a claim that he has recognized the caller and move on to the next action sequence, or he will make a claim that he hasn't recognized the caller in T3 and request additional information. In T3, the receiver overlaps the speech of the caller and then repairs this overlap by starting his sentence over. His claim that he has recognized the caller is not overt, but is implied since he moves the conversation forward by requesting the caller to introduce the topic of conversation. Please note that regardless of the actual accuracy of the identification, T3 is still making a claim that the receiver has recognized the caller.

In T4 the caller says, "I am housekeeping," a repair of his attempt to identify himself as a housekeeper during his uncompleted turn in T2, which he lost when he hesitated. However, based on the receiver's response in T5, the receiver appears to interpret this as an answer to his T3 request for an introduction of topic, in other words, the receiver sees this as a second, an introduction of topic: an answer to his request, and also as a first, a request for housekeeping.

In T5 the receiver, who has understood T4 as a request, offers a dispreferred second—an answer regarding how to reach Housekeeping, rather than a granting of the request which would be the preferred second. From the receiver's perspective, T5 is also a first, a directive to call housekeeping.

From the caller's perspective, a different set of actions has occurred. The caller views this as an answer to the repair, an answer that indicates the repair was unsuccessful. This is evidenced by the fact that in the caller's next turn he again attempts another repair, indicating that he realizes his first repair was unsuccessful.

In T6 the caller again attempts a repair at identification, and then proceeds to the next action sequence—the introduction of topic, a request for a pick up. The receiver, however, again fails to interpret this as a repair of the identification sequence or as an introduction of topic: a request for a pick-up. Instead, he seems to see it as a rejection of the dispreferred second, the directive, and as a renewed request to speak to Housekeeping.

In T7 the receiver responds to the request in T7 with a reiteration of his answer, a directive to dial 52. The caller realizes that the repair has again been unsuccessful and that the receiver has not taken up the topic he has introduced.

In T8 the caller again attempts a repair, reintroducing the topic. The receiver, however, sees this again as a rejection of his directive and a request for housekeeping in room 1717.

In T9 instead of offering a second, the taking up of the caller's topic which would have required the receiver to determine anew the caller's topic, the receiver seems to offer a second to his own first from T8, responding to his own directive. Another possibility is that the receiver is offering what he perceives to be a more preferred second to the caller's apparent request for housekeeping, a promise to call housekeeping for the caller. The conversation ends abruptly without a preclosing sequence[6] when the receiver nominates himself for a second turn constructional unit in T9 and says "Good-bye" without consultation with the caller.[7]

In T10 the caller again attempts a repair, until he realizes there is no one on the other end of the phone.

In a subsequent interview the employee in Convention Services said "there hasn't been a call from Housekeeping all morning." He believed he was talking to a guest in the transcript above. The novice speaker was too embarrassed to allow the tape to be played for other employees, so no data was collected about this transcript in the lunchroom.

In Example (8) we again see the novice speaker trying to identify herself in T2. She uses the departmental name, rather than the person form "housekeeper"—an extremely common mistake among LPES housekeepers who were frequently referred to with this form in phrases like "go tell housekeeping" or "get housekeeping." The "No" response in T3 suggests that the receiver has

---

[6] See Schegloff and Sacks (1973) for more information about closings and presequences.

[7] A reviewer suggests that the use of "Good-bye" by the receiver also provides internal evidence that the receiver believes he is speaking with a guest, since in the example with the expert English speaker supervisor there is no overt closing sequence at all and this is true. However, I am not confident about the role of various types of closings. In Example (10), which is successful, there is also a closing sequence after a negotiation of meaning. It seems possible that longer conversation duration or negotiation of meaning may also trigger the use of a closing. The same reviewer also points out that, contradictorily, if the receiver believes he is talking to a guest he cannot, no matter how tortured the call has become, hang up on a guest. I suspect that if we look at interactions between native and nonnative speakers, we will find that such politeness gestures are frequently violated, either by sales clerks who change their attention from nonnative speakers to native speakers, leaving the nonnative speaker unattended, to people who hang up when an impasse is reached. One particular testament to this as a strategy for ending difficult meaning negotiations was illustrated a couple of years ago on Jay Leno when he telephoned random numbers to survey people. After reaching one nonnative speaker whom he was completely unable to communicate with, he abruptly hung up. This action didn't seem to strike the audience as odd, though he didn't hang up on anyone else. To me this suggests that hanging up may be seen as an acceptable strategy for ending a difficult meaning negotiation. Certainly, this is something to investigate more carefully.

interpreted this as a ((Claim not to have recognized the receiver)) rather than as a ((Claim that the receiver can recognize the caller)). Thus, we see an identification attempt in T2. We also notice that the caller never gets to introduce her topic of conversation before the call ends in T8.

(8) Second novice speaker: Unsuccessful call-in

        T0: C: (Ring)
        T1: R: Hello. Convention Services. How can I help you?
        T2: C: This is housekeeping
        T3: R: No. This is Convention Services. Shall I transfer you.
        T4: C: (.)
        T5: R: Let me transfer you?
        T6: C: (mumbled) housekeeping.
        T7: R: Uh. Let me transfer you.
        T8:   (Ring, Ring)
        T9: C: (Hang up)

(Transcript of T. recorded in April, 1998)

In T2 of Example (9), the novice speaker tries to identify herself. In T4 she tries to introduce the topic, and is hindered by her inability to keep the floor. In T5 the receiver demonstrates an understanding of the request which is different from the intended request. In T6 the LPES housekeeper is unable to change what has been understood.

(9) Third novice speaker: Unsuccessful call-in

        T0: C: (Ring)
        T1: R: Convention Services. How can I help you?
        T2: C: This is L.
                (.)
                Room 717
                (.)
        T3: R: How can I help you?
        T4: C: need
                (.)
                refrigerator
                (.)
                [pick uh-]
        T5: R: [You—] You need a refrigerator?
        T6: C: No. pee cup.
        T7: R: Ahhh, what?
        T8: C: Ping up'.
                (.)
                refrigerator. Ping up'.
        T9: R: Hhhh. Can you say that again please?

```
T10:  C:  Ping cup.
          (.)
          717.
          (Tries to hand phone to the teacher who refuses it.)
T11:  R:  Uhh. 717.
T12:  C:  Wait, please.
          (Tries to hand phone to the teacher again who refuses it.)
          Thank you. Good-bye.
          (Hangs up)
T13:  R:  ((Ring)) ((Ring)) ((Ring))
T14:  T:  (Teacher answers the phone after a short negotiation with the student and
          clarifies the request.)
```

(Transcript of L. recorded in April, 1998)

In T2 of Example (10), this novice speaker identifies herself as housekeeping. It is nearly idiomatic usage of this term to refer to herself, except her intonation which may have been a little bit off. The receiver begins to respond, although there is no way to know what he was going to say. She maintains the floor, however, and introduces her topic before ending her turn.

(10) Fourth novice speaker: Successful call-in

```
T0:   C:  (Ring)
T1:   R:  Convention Services. How can I help you?
T2:   C:  Housekeeping. Pl[ease] pick-up roll-away.
Tx:   R:                    [Thi-]
T3:   R:  Pick up roll-away?
T4:   C:  Yes.
T5:   R:  Which room?
T6:   C:  906.
T7:   R:  906?
T8:   C:  Ok.
T9:   R:  Ok. Bye. (Hangs up)
T10:  C:  B--ai.
```

(Transcript of N. recorded in April, 1998)

In Example (11), the novice speaker identifies herself in T2 and is personally identified in T3 by the receiver who tells her where her husband is. In T4 she successfully introduces her topic despite a word choice error.

(11) Fifth novice speaker: Successful call-in

```
T0:   C:  (Ring)
T1:   R:  Hello. Convention Services. How can I help you?
T2:   C:  Is S.
T3:   R:  Hi. R is in the ballroom.
T4:   C:  Ee. No. I need roll-away take out.
T5:   R:  Hh. Is it a check-out?
```

T6: C: Si. Check-out.
T7: R: Room number?
T8: C: One One Zero One.
T9: R: Alright.
          (.)
          See ya.
T10:C: Bye. ((Hangs up.))

(Transcript of R. recorded in April, 1998)

Recording of the Novice Call-in After Modeling

The following model dialogue was created based on the expert speaker's transcript in Example (6).

(12) Dialogue based on the expert speaker's transcript

T0: C: *Rings*
T1: R: Hello.
T2: C: Pick up in room_____, _____.
                          number   *item name*
T3: R: _____.
           number
T4: C: Yep. (Hang up)

Using a sheet of paper with the dialogue in Example (12), the same novice speaker who was unsuccessful in Example (7) called Convention Services and produced the transcript in Example (13), and the same unsuccessful speaker seen in Example (9) produced the transcript in Example (14).

The action sequences in (13) and (14) are nearly identical to the action sequences produced in Example (6) by the expert speaker. There are only two differences between Example (6) and Example (13). First there is a request for the topic in T1 by the receiver, and there is an appeal to politeness in T5 by the receiver.

(13) First novice speaker: successful

T0:	((*Rings*))		((Summons))
T1:	R:	Hello.	((Answer))
		Convention Services.	((Display for recognition))
		How can I help you?	((Request for intro. of topic))
T2:	C:	Pick up refrigerator,	((Claim C has recognized R))
		Room 1215.	((Claim R can recognize C))
			((Answer to request for topic))
T3:	R:	Room 1250?	((Granting of request/
			Uptake of topic))
			((Claim R has recognized C))
			((Question))

T4:	C:	Yes. Room 1215.	((Answer))
T5:	R:	Thank you.	((Appeal to politeness))
		Good-bye. (Hangs up)	((Closure))
T6:	C:	Good-bye. (laughter)	((Closure))

(J., May 1998)

In Example (14) the action sequences are again very similar to the action sequences in Example (6). Despite severe pronunciation difficulties in T2, the receiver is able to understand that it is an employee calling in and he responds appropriately. The only real difficulty seems to be in T4 when the novice speaker repeats the room number as a means of agreement instead of saying "yes" or "okay." This seems to confuse the receiver a little bit who then repeats his request for confirmation of the room number.

(14) Third novice speaker: Successful

T0:		*((Rings))*	((Summons))
T1:	R:	Hello.	((Answer))
		Convention Services.	((Display for recognition))
		How can I help you?	((Request for introduction of topic))
T2:	C:	Ping up. Room 709.	((Claim C has recognized R))
			((Claim R can recognize C))
			((Answer to request for topic))
T3:	R:	709?	((Granting of request/Uptake of topic))
			((Claim R has recognized C))
			((Request for Confirmation))
T4:	C:	709.	((Answer))
T5:	R:	709?	((Repetition of request for confirmation))
T6:	C:	Yes.	((Answer))
		Good-bye.	((Closure))
T7:	R:	Yeah.	((Closure))

(L., May 1998)

The unsuccessful recordings are all characterized by frustrating exchanges in which the LPES housekeeper loses the floor and the Convention Services employee misidentifies the caller as a guest which the LPES housekeeper is unsuccessful in correcting due to an inability to regain control of the conversation and/or due to pronunciation or grammatical errors. The successful recordings also have pronunciation and grammatical errors in them, but the participants are all successfully identified as employees at the end of T2 and they are able to coordinate a mutual goal.

Comparison of the Expert Speaker's Call-in and Canonical Structure

A comparison of the structure of the expert speaker's call-in in Example (6) with the canonical structure of a social phone call (Schegloff, 1986), illustrated

Table 7.1. Action sequences of a call-in compared to the canonical structure

Expert Call-in Structure	Canonical Conversational Structure

T0: C: 1st :   Summons
               Ring
	T0: C: 1st: Summons
	               Ring

T1: R: 2nd :   Answer
        1st:   Claim   that   the   caller   can
               recognize the receiver
               Hello
	T1: R: 2nd : Answer
	        1st : Claim that the caller can recognize
	               the receiver
	               Hello

T2: C: 2nd :   Claim C recognized R.
        1st:   Claim R can recognize C
        1st :   Introduction of Topic
               *Pick   up   in   room   936,
               refrigerator.*
	T2: C: 2nd : Claim C recognized R
	        1st: Claim R can recognize C
	        1st: Greeting
	               Hi.

T3: R: 2nd :   Claim R recognized C
        2nd :   Up-take of Topic
               936
	T3: R: 2nd : Claim R recognized C
	        2nd: Greeting
	               Oh hi.:

--end of call--	T4: C: 1st : Introduction of topic
	T5: R: 2nd: Up-take of topic

in Table 7.1, reveals three main differences. First, in the expert's call-in, the topic is introduced preemptively at T2 before the identification sequence is even completed. Second, there is no personal identification of the caller and receiver and the identification sequence is a nonovert sequence. Third, there is no greeting sequence in the hotel data.

Although there is a *hello* in T1 of Example (6), it is not considered a greeting for reasons that Schegloff (1986) takes up in detail. Briefly, it is considered an answer to a summons. (That is why, according to Schegloff, there are usually three *hello*s at the beginning of a phone conversation. The first *hello* is an answer to a summons and not a greeting. The second and third *hello* are the greetings.) In this institutional data, in the expert speaker's transcript, there is nothing that is construable as a greeting.

Inasmuch as I am claiming that there is not a greeting sequence in the hotel data, based on the omission of any overt statements that seem like true greetings, one might wonder whether there is also really an identification sequence. The existence of the identification sequence is primarily based on the same logical argument provided before by Schegloff, but with one modification: In the hotel data, people are not being identified as particular individuals. Rather, they are being identified as belonging to a particular group (such as Housekeepers, Convention Service Employees, Room Service, or Guests). The exception to this is Example (11) in which R is recognized as an individual, but the response to this is fascinating. The receiver immediately tells R where her husband is, suggesting that he has oriented to the caller as an outsider—a colleague's wife—not as a colleague herself seeking to coordinate collegial duties.

The fact that group identification has occurred in the collegial exchanges was also confirmed by the interviews after the phone conversations. After each phone conversation, the participants had a clear understanding as to whether or not they had been talking to an employee or to a guest. It should be noted, however, that in the collegial exchanges participants generally did not seem to have a name or face attached to the person they were talking to.

Speech Events Compared:
The Expert Speaker vs. the Novice vs. Schegloff

Table 7.2 allows us to compare the structure of the novice speaker's unsuccessful call-in from Example (7) with the structure of the expert speaker's call-in from Example (6) with the canonical structure. Like the expert speaker's call-in, the novice speaker omits the greeting sequence. Unlike the expert speaker's call-in, the novice speaker follows the canonical structure in having an overt identification sequence and identification of person. Finally, and perhaps crucially, while the expert speaker's call-in introduces the topic preemptively in T2 before the identification sequence is complete, the novice speaker does not introduce the topic until T6, after trying to complete an identification sequence, just as in the canonical telephone call.

Misidentification of the novice speaker seems to occur when T2 passes without introduction of the topic and without the Convention Services employee orienting to either the housekeeper or the need to coordinate a task. In addition to T2 passing without introduction of the topic by the novice, the personal identification sequence offered by the novice in T2 corresponds to the canonical telephone call examined by Schegloff, but not to the call-in genre. While a novice native speaker might have been able to repair this misidentification, this LPES novice speaker was unsuccessful in his repair attempts.[8]

Effect of an Accurate Model

Providing the novice speaker with an accurate model did in fact result in a successful *call-in*, despite the persistence of marked phonological difficulties, since the phone call resulted in an employee from convention services coming to the requisite floor where the housekeeper directed him to the correct room. The success of the novice speakers when using the model produced by the expert speaker adds validity to the idea that genres do have unique rules that are utilized by expert members of the discourse community to accomplish their goals, rules that can be taught to novices.

During the first recording, the students in this study were using a structure that included an overt identification sequence and they were not immediately

---

[8] For more about why he was unsuccessful in repairing the misidentification, see Gibbs (2002).

Table 7.2. Expert and novice hotel calls compared to a social call.

Hotel data: Expert supervisor	Hotel data: LPES speaker	Social call: Schegloff data
T0: C: 1st: Summons **Ring**	T0: C: 1st: Summons **Ring**	T0: C: 1st: Summons **Ring**
T1: R: 2nd: Answer 1st : Claim that the caller can recognize the receiver **Hello**	T1: R: 2nd: Answer 1st : Claim that the caller can recognize the receiver **Hello. Convention Services.**	T1: R: 2nd : Answer 1st : Claim that the caller can recognize the receiver **Hello.**
T2: C: 2nd: Claim that C has recognized R 1st : Claim R can recognize C 1st : <u>Introduction of topic</u> **Pick up in room 936, refrigerator.**	T2: C: 2nd: Claim that C has recognized R 1st: Claim R can recognize C **This is J. I'm- (.8) [housekeeping]**	T2: C: 2nd: Claim that C has recognized R 1st: Claim R can recognize C 1st : Greeting **Hi.**
T3: R: 2nd: Claim that R has recognized C 2nd: Up-take of topic, granting of request **936**	T3: R: 2nd: Claim that R has recognized C 1st: Request for topic **[How can-] How can I help you?**	T3: R: 2nd: Claim that R has recognized C 2nd : Greeting **Oh hi::**
--end of call--	T4: **C: 1st: Repair of T3** R: 2nd:*Intro. of topic: answer* 1st:*Request for housekeeping* **I am housekeeping.**	T4: R: 2nd: Answer 1st: How are you **Fine. And you?**
Speech acts which are perceived differently by **the caller** and *the receiver* are indicated with **bold** and *italics* respectively.	T5:*R: dispreferred 2nd: Uptake of topic* 1st:*Directive* **C: dispreferred 2nd : an answer to the repair which indicates that the repair was unsuccessful To call housekeeping you need to dial 52.**	T5: C: 2nd: Answer 1st : Intro. of topic **Fine. Say, are you busy later?**
	T6: C: **1st: Repair of T3: Claim that R has recognized C: assertion: Claim that R can recognize C 1st: Introduction of topic: request for pick-up** 2nd:*Rejection of directive to call housekeeping* 1st:*Request for housekeeping* **Housekeeping. Pick up.**	T6: R: 2nd : Up-take of topic **No. What's up?**

introducing the topic. Perhaps this was because an overt sequence is required in social phone calls and topics are not introduced until after identification has occurred. It also could have been an effect of prior training on incorrect models. Both the dialogue practiced in the previous ESL class, Example (15), and the New Employee Orientation video, Example (16), included overt identification sequences which the expert speaker did not use, and both waited to introduce the topic until after identification had occurred. This suggests that it is important to base instructional materials on talk produced by expert members of the discourse community so that the rules of the genre can be incorporated in the training model.

(15) Dialogue from previous course materials

> C: ((Ring))
> R: Hello. Conference Services, this is <u>Jeff</u>.
> C: Hi. This is <u>Mary.</u>
> R: How can I help you?
> C: I am in room <u>100.</u> Can you come get a <u>refrigerator</u>, please?
> R: Sure.
> C: Great. Good-bye.
> R: Good-bye.

(16) In-house, new employee orientation video script

> T0: C: ((Ring))
> T1: R: Hello, Conference Services.
> T2: C: Hello, this is Mary from Housekeeping. I'm in room 214. There is a wet bar and a refrigerator here which need to be picked up.
> T3: R: Thank you, Mary. Do you need the room right away?
> T4: C: Yes, I do.
> T5: R: Ok. We'll send someone up. Can I do anything else for you?
> T6: C: No. Thank you. Good-bye.
> T7: R: Good-bye.

(Training video for new housekeepers, circa 1997)

New employees usually learn the genre by following around a senior housekeeper for 3 days, listening to their mentor perform call-ins, and practicing call-ins themselves. The LPES housekeepers are usually trained by a native speaker of their language (so new Vietnamese housekeepers are trained by senior Vietnamese housekeepers). Because most of the nonnative speakers of English were not successful in making call-ins, new LPES housekeepers lacked good mentorship for learning the call-in, although they probably did hear their supervisors making call-ins. As the LPES housekeepers may have been influenced by the incorrect models displayed during the new employee orientation and in a prior ESL program, it is not clear whether they would have learned the genre on their own if they hadn't had bad models in their environment or whether this genre was inaccessible for other reasons.

Comparison of the Call-in with the Doctor's Office Call and the 911 Call

Table 7.3 compares the sequences found in the hotel data with the sequences in institutional phone calls studied by Hopper et al. (1990) and Wakin and Zimmerman (1999).

All of the institutional samples show preemptive introduction of topic, so this may be a feature of institutional telephone calls. Overt vs. nonovert identification seems to vary by institution and may be specific to the individual genres. In all of the transcripts of telephone calls to a work place shown here, the greeting sequence is omitted. The idea that the greeting sequence may not be mandatory actually receives some support from Schegloff (1986). Schegloff notes that he finds the job of the greeting sequence difficult to define.[9] However, he suggests, it seems to be a ritual whose purpose is orienting the caller and receiver to one another and it is used to establish cooperation toward a shared goal. Since genres have their own sets of rules, it seems logical that an orientation to the genre must occur. Thus, it might be more appropriate to say that at T2 an orienting process occurs. In the social, hello–hello sequenced phone calls this orienting process between individuals is realized by a "greeting" sequence. In the case of the call-in, however, this orienting may have to do with displaying themselves as employees making a call-in by introducing the topic preemptively with a directive.

The how-are-you sequence is also not in any of the transcripts recording institutional interactions. In fact, it seems likely that the how-are-you sequence is only tangentially part of the opening sequence even in social calls, in that it seems to be some sort of presequence to the introduction of the topic in social

Table 7.3. Comparison of Various Institutional Telephone Calls

Feature	Hotel employee-expert	Hotel employee – novice (Unsuccessful)	Client-to-doctor	Client-to-911
Summons-answer	Yes	Yes	Yes	Yes
Identification sequence	Yes	Yes	Yes	Yes
Overt	No	Yes	Yes	No
Nonovert	Yes	No	No	Yes
Greeting	No	No	No	No
How are you?	No	No	No	No

---

[9] This is an oversimplification of Schegloff's analysis. He writes "the jobs attributed to greetings defy listing, let alone description, here; at a minimum, they put the parties into what Goffman (1963, p. 100) has called a ritual state of ratified mutual participation, and in doing so may accomplish other work for the interaction and its parties as well" (Schegloff, 1986, p. 118).

phone calls displaying intimacy. Hopper observes that intimate social calls contain substantially more presequences than phone calls between nonintimates. Thus, the institutional phone calls seem to display canonically a summons–answer sequence and an identification sequence with introduction of the topic prior to the completion of the identification sequence. The orientation sequence seems to be achieved in unique ways by different genres. Different genres also may differ in regards to whether the identification sequence is handled overtly with its own turn constructional unit, or nonovertly.

CONCLUSION

These data are in agreement with the notion that genres have their own rules for (1) which actions are engaged in and (2) the sequence in which the actions are engaged in, and that training materials need to be designed with this awareness in mind since not following the rules of the genre can result in unsuccessful speech events. Unlike Schegloff's social telephone calls where preemptive introduction of topic before completion of the identification sequence might indicate irritation, preemptive introduction of topic in the call-in genre seems to indicate that the caller is a fellow employee, rather than a guest. Failure to understand and follow the rules of the genre seems to result in an unintended meaning being transmitted: specifically "I am a guest" rather than "I am a fellow employee." Due to the difficulty experienced by the LPES housekeepers in controlling the talk, such a misidentification became difficult for them to repair.

This work suggests that there are phone call genres that have features different from the call features described in Levinson (1983) and Schegloff (1968, 1979, 1986). In particular, work needs to proceed on the differences between employees and clients when they call a business. Recordings of new employees acquiring discourse competence in the rules of their new speech community may also yield interesting insights on acquisition and proto-typicality. Finally, the generality of the preemptive introduction of topic in institutional data, the meaning of overt–nonovert identification sequences in institutional data, and processes for orienting to the type of call needs to be established across genres.

REFERENCES

Atkinson, J. M., & Heritage, J. (Eds.). (1984). *Structures of social action*. Cambridge, England: Cambridge University Press.
Gibbs, T. L. (2002). *Misidentification of limited proficiency English speaking (LPES) employees in hotel call-ins*. Unpublished Plan B paper, University of Minnesota.
Goffman, E. (1963). *Behavior in public places*. New York: Free Press.
Fairchild, M. (1995). *Mind your modals: The telephone request in a business context*. Unpublished Plan B paper, University of Minnesota.
Hopper, R., Doany, N., Johnson, M., & Drummond, K. (1990). Universals and particulars in telephone openings. *Research on Language and Social Interaction, 24,* 369-387.
Levinson, S. (1983). *Pragmatics*. Cambridge, England: Cambridge University Press.
Markee, N. (2000). *Conversation analysis*. Mahwah, NJ: Lawrence Erlbaum Associates.

Psathas, G. (1995). *Conversation analysis.* Thousand Oaks, CA: Sage.

Sacks, H., Schegloff, E. A., & Jefferson, G. (1974). A simplest systematics for the organization of turn taking in conversation. *Language, 50,* 696-735.

Schegloff, E. (1968). Sequencing in conversational openings. *American anthropologist, 70,* 1075-1095.

Schegloff, E. (1979). Identification and recognition in telephone conversation openings. *Everyday language: Studies in ethnomethodology* (pp. 23-78). New York: Irvington.

Schegloff, E. (1986). The routine as achievement. *Human Studies, 9,* 111-151.

Schegloff, E. (1992). On talk and its institutional occasions. In P. Drew & J. Heritage (Eds.), *Talk at work: Interaction in institutional settings* (pp. 101-134). Cambridge, England: Cambridge University Press.

Schegloff, E. (1996). Turn organization: One intersection of grammar and interaction. In E. Ochs, E. Schegloff, & S. Thompson (Eds.), *Interaction and grammar* (pp. 52-125). New York: Cambridge University Press.

Schegloff, E., & Sacks, H. (1973). Opening up closings. *Semiotica, 7,* 289-327.

Swales, J. (1990). *Genre analysis.* Cambridge, England: Cambridge University Press.

Wakin, M., & Zimmerman, D. (1999). Reduction and specialization in emergency and directory assistance calls. *Research on Language and Social Interaction, 32,* 409-437.

Whalen, M., & Zimmerman, D. (1987). Sequential and institutional contexts in calls for help. *Social Psychology Quarterly, 50,* 172-85.

Whalen, M., & Zimmerman, D. (1990). Describing trouble: Practical epistemology in citizen calls to the police. *Language in Society, 19,* 465-492.

Zimmerman, D. (1992). The interactional organization of calls for emergency assistance. In P. Drew & J. Heritage (Eds.), *Talk at work: Interaction in institutional settings* (pp. 418-469). Cambridge, England: Cambridge University Press.

8

Practical Considerations

Kathleen Bardovi-Harlig
Beverly S. Hartford
Indiana University

This chapter discusses the practical concerns of getting started in research that explores interlanguage pragmatics through institutional talk. Rather than drawing solely on our own experiences, we have asked colleagues to share their experiences with us, and we report these in this chapter. Some have conducted research in the institutions represented in this volume, but some have done their work in other institutions as well, allowing for a broad perspective.[1]

The institutions represented in this chapter include universities— specifically, the writing center (Williams, chapter 2, this volume), classrooms (Davies & Tyler, chapter 5, this volume), university advising sessions (Bardovi-Harlig & Hartford, 1990, 1993, 1996; Hartford & Bardovi-Harlig, 1992)— secondary schools (Yates, chapter 3, this volume), employment agencies (Kerekes, chapter 4, this volume), a four-star conference hotel (Gibbs, chapter 7, this volume), the INS (the United States Immigration and Naturalization Service; Johnston, 2003a, 2003b, in press; Seig & Winn, 2003; Winn, 2000, under review), hospitals and clinics (Cameron, 1998; Cameron & Williams, 1997), and a variety of workplaces (Clyne, 1994). Most of the research settings were in the United States, but information from Yates and Clyne suggests that the process of setting up research on institutional talk is similar in Australia. The guidelines presented here are intended to help researchers get started; we acknowledge that specific requirements may vary by institution and local practices. Comprehensive reports such as Clyne (1994) contain detailed information and should also be consulted. We have organized this chapter by the approximate sequential order of steps that one may take in organizing such a project. These include identifying the institution, getting permission from the institution, completing a review process, collecting data, and winding up the project. Necessarily there is some overlap among the sections which reflects overlapping considerations at different points in a project.

---

[1] We thank the following colleagues for their expertise: Tara Gibbs, Julie Kerekes, Andrea Tyler, Jessica Williams, Lynda Yates, Michael Clyne, Richard Cameron, Alexandra Johnston, Mary Theresa Seig, and Michelle Winn.

In the remainder of this chapter, any unattributed quotation should be understood as a response to a set of questions sent out through e-mail in July and August, 2003. These questions were sent to the authors whose work is included in this volume as well as to other researchers who have studied institutional talk of L2 speakers.

IDENTIFYING THE INSTITUTION

There seem to be two main orientations to studying institutional talk. In one, researchers study their local institutions, making an investigation of the interactions around them. In the other, investigators seek out new institutions with which they have no official relationship.

Guideline 1. Make your institution work for you. Look at your local setting as an outsider. Evaluate the interaction patterns. What are the services offered by your unit and who uses them? What type of talk occurs there?

Our own research on the academic advising session has been of the first type, a study of the local institution. The academic advising sessions that we studied were meetings between faculty members serving as academic advisors for graduate and undergraduate students in the department of linguistics (Bardovi-Harlig & Hartford, 1990, 1993, 1996; Hartford & Bardovi-Harlig, 1992). We began work on the academic advising session because we were intrigued by the different outcomes of the sessions and were interested to learn how talk during the sessions influenced or determined those outcomes. Natural local settings for academic researchers who teach at universities are often (but not always) the universities themselves and this means studying institutional talk at the university. It is important to keep in mind, however, that university talk—like the university itself—is made up of talk in many different settings. Universities offer many services and, consequently, offer many different opportunities to investigate talk in different local settings including some described in the present volume such as the university writing center and lab sessions. In addition to these and the faculty advising sessions already discussed, other university settings include peer advising (He, 1994), class lectures (Tyler, 1992), the local Intensive English Program (Bardovi-Harlig & Hartford, 1997; Hartford & Bardovi-Harlig, 1996b) and office hours (Tyler, 1995) Not all insider research is done at universities, however: In this volume, Gibbs reports on data that she collected when she was teaching ESL at a four-star conference hotel.

Guideline 2. Consider a range of institutions.

Research done outside researchers' own institutions shows a remarkable array of settings. We were intrigued to find not one, but two studies presented on talk during INS interviews at the 2003 meeting of American Association of Applied Linguistics (AAAL). These studies took place in different states (Johnston, 2003a, 2003b, in press; Seig &Winn, 2003; Winn, 2000). Other studies involving native and nonnative speakers were set in a psychiatric ward of a major metropolitan hospital (Cameron & Williams, 1997), a variety of factories (Clyne, 1994), a social services office (Tarone & Kuehn, 2000), and secondary-school classrooms (Yates, chapter 3, this volume). Readers are encouraged to consult Clyne (1994) for a detailed discussion of selecting work sites and participants.

Guideline 3. Make use of your social network.

Conducting research away from one's home institution requires making contacts. This ranges from relying on one's network of friends to help make contacts to making "cold calls," that is, approaching an institution without a prior personal relationship. Many researchers report that friends helped them make contacts within the targeted institution. Yates, who studies the talk of teachers in secondary classrooms, was involved in teacher training at the university level (this volume, Chapter 3). Her department sent some of its students to some of the schools that she eventually studied. She explains, "I developed a relationship with people from other universities who were coordinating practicum placements in school. Through these I identified participants. When they were assigned to schools for their practicum placements, I contacted the principals of the schools and the relevant teachers to request their permission." Like Yates, Cameron, whose research followed nurses at four different hospitals and clinics, developed his contacts through faculty colleagues. Cameron reports, "I found out names of contacts through different faculty members in the School of Nursing at Penn. Then, I called on the phone and went in person to explain the project."

Kerekes' contact in the employment agency industry began with a friend whose sister lived in another state. Kerekes recalls, "I had a friend whose sister worked in the employment agency industry as a staffing supervisor in Seattle. She and I communicated by e-mail and phone and she expressed interest in my study, so she connected me with some of her colleagues in a San Francisco Bay Area branch of the same employment agency for which she worked."

Guideline 4. Treat the institutional representatives as experts.

Treating the institutional representatives as the experts regarding the institution and not as hindrances to the study helps in obtaining permission. It is important to keep in mind that the researchers may have much to learn from the institutional representatives themselves (cf. Douglas and Selinker's, 1994, use of the subject specialist informant).

Guideline 5. Once you have a contact at the institution, learn the chain of command, and then follow it.

Making contacts and checking with supervisors is important whether working in your own institution or an outside institution. Don't assume you will automatically be granted access to interactions either in your immediate department or affiliated departments. Take the time to make the right contacts even at home; securing permission at all steps along the way helps the research proceed more smoothly.

Interestingly, the research chain of contact often seems to start with an individual at the institution, then move up to a supervisory or higher institutional level (or levels), and then return to the level of the client. Cameron explains that his approach to clinics and schools is similar: "I arranged it first with a local administrator and then with the specific individuals in the clinic where I was going to do the research. I have done similar work in schools. First, permission from the principal and school district. Then, permission from individual teachers. Then, permission from parents and kids. But, where possible, I tried to make a local contact first, then sought out the higher up administrator. In my experience, if I can go to a higher up administrator, saying that I had spoken with a nurse (who had approved the idea), I seemed to have a smoother ride in obtaining permission."

Clyne conducted his research on workplace talk in eight different settings, a car factory of American origin, a car factory of Japanese origin, a textile factory, an electronics factory, a catering department, an education office of a government operation, an employment office, and a meeting at a multicultural parents' group at a high school. Clyne reports that they "discussed the project, what was required, and our responsibilities (anonymity, confidentiality, opportunity to withdraw, possibility of receiving information on the findings) with management, union representatives, shop stewards, and workers themselves."

Yates presents the order of contacts that she used when researching secondary schools in her position as a researcher at a university, "I had to get ethics clearance from my university (filling out appropriate form), then permission from the regional director (by letter with accompanying outline of the project), then from the principal (letter plus details), then the supervising teacher (phone) and then from the parents of all the students in each class (permission slip to be given out to students in advance and returned by the date of the taping)."

Guideline 6. Be persistent and patient.

Johnston's account of her contacts with the INS illustrates several points: that research can be conducted in a full range of settings, that researchers can cultivate a relationship through cold calls when necessary, and that the chain of command is very important. Most of all, Johnston's account emphasizes that persistence and patience pay off. Johnston recounts, "I made 41 telephone calls to the Public Affairs Office, sent five letters describing my project to different levels of managers up to the District Director, and presented my project at three meetings with INS personnel before I won permission to present my project to the entire staff of District Adjudications Officers. The process took over six months."

Guideline 7. Consult with other researchers, but don't let nay-sayers discourage you.

All researchers benefit from the expertise of colleagues, just as we have done in this chapter! Colleagues who have done institutional research can offer many practical suggestions. However, as Johnston learned, some advice can be unnecessarily discouraging. She writes, "Don't get discouraged if other researchers tell you that a certain approach to gaining access won't work. I sought help from several researchers who had successfully gained access to the INS, which rarely grants permission for on-site research. All of those whom I contacted had gotten in through connections or a friend-of-a-friend. They told me this was the best way and that cold calling the Public Affairs Office wouldn't work because it's the job of Public Affairs to screen people out (they are the gatekeepers to the gatekeepers). That may be true, but I think persistence, courteousness, and a willingness to provide a service in exchange for access goes a long way. It worked in my case."

GETTING PERMISSION TO CONDUCT THE STUDY

Once contact is made, the next step is to convince the institution to give permission to conduct the study. We asked what the researchers felt were the convincing factors for their gaining permission to do their studies. The most important, reported by all, was that they stressed the benefits of their project to the institution. In many cases, there were direct benefits, such as designing a training course for institutional members, or materials development for those members to use. In others, offering to share the results with the institution and pointing out how the results might be used to help institutional members were convincing factors. In all cases, some offer of help to the institution as a result of the study was felt to be a major factor in obtaining permission.

Guideline 8. Cite the benefits to the institution.

Yates explained to the school board and the candidate schools the benefit of learning more about the language needs of teachers. Such knowledge has the potential of improving teacher education to the potential benefit of both schools and teachers. A second type of benefit accrues directly to the participating institution rather than to the field or profession more generally. Like Johnston, Winn also studied immigration interviews at the INS. They took slightly different approaches. Johnston convinced her point of contact that her primary goals were to help the INS and to complete her degree. Winn involved the institution in the planning process by asking them what they would like to learn from the research, "I wrote a letter outlining my reasons to study the naturalization interview and asked if the INS wanted me to focus on any question in particular in my research. I explained the personal stake I had in the research—having been a U.S. citizenship preparation teacher."

A different type of benefit to the institution is the researcher's offer to help out in some way. In this way, the researcher also learns more about how the institution works. Kerekes, for example, volunteered at the employment agency where she collected her data. She helped out at the front desk, helped with filing in the back room, and answered phones. She reports that she offered to do some volunteer work in order to get a partial insider's perspective while collecting data.

Guideline 9. Be personally invested.

Winn, in her discussion of working with the INS, suggests that researchers "be personally invested." As Winn's advice suggests, it is also helpful to let the institution know that you are invested in the field. Teacher-researchers often have an obvious link to various institutions. Winn's link to the INS as a citizenship teacher might have made her interest in the INS more tangible to the approving officer. Similarly, as a teacher educator, Yates also had a demonstrable interest in the language that teachers need, as Cameron did when he was developing courses for nursing students who were nonnative speakers of English.

Guideline 10. Do not hinder the everyday workplace activities.

The researchers noted that assurances of unobtrusiveness on their part while conducting the study were also important. Institutions have goals to accomplish and work days which are allocated to a variety of activities, and they are not eager to disrupt the flow of work. Thus, unobtrusiveness in the form of not affecting the organizational practices in any major way was appreciated. People could essentially carry on with what they would normally do without having to change time-lines, spatial locations, and so forth. At the same time, an actual low level of intrusion on the part of the investigator seemed desired. Setting up recording equipment ahead of time, locating oneself in a fairly unobtrusive part of the room (or not being present at all), not participating in the process at hand, were assurances of noninterference that various researchers gave which they felt helped to persuade the institutions.

Sometimes the agreement for unobtrusiveness is general as Kerekes reports, "My presence was welcome under the condition that my work would in no way slow down or impede on FastEmp's normal procedures regarding the selection of job candidates." In other cases, unobtrusiveness relates to the recording equipment that researchers use. Cameron could only use audio recorders, without attaching microphones directly to the patients. The student-teachers in Yates' study wore portable recorders that she describes as a "walk person" plus mini mike for each class recorded, and she worked the video camera from the back of the room. When we recorded the advising sessions we quickly learned that both advisors and students preferred a small tape recorder with an omni-directional microphone to a larger, higher quality stereo recorder with separate lapel mikes for each participant. (We return to the topic of equipment later in this chapter; see Guideline 19). Setting up equipment in advance of the institutional event is often part of being unobtrusive. This minimizes the disruption to the normal flow of the event.

Guideline 11. Be accessible.

Make your proposal accessible to the institution. Researchers may often forget that others do not necessarily share our interest, expertise, or vocabulary for talking about language. Bringing the institution into the research as a partner is an important step. As Johnston suggests, "translate your research agenda into accessible language that dovetails with the internal concerns of your target institution. Show them that you understand (or want to learn about) their concerns and questions. Offer your problem-solving services, without compromising your goals or ethics."

Guideline 12. Guarantee and deliver fair treatment.

Some institutions may be particularly sensitive to public opinion. Such may be the case at schools which have recently been in the news, medical institutions, and government agencies. For example, Johnston reports that "the INS has received a great deal of criticism from government and the media for its inefficiency and errors. Representatives of the institution are understandably wary of outsiders who request to research and write about its practices. This wariness was apparent in my initial contacts with Public Affairs Officer, Management, and District Adjudications Officers. Therefore, I was careful to present my research as an instrument that might provide benefit to the INS in terms of improving service to clients and reducing miscommunication with clients. I offered to use my results to create a training module for the officers. And I reassured them that I was not affiliated with the press or any association advocating immigration reform (a question I was asked more than once). After reading my confidentiality forms and engaging in multiple interviews, I finally convinced my point of contact that my primary goal was (1) to help the INS and (2) to complete my degree (and not to excoriate the INS in my future publications, which I intended for an academic audience, not the mass media)."

Guideline 13. Contact the institutional representatives.

Once the institution has approved the study, then permission remains to be secured from two more groups, the institutional representatives and the clients. These are the people whose interactions will be recorded. Generally the first step is to contact the institutional representatives. Sometimes these are the same individuals that were contacted informally at the outset of the study, but this step secures their official permission.

In our observations of the academic advising sessions, we presented our case at a faculty meeting, because in our department, all faculty members participated equally in the advising of graduate and undergraduate students. We recruited five faculty participants in addition to ourselves. As experienced advisors, we participated in the first year of advising prior to data analysis. Once we began to analyze the data, we no longer took part in the tape-recorded interviews. The five volunteers constituted more than half of the faculty at the time.

Williams had the advantage of being the faculty director of the writing center in which she conducted the research, although she reports that the tutors were quite eager to participate. (There was also an administrative director who was interested in having research conducted in the center). They were recruited by word-of-mouth from among the tutor-staff. There was no problem finding tutors who wished to participate. Williams is the only researcher we contacted who reports being able to pay her tutors for participating. The Vice Chancellor's office had also funded the project. As a result, she had not only institutional permission, but institutional support, much as Gibbs had at the hotel.

While word of mouth recruiting worked among the writing center tutors, other institutional participants were recruited by face-to-face meeting or by phone calls. Kerekes met with staff personally: "After the proposal was accepted, I spoke with all of the FastEmp staff to ask them if they were willing to participate in my study, and then had them sign consent forms." Johnston also made a face-to-face appeal for participation at a staff meeting. She reports, "After receiving approval from management, I was allowed to present my project at a staff meeting of the nine District Adjudications Officers in order to invite their participation. One officer volunteered."

Yates contacted her participants by phone using contact details that were provided by the practicum placement coordinators in each university where they were undertaking their teacher training. One of the factors that leads to different approaches is whether the research is located in a single or in multiple settings. Johnston's and Kerekes' studies took place in a single office of the INS and FastEmp, respectively, whereas Yates' prospective student–teacher participants attended different universities and would be assigned to different secondary schools.

Guideline 14. Contact clients of the participating institutional representatives.

The institutional representatives form the bulwark of the project. Once the institutional representatives have agreed to participate, then the task of contacting the institutional clients begins. As we discussed earlier in chapter 1, clients are identified through their interaction with the participating institutional representatives. Thus researchers variously approach students who come to participating advisors, instructors, or tutors, patients who seek the services of participating nurses, or visa applicants who are assigned to a particular INS officer. Most of the contacts with clients were done face-to-face in the institution, where potential participants could be asked if they would take part in the study. This might be done in a one-on-one context, or in a more general meeting of possible participants where the researcher would present the project. If the parties agreed, they were usually given a consent form of some type to sign. In those cases where the researcher was also a member of the institution often the potential participants were initially contacted through recruiting measures such as distribution of flyers and announcements, but were still asked to sign a consent form. In only one case discussed in this book (Williams, chapter 2, this volume), was payment offered for participation in the study. Payment did not seem to be a primary motivating factor in these studies, however.

The writers in Williams' writing center studies were one group that could be recruited by group contact. Williams recruited student participants (the institutional clients) through undergraduate composition classes by sending flyers to the classes, after which her graduate assistant would "talk it up." Such recruitment procedures paralleled the general practices for encouraging students to use the writing center. In contrast, Kerekes, Cameron, and Johnston met their prospective client-participants at the time of the institutional encounter and asked them each to participate face-to-face. Their approaches varied according to the institutions. Cameron used slightly different approaches in the hospitals and clinics that he studied. At three of the sites Cameron reports, "I asked them face to face and had them sign short, small consent forms. For patients, in the HMO [Health Maintenance Organization] clinic, the nurse would first enter and ask if I could speak to the patient about the project."

Kerekes outlines what approaching a prospective participant entails: "I contacted job candidates individually, at the time that they had their FastEmp job interviews. At that time, I introduced myself, described my project in general terms ('I am a graduate student at Stanford, working with FastEmp to understand how the interviewing process can be improved'), explained that their participation in my study was voluntary and would not affect their success or failure, and then I asked them if they would like to participate."

Because applicants at the INS are routinely informed by INS that their interview will be taped, Johnston secured permission to use these taped interviews after the session (Johnston) When the officer led an applicant into the office for their interview, he turned on both the camcorder and audiocassette recorder in view of the applicant (and their spouse, children or attorney). (All INS officers have the prerogative to videotape and otherwise record interviews, and all applicants are apprised of this in the official INS letter that notifies them of their interview date and time in a sentence that reads: "This interview will be videotaped.")

After the officer concluded the official interview, he asked the applicants if they would please step into the office next door, where I was waiting. (I was given the use of an empty office to conduct my interviews and to stay throughout the workday.) He told the applicants that I would like to use the videotape in my research, and that I would explain further. All applicants (60) obligingly stepped into my office for a 5 minute explanation. If they did not agree to participate, I erased their video and audiotapes.

If they agreed to participate, I explained the consent form and its contents (right to confidentiality and anonymity, right to withdraw, right to contact the researcher at any point, etc.). After they read the form and signed it, I conducted a brief interview about their experience communicating with the INS officer and their INS experience in general. In all, 51 of 60 applicants agreed to participate."

Guideline 15. Note that post-interviews may be possible.

Kerekes (chapter 4, this volume) and Johnston (2003a, 2003b) not only recorded the employment and INS interviews, respectively, but they also conducted postevent interviews with the participants, a step that involves an even higher level of participation by both representatives and clients. Johnston's account of her procedure was reported in the immediately preceding section.

STANDARD REVIEW PROCESS

Universities have review processes that protects human subjects. At some institutions this is called the Human Subjects Committee, in others the internal review board or IRB. The institution at which you plan to work may also have its own version of such a process (this is true of public school districts, for example). This should not discourage situated research. A researcher must also seek approval from the review board for any study in interlanguage pragmatics, including, for example, the completion of questionnaires.

You will need a consent form for all parties involved, specifically, the institutional representative and the client. Very often, IRB procedures specify the format of a consent form and will provide a template for you to use. These can be difficult for nonnative speakers to understand, and outside the university, such consent forms may be difficult for any participant to understand. To that end, where permitted, Winn suggests writing the consent form in "PLAIN ENGLISH" (emphasis in original). Researchers whose institutions do not have such requirements should consider following similar general guidelines out of courtesy for the participants.

Included in considerations when working with human subjects are confidentiality and anonymity. It is standard to guarantee anonymity to both institutional clients and representatives. This often involves using code names and destroying identity markers, not showing the raw data to anyone outside of the investigators, keeping the data locked away, among others. As an illustration, Johnston reports that "the applicant consent form and the officer consent form promised both applicants and officers confidentiality and anonymity. They affirmed that the results of the study were intended for academic publication and presentation, and that no names, personally identifying characteristics or locations would be revealed. . . . The tapes became the property of the researcher and were to be kept in a safe place with restricted access."

Johnston also reports creating a third type of confidentiality that extended to the INS, allowing the institution the same rights as the individual participants: "to view the tapes and request partial or full erasure in the interest of safeguarding the confidentiality and anonymity of both the INS and the INS officers involved. This form allowed an institutional representative (or representatives) named by the INS to have access to the raw video, audio and written field data in which any INS officers appeared." The same approach could be taken with other institutions. Institutions that have not previously participated in research may be wary of having interactions taped. Such a measure might help reassure them.

Researchers also often create a pseudonym for the institution, providing anonymity for the institution as well as for the institutional representatives and clients. Kerekes named the employment agency "FastEmp," a pseudonym that captured the type of institution and the potentially fast placements that the industry and the clients sought. Clyne (1994) refers to his workplace locations by generic types such as Catering, Weavers, Education Office, and Employmant Office. Cameron describes his research sites by their main characteristics: a psychiatric unit of a major metropolitan hospital, a community-based HMO (health maintenance organization), a neurotrauma unit of a major urban hospital, and a gynecological and birthing clinic of a smaller metropolitan hospital.

Internal review approval also typically requires that participants be able to withdraw from the study at any time. In the case of single institutional interactions (as opposed to longitudinal studies), we generally offer participants the option of turning off the recorder at any time during an interaction. Occasionally students took us up on this option during advising sessions or immediately following the advising session proper in order to discuss sensitive issues.

Participants may also request that their tape(s) be returned to them or destroyed. (These are standard items on internal review board applications for approval.) Although 51 of the 60 applicants that Johnston approached agreed to participate in her study, 9 did not, and their tapes were erased.

Review procedures differ in detail at different universities, and we encourage researchers who are unfamiliar with their review process to contact their campus offices.

COLLECTING DATA AT THE INSTITUTION

In this section we consider some of the steps involved in actual data collection, once all necessary permissions have been secured.

Guideline 16. Take advantage of institutional practices.

Many institutions have practices that make it easier for researchers to collect data. For example, writing centers often keep copies of the essays that were discussed (Thonus, 1999; Williams, 2002). In some cases, having one's work or talk recorded is a condition of a class, program, or employment. The studies by Gibbs of hotel employees (this volume, chapter 7), Davies and Tyler of international teaching assistants (this volume. chapter 5; Tyler & Davies, 1990), and Johnston of immigration interviews (2003a, 2003b, in press, discussed earlier) took advantage of situations of this type. In Gibb's study the shadowing of housekeeping employees and the collection of natural data was part of her job as a materials developer and teacher for the hotel, and it was part of the employees' jobs to participate. In fact, the data collection for the job went beyond what Gibbs used for research and included photos, video-taping, audio-taping, copying written materials that employees both received and produced. Similarly, Davies and Tyler report that the requirements of the university were such that ITAs [international teaching assistants] and students were required to participate in the videotaping for instructional purposes. Tyler writes, "Gathering the data was part of the ongoing activities of the program. The subject was enrolled in an ITA class in which his classroom teaching was videotaped and analyzed on a regular basis."

Once researchers move from using tape-recorded interactions for instructional purposes to research purposes, researchers are required to have the participants sign release forms. Davies and Tyler report that "the researcher directly involved in the videotaping asked the participants for permission to use the transcript of the videotape for research purposes. Both participants readily agreed. (In fact they also agreed to let us show the videotape to academic audiences)."

Guideline 17a. Be prepared for some restrictions.
Guideline 17b. Be flexible.

In granting permission for the studies to be carried out, the institutions sometimes place restrictions or requirements on the researchers. These requirements are often those of the human subject approvals process. Common restrictions included the guarantee of anonymity of the participants and not allowing unauthorized persons access to the data. However others may be particular to the individual institution such as the restriction of the research solely to the portion of the institution under study by the project and not to other departments or locations where non-participating and/or non-institutional members might appear. An example of this is Gibbs's work done in a hotel, where the participants in the study were hotel employees, but where there was a stipulation that no data could be collected where hotel guests might be involved, and permission for taping outside of the housekeeping department had to be secured.

Kerekes and the supervisors at FastEmp negotiated changes at the time that the study was proposed. Kerekes reports, "I had a meeting with two of the FastEmp staff and presented them with a preliminary proposal. At our meeting we negotiated possible changes, after which I submitted a revised written proposal to them and their supervisors."

Whereas some institutions restricted access to clients, others restricted the reporting of certain phases of the institutional event. Kerekes's work involved some aspects which might be viewed as having legal sensitivity, and so she was asked not record those portions of the interview, as she reports: "I was not allowed to use as data one portion of the job interviews—the part during which legal papers were signed and/or discussed (regarding legal residence, citizenship, and taxes)."

Negotiation and flexibility are key in this type of research. Winn felt conducting post-interviews at the INS office where her research was located was a potential stumbling block to approval. She told us, "I had originally wanted to do post interviews with immigrant applicants but realized that was a sticky issue so backed down on that." This flexibility allowed her to go ahead with the larger project. There may be no absolutes as to what is allowed; recall that at another INS office, Johnston was permitted to conduct such interviews.

Although we already mentioned Cameron's use of audio-recorders as an example of unobtrusiveness in the medical setting, this is also an example of a restriction that is institutionally-based. For reasons of client confidentially, no videotaping was permitted.

Guideline 18. Use common sense about what to tape.

We have just discussed aspects of interviews that might be omitted from the published data. In addition, in those institutions where personally, politically, or legally sensitive interactions are undertaken, the researcher might have to ask someone else to collect the data or might need to forego the data entirely. This may be particularly true of medical institutions where, for reasons of privacy or modesty, a researcher of a different gender might have to gather data, or in potential health-threatening situations, such as possible contagion in either direction, in which case some other person actually gathers the data. In the course of his work at hospitals and clinics, Cameron encountered both of these situations. In these cases, where possible, trained assistants who were already members of the institution gathered the data.

As Cameron's work demonstrates, there are situations from which a researcher may wish to exclude him- or herself. Cameron enlisted the assistance of a trained female nurse to work at the OB/GYN clinic (because of gender) and at the neurotrauma unit (because of her medical training). Cameron writes: "Also, being a man, I excluded myself from fieldwork and observations in the gynecological clinic and from observations with teenage girls in the HMO clinic when it became apparent to the nurse that they were going to have to discuss issues of sexuality. . . . I also tried to stay out of consultations with individuals who the nurses felt might be highly contagious with something like the measles, even though I had had the measles as a kid. I recall one case where this occurred, but it occurred after I was already in the consulting room and had shaken hands with the patient. So, they let me stay. I also did not do work in the Neurotrauma unit as the setting seemed highly technical and precarious. Hence, the nurse who I trained did the observations there. It turns out that I probably could have done these observations."

Although often a condition of IRB approvals, offering institutional clients the opportunity to request that the recording of the event be terminated is also a common sense approach to research whether it is required or not. In our research on advising sessions, we found that students occasionally requested that the portion of the interview following the official advising business not be taped. Once in a while when students were having real difficulty in school, they requested that a session not be taped, even though they had signed up for the longitudinal study. Accommodating participants ultimately benefits the research.

Guideline 19. Know the environment and use appropriate equipment.

Scope out your setting before recording data. Michael Clyne (1994) reports that locating areas that were quiet enough to tape in was essential in the factories that he observed. Williams reports moving the writing tutorial upstairs for better recording: "We decided that videotaping in the WC itself would be too disruptive to other writing tutorials (it's a very open space), so we did the sessions in a room upstairs from the center." An open space can also yield poor tape quality, with significant background noise.

In the case of the advising sessions, we experimented with our equipment. We had purchased two excellent high quality dual track tape recorders with lapel microphones. We had asked advisors to take a tape recorder from the office when they picked up the student files for advising. We quickly learned that the advisors were not comfortable with these large and obviously expensive tape recorders, and that, furthermore, no one really wanted to wear a lapel microphone, no matter how small. We replaced these tape recorders with inexpensive but good quality portable tape recorders (about 5 x 4 x 1 1/2") with omni-directional microphones. The advisors were much happier with the smaller units and the data were sufficiently clear without the somewhat intrusive microphones (which, although small, were attached to the recorder with a wire, and probably reminded participants that they were being recorded).

As we have already noted, in many cases, the equipment is set up in the offices in which the interactions were scheduled to take place prior to the event. Not only is this less obtrusive as we discussed earlier, it also assures that the equipment is ready to go when the participants are ready to begin. As Kerekes says, "I had recording equipment set up in the room in which interviews took place, and I explained this to the participants before they decided whether or not they wanted to participate in the study." Johnston reports that after the officer agreed to participate, "I set up his office for videotaping interviews. One handheld Sony DCR-PC100 mini digital video camcorder was placed on the windowsill to capture a side-view of the desk across which the officer and the applicant spoke during the interview. On top of the desk was a handheld audiocassette recorder."

Other times portable equipment, such as Yates used, is the most desirable. She bought portable mini recorders and borrowed a video camera from her university.

Guideline 20. Listen to your tapes immediately.

This advice can be found in any field manual, but we include it here so it doesn't go unsaid: Check your tapes immediately. This stems from at least two concerns: equipment failure and interpretation. There could be a problem with the recording equipment or the setting that you may not have recognized. Checking your tapes will prevent the loss of valuable data. A very common problem is old batteries. Put fresh batteries in the tape recorder every day or every session. Recharge rechargeable batteries and have a backup charged and ready to go. Batteries are not the only problem, however. Equipment needs to be monitored frequently. One of our transcribers pointed out to us that when the voice activation was set to "on," we were losing important information. Not only were the beginnings of turns being cut off, but we were losing the information on pauses. We made sure that the voice activation was always turned off once the problem was identified.

Clyne emphasizes the importance of listening to the tapes immediately for reasons of interpretation, "We found it useful to listen to the tapes immediately so that any questions of clarification, identification or interpretation could be attended to as soon as possible."

Johnston pointed out another reason to listen to the tapes immediately: in cases where the participants are doing their own taping, to make sure that the participants' and the researchers' concepts of the event boundaries are the same. As we reported earlier, the INS officer recorded his own interviews. When Johnston reviewed the tapes from the first day, she realized that he had turned off the camera when he judged that the official interview was over, which was after he received a negative answer to "Any more questions?" As Johnston learned, this was sometimes a few minutes before the applicants left the office. She reports, "He was capturing the end of the interview in his judgment, but not the end of the interaction, which was what I wanted. Reviewing the tapes allowed me to realize that I had not been specific enough in my instructions to him." Fortunately, the researcher and the interviewer were able to correct this the next day, and no further data were lost.

Johnston's story reminded us of our own experience with one of the advisors who took part in the advising session study. Like Johnston's interviewer, he too turned the tape recorder off at the conclusion of the official portion of the advising session, after the student had received the signed registration form (Hartford & Bardovi-Harlig, 1992). Like Johnston, we had hoped to study the closing of the session and any co-membership talk that might occur, but unlike Johnston we did not review our tapes immediately, and thus were unable to make adjustments with that advisor.

Guideline 21. Thank the institution.

When you have completed your study, be sure to thank the institution for its participation. As Dörnyei (2003) observes, thanking participants is a basic courtesy which is often overlooked. The institutions do us a favor to allow us to observe their daily practices, and they may be more inclined to accommodate other researchers if the basic social courtesies are observed. In addition to writing thank you letters to the participants, Johnston suggested including the participants' supervisors as well. In writing to the district supervisor Johnston thanked him for allowing her to carry out her project and also let him know how helpful his staff was. She wrote, "I felt that it was good to let him, as a supervisor, know how capably they managed their participation in the project while at the same time performing their regular work duties. I hoped it would show him how research participation can be smoothly integrated with work routines, and also how professionally his staff treated me." This last point, pointing out that research can be smoothly integrated into work routines, like the extra consideration of writing a thank you letter, helps open the channels of cooperation with institutions for our own future research as well as that of other scholars.

AFTER THE STUDY

Once the study has been completed, we approach the issue of dissemination. We see at least three types of dissemination. The first is the standard academic publication, conference presentation, or report, and we will not go into those here. The next two might be particular to the setting: sharing information with the institution and developing practical applications.

Guideline 22. Offer to share information with the institution.

As Sarangi and Roberts (1999, pp. 41-42) point out, there is concern among researchers about whether or not institutional research should have tangible benefits for the people being studied. Sometimes sharing information is used as a selling point. Sometimes institutions are interested in the information and sometimes they are not. This takes various forms and has different effects. Tyler, Winn, and Johnston all met to share information with officials from the various institutions in which their research was located. However, not every study results in a sharing of the data with the institution.

In some cases, sharing information with the institution is done through reports. Winn wrote reports for all parties involved, including INS officers and Citizenship teachers and tutors. Tyler and Davies were part of the institution that was being studied. Tyler writes: "I did show portions of the tape to the Physics Lab supervisor (a faculty member) and the dean of the graduate school. They took it as strong indication of the need to continue to support the [ITA] program." Johnston's plan for sharing the data with the institution was twofold, including an informal discussion immediately following the data collection followed by materials development at a later stage. She writes, "My last day included an informal discussion of my impressions and suggestions for change with my point of contact. After completing data collection, my goal was to analyze the data for future presentation to academic audiences and to complete my dissertation. I planned to reinterpret my findings with the goal of creating training materials for INS officers and presenting to the INS following the completion of my dissertation."

Benefits and Practical Applications

Delivering or developing a practical application for the participating institution is a specialized form of sharing the information. As we pointed out earlier, one part of pitching one's project to an institution may be to point out the potential benefits of the intended research to the institution itself. This seems to be particularly true when the researcher is part of the institution.

Although nonnative speakers are often the clients in much institutional research (in this volume see Kerekes, Williams; Bardovi-Harlig & Hartford, 1990, 1993, 1996; Hartford & Bardovi-Harlig, 1992; Tarone & Kuehn, 2000; Thonus, 1999; Winn & Seig, 2003), they are increasingly also institutional representatives in studies of institutional talk and employees in work place talk (in this volume see the chapters by Davies & Tyler, Gibbs, Tarone, and Yates; in other publications, see Cameron & Williams, 1997; Clyne, 1994; Tyler, 1995; Tyler & Davies, 1990), and institutions may be particularly interested in assisting their employees with aspects of language use required by their jobs.

Most of the researchers that we contacted saw a practical application for their research, particularly when they teach in the same area as they conduct research. Winn reports that her work with Seig informs the teaching of U.S. Citizenship (Seig and Winn, 2003). Yates's study of native and nonnative English speaking teachers in Australian secondary schools informs the advice that she gives teachers.

The data collected by Tyler and Davies at the physics lab and by Gibbs at the hotel directly informed teaching and teaching materials. This may be due to the fact that they were collected in an educational setting. Tyler reported regularly using the tape itself in subsequent ITA classes. She writes, "I believe the program continues to use it. I also developed a series of strategic role plays based on the interaction" (See Tyler, 1994.)

Gibbs collected data for the expressed purpose of solving an institutional problem (the failure of the novice call-ins) and correcting it through instruction, as part of her job as an ESL teacher at the hotel. Thus the benefits to the institution were prearranged as a requirement of her employment. Gibbs used the call-ins of the expert English speaking supervisor as an authentic pedagogical model for novice housekeeping employees. Call-ins made by novices were played in class to help novices identify differences in their call-ins and they were also used to develop worksheets. As Gibbs reports, "The worksheets became part of the curriculum which was passed on to other teachers and presented at in-house teacher training sessions to other ESL teachers in the project. (There were 27 teachers at 43 sites around the Twin Cities involved in similar teaching scenarios.)"

When asked to reflect on the potential applications of her study of placement interviews at the employment agency, Kerekes wrote "the findings are applicable both to the FastEmp (and other employment agency) staff, who can learn from my analyses how preconceived notions of communicative styles contribute to the outcomes of these gatekeeping encounters. The findings can also be used in ESL and other communication and/or job training courses."

Not all offers of practical application are accepted. Johnston notes that practical applications of studying the INS green card interview include applications "both for the officers who perform interviews (improving officer training) as well as the applicants who are interviewed (information on how green card interviews are conducted, tips on communicating clearly and helping the officer do their job)." Johnston also reports that when her offers of assistance were not ultimately accepted, she was disappointed, "Interestingly, once I received permission (it took over six months and was very touch and go), there were no restrictions placed on me—and no requirement to fulfill the offers of assistance I had made. Once I got through the gate, I was free, both to investigate as well as to leave without follow-up. The latter was disappointing; I had hoped that once I was finished that there would be interest in what I had found or requests for formal follow-up rather than the off-the-cuff discussions that concluded my time on site. However, I realize that the INS has enough on its plate without attending to the suggestions of a graduate student. (Note: my data collection was completed in May 2001, before the repercussions of September 11, 2001 or the massive institutional reorganization of March 2003, when the division was moved to the Department of Homeland Security.)"

Direct assistance to a particular institution is not the only benefit that can be realized from an institutional study, and thus not a researcher's only chance to put research to practical application if desired. Another type of practical application are published materials or reports such as that written by Cameron (1998), "A language-focused needs analysis for ESL-speaking nursing students in class and clinic," and the public presentation by Seig and Winn (2003, March), "Guardians of America's Gate: Discourse-Based Training Lessons from INS Interviews." Such reports reach a much larger audience than the individual participating institutions. Dissemination of findings and their practical interpretation assists practitioners in helping both institutional representatives and employees and, in turn, their institutional clients. Whether the researchers propose the application themselves (Cameron, 1998; Seig & Winn, 2003) or whether they make their results available for others to draw on, dissemination is an important step in the research process.

REFERENCES

Bardovi-Harlig, K., & Hartford, B. S. (1990). Congruence in native and nonnative conversations: Status balance in the academic advising session. *Language Learning, 40*, 467-501.

Bardovi-Harlig, K., & Hartford, B. S. (1993). Learning the rules of academic talk: A longitudinal study of pragmatic development. *Studies in Second Language Acquisition, 15*, 279-304.

Bardovi-Harlig, K., & Hartford, B. S. (1996). Input in an institutional setting. *Studies in Second Language Acquisition, 18*, 171-188.

Bardovi-Harlig, K., & Hartford, B. S. (1997, April). *Academic advising sessions with students in an intensive English program.* Paper presented at the Eleventh International Conference on Pragmatics and Language Learning; Urbana, IL.

Cameron, R. (1998). A language-focused needs analysis for ESL-speaking nursing students in class and clinic. *Foreign Language Annals, 31,* 202-218.

Cameron, R., & Williams, J. (1997). Senténce to tén cents: A case study of relevance and communicative success in nonnative-native speaker interaction in a medical setting. *Applied Linguistics, 18,* 415-445.

Clyne, M. (1994). *Inter-cultural communication at work: Cultural values in discourse.* Cambridge, England: Cambridge University Press.

Dörnyei, Z. (2003). *Questionnaires in second language research: Construction, administration, and processing.* Mahwah, NJ: Erlbaum.

Douglas, D., & Selinker, L. (1994). Research methodology in context-based second-language research. In E. E. Tarone, S. M. Gass, & A. D. Cohen (Eds.), *Research Methodology in Second-Language Acquisition* (pp. 119-131). Hillsdale, NJ: Lawrence Erlbaum Associates.

Hartford, B. S., & Bardovi-Harlig, K. (1992). Closing the conversation: Evidence from the academic advising session. *Discourse Processes, 15,* 93-116.

Hartford, B. S., & Bardovi-Harlig, K. (1996b, August). *Cross-sectional study of the acquisition of speech acts by non-native learners of English: The use of natural data in an intensive English program.* Paper presented at the 11th World Congress of the International Association of Applied Linguistics (AILA), Jyvaskyla, Finland.

He, A. W. (1994). Withholding academic advice: Institutional context and discourse practice. *Discourse Processes, 18,* 297-316.

Johnston, A. (2003a) *A mediated discourse analysis of immigration gatekeeping interviews.* Unpublished doctoral dissertation, Georgetown University. Georgetown, Washington, DC.

Johnston, A. (2003b, March). *Comembership in immigration gatekeeping interviews: Construction, ratification and refutation.* Paper presented at the annual conference of the American Association of Applied Linguistics, Arlington, Virginia.

Johnston, A. (in press). Files, forms and fonts: Mediational means and identity negotiation in immigration interviews. In R. Scollon & P. LeVine (Eds.), *Proceedings of the Georgetown University Round Table.* Washington, DC: Georgetown University.

Kerekes, J. (2000, April). *The co-construction of a successful gatekeeping encounter: Strategies of linguistically diverse speakers.* Paper presented at the annual conference of Pragmatics and Language Learning, Urbana, Illinois.

Kerekes, J. (2001) *The co-construction of a successful gatekeeping encounter: Strategies of linguistically diverse speakers.* Unpublished doctoral thesis, Stanford University, Stanford, California.

Kerekes, J. (2003). Distrust: A determining factor in the outcomes of gatekeeping encounters. In S. Ross (Ed.) *Misunderstanding in Spoken Discourse.* London: Longman/Pearson.

Sarangi, S., & Roberts, C. (Eds.). (1999). *Talk, work and institutional order: Discourse in medical, mediation and management settings.* Berlin: de Gruyter.

Seig, M. T., & Winn, M. (2003, March). *Guardians of America's Gate: Discourse-Based Training Lessons from INS Interviews.* Paper presented at the colloquium on High-stakes Gatekeeping Encounters at the American Association of Applied Linguistics, Arlington, Virginia.

Tarone, E., & Kuehn, K. (2000). Negotiating the social service oral intake interview: Communicative needs of nonnative speakers of English. *TESOL Quarterly, 34,* 99 126.

Thonus, T. (1999). How to communicate politely and be a tutor, too: NS-NNS interaction and writing center practice. *Text, 19,* 253-279.

Tyler, A. (1992). Discourse structure and the perception of incoherence in international teaching assistants' spoken discourse. *TESOL Quarterly, 26,* 713-730.

Tyler, A. (1994). Effective role-play situations and focused feedback: A case for pragmatic analysis in the classroom. In C. Madden & C. Meyers (Eds.), *Discourse and performance of international teaching assistants* (pp. 116-131). Alexandria, VA: TESOL.

Tyler, A. (1995). The co-construction of cross-cultural miscommunication: Conflicts in perception, negotiation and enactment of participant role and status. *Studies in Second Language Acquisition, 17,* 129-152.

Tyler, A., & Davies, C. (1990). Cross-linguistics communication missteps. *Text, 10,* 385-411.

Williams, J. (2002). Undergraduate second language writers in the writing center. *Journal of Basic Writing, 21,* 73-91.

Winn, M. (2000). Negotiating borders and discourse: A study of interaction in the US naturalization interview. Unpublished manuscript. Honolulu, HI: University of Hawai'i at Manoa.

Winn, M. (under review). Collecting target discourse: The case of the U.S. naturalization interview.

Author Index

223

Subject Index